Revealing Antiquity

· 3 ·

G. W. Bowersock, General Editor

Greek Virginity

GIULIA SISSA

Translated by
Arthur Goldhammer

HARVARD UNIVERSITY PRESS
Cambridge, Massachusetts
London, England
1990

Originally published in 1987 by Librairie Philosophique
J. Vrin as *Le corps virginal*

This book is printed on acid-free paper, and its binding
materials have been chosen for strength and durability.

Designed by Joyce C. Weston

Library of Congress Cataloging-in-Publication Data

Sissa, Giulia, 1954–
[Corps virginal. English]
Greek virginity / Giulia Sissa; translated by
Arthur Goldhammer.
p. cm.—(Revealing antiquity; 3)
Translation of: Le corps virginal.
Bibliography: p.
Includes index.
ISBN 0-674-36320-5 (alk. paper)
1. Women—Greece. 2. Virginity. I. Title. II. Series.
DF93.S5313 1990   89-15466
305.4′00938—dc20   CIP

CONTENTS

*Painting inside the Vulci Cup. Antikenmuseum,
Staatlich Museen, Berlin.*

Introduction

THIS BOOK has three parts, but just one subject: the female body as it was conceived in ancient Greece.

First comes the Pythia, Apollo's priestess at Delphi, whose mystery for us resides not so much in her language as in the relation of her virginal state to her oracular function. The Danaides in the underworld, who occupy the final chapter of the book, pose a problem of interpretation that can be solved once we are clear about Greek images of the maternal and virginal body. The central chapter of my triptych concerns the question of virginity in the most basic sense: Did the hymen exist according to the Greek perception of anatomy (among laymen as well as physicians)? It is central because the ancients' conception of virginity provides the key to resolving the questions I have raised.

The hymen today is a part of the body whose function as sign, or *signaculum,* hence as seal, is alleged to be valued and whose actual existence is not questioned. It is a sort of biological undergarment protecting the female genitals. But the conviction that this membranous veil is as natural a part of the female body as the clitoris and that its rupture is universally acknowledged to be a bloody injury is seriously shaken when one attempts to find traces of it in Greek literature from Euripides to the late lexicographers, from the *Corpus Hippocraticum* to

1

Galen. When judged by the light of ancient gynecology, more-over, it is western secular medicine that turns out throughout its history to have displayed an astonishing reserve in its atti-tude toward the hymenological vulgate.

Is the hymen perhaps a hypostasis, a fetish, an article of faith? Neither mariology nor psychoanalysis nor forensic med-icine nor erotic literature can renounce belief in this material token of female intactness, which makes it possible to conceive of a woman's first act of sexual intercourse as a definite, recog-nizable wound. Medical descriptions of the hymen prudently depict it as nothing more than a lunule bordering the labia mi-nora.[1] Yet the hymen that is spoken of as being torn or de-stroyed, the membrane that is associated with defloration, evokes the image of a thin skin stretched tightly across an open-ing, which is thereby obstructed. As an organ of virginity, the hymen of imagination is a cover. Moreover, in order to explain the narcissistic humiliation of the deflowered woman, Freud actually says that the first penetration of her genitalia *destroys an organ*, a destruction that is supposed to account for the hos-tility that every woman allegedly feels toward her first lover.[2]

In which representations of the female body and of female sexuality does the hymen play a central role? What are the ef-fects and advantages of this unduly generalized way of envi-sioning the intact woman? This book offers no answers to such questions. It limits itself to an exploration of the ancient world, a world in which the marriage song was called the hymeneal but in which there was no proof of the hymen's existence, a world in which the young woman who had yet to experience love lived behind a barrier of a different kind. In Italy, in Rome, the problem of the hymen was raised explicitly. But in Greece the female body appears to have been conceptualized in a dif-ferent way.

In describing my research it was inevitable that I should resort to the metaphor of exploration. The structure of the book faithfully reflects the progress of the work. Hence the priestess

2

of Apollo is not simply a case of Greek virginity; she discreetly fills a leading role. It was because of her and for her that the question of the hymen was raised. I therefore judged it best not to limit her appearance to that of one example among others; instead I have reproduced the sinuous path of the work as it proceeded, leaving the broad questions regarding the priestess of Apollo as they were stated at the outset.

The priestess of Apollo at Delphi has been the victim of great volumes of rumor and hearsay. Had Pausanias, who knew the sites, described her gestures, had Herodotus described the nature of her ceremonial, then perhaps we would have access to the ethnographic facts. But we do not. The geographer Strabo reported what was said and believed about the oracle in the vicinity of Delphi, while Diodorus Siculus recounted a local legend.[3]

To approach the oracle from the point of view of the beliefs that gave it a literary existence: this, in Marie Delcourt's view, was the aim of the leading specialist in divination, A. Bouché-Leclercq.[4] To take tradition seriously for what it reveals about the thought that underlies it: the method has been well tested. But it is not my intention to adopt a religious-historical model in the manner of J. J. Bachofen, nor is it my wish to transform the Pythia into an emblem of feminine and mystical grandeur. My point is much simpler: that the scattered but richly suggestive fragments of ancient literature concerning this singular priestess do not deserve to be dismissed as nonsense simply because excavations at Delphi have failed to find any geological basis for them. Surely Plutarch, when he describes the light of truth as radiating out upon Parnassus "through the breast of Themis," is not simply using a superfluous metaphor;[5] surely his words are more than the fantasy of a fanatical devotee of Delphi.

The image of the priestess-voice, the idea of oracular speech taking on palpable form inside the body of a virgin, the image of a lunar soul, the art of assisting in the birth of signs—

all these characteristic features of the Pythia's role did admittedly attract my attention. My interest was aroused not so much by the literature concerning or the words uttered by the oracle as by the inception of a form of language that was at once divine and feminine. This was of course a question for theologians, philosophers, and mythologists; but it was also a Greek question, a pertinent one at that, since Plutarch devoted two dialogues to answering it.

In the first place, in order to understand what took place when the oracle was consulted one has to understand the structure of enthusiasm. Obviously the Pythia said what the god inspired her to say, and a disturbance took place within her body. But scholars have clashed over the nature of the Pythia's delirium: Was it madness or contemplation? ritual or hysteria? It took many readings of Plutarch before I understood his thinking on the subject, even though it is clear and consistent. I read the dialogue of Theon and Lamprias more than once before realizing that even a history of the oracular style would have to be based on a psychology of inspiration and that this psychology, constant through time, explains, as an always latent virtual presence, the poetry and the prose, the enigma and the transparency, the agitation and the tranquillity. The very structure of the Pythia's language, no less than its expression in verse, then appears intrinsically linked to the state of her soul, to be sure, but also to the purity of her body, which no mortal has known: it is intact. The virginity of the prophetess is not merely an accessory quality, as it would be if it were merely a cultural precaution to ensure cleanliness; it is that which makes reception of the god possible. If the priestess can surrender, accessible and intact, to her husband and master, it is by virtue of that integrity, which symbolizes that her body is in tune and capable, like a musical instrument, of full and faithful rendition.

Sexuality is therefore implicit in divinatory speech. One scene of consultation at Delphi shows a woman seated on a raised tripod as vapors emanating from the earth rise toward her body. Thinking about various versions of this image and about the Pythia's eloquent enthusiasm suggested two distinct ways of approaching the subject: first, by analyzing the symbolic analogy between the mouth that speaks and eats and the other female *stoma* (the cervix of the uterus and the labia of the vulva), and second, by examining the Greek concept of virginity. On the one hand, in the works of the physicians on fertility and of the philosophers on the morality of women, we see a wide-open female body that brims over with truth as it is invaded by a divine spirit. On the other hand, we find that same body hermetically sealed, untouchable, and silent when not in proximity to men. What accounts for this strange virginal silence?

Finally, as if the model of the female body developed in these pages required proof by contradiction, I investigated a well-known and much studied allegory, proverbially attributed to the philosophers: the perforated jar or sieve used for carrying or drawing water and associated with those uninitiated in the mysteries of Eleusis and above all with the Danaides. The infernal punishment meted out to women who prevented the fulfillment of marriage in motherhood, to murderesses who slit their husbands' throats, reveals the extent to which women's bodies were represented in terms of constant alternation between the closed and the open, void and plenitude. These incomplete women, who experienced penetration by a male but whose wombs did not close around a living seed, are condemned to carry water in a leaky jar and to draw it with a sieve.

Will I then conclude by returning to the Pythia, as if in traveling toward Argos by way of Artemisian Arcadia I had wandered far from Delphi? No, for in the meantime I shall have woven around her, mysterious in the middle of the world, a web of analogies, similes, and suggestions.

I

The Enigmatic Virgin

～ 1 ～

A Luminous Pit

I N PINDAR'S *Pythian Odes* and Plutarch's *Pythian Dialogues* Delphi is a source of knowledge unsullied by falsehood, knowledge that is communicated to men in their own language: in Strabo's words, "through discourse" and not "through symbols."[1] A god of few words, fond of clear, concise expression, the oracular Apollo was called *Loxias,* not because of his lack of clarity but because he avoided idle talk.[2] By condensing his messages into an "oblique," abbreviated form, the god of Delphi set the highest example of that wisdom whose original apothegms were inscribed on the pediment of his temple.[3] Unlike an ordinary interlocutor, who must reflect a moment after being asked a question, the Pythia could formulate her answers even before a question was asked. There was a profound difference between a human speaker and this woman inspired by Apollo who "understood the deaf-mute and heard the man who said nothing." The crucial point, however, is that Plutarch likens a consultation with the Delphic oracle to a dialogue.[4] Thanks to him we understand the analogy between divination and dialectics: "The fact that the god is no less a philosopher than a soothsayer, according to Ammonius (and we all thought that he was right), explains each of his surnames. He thus explained that Apollo is *Pythian* (Seeker) for those who are beginning to learn and to search, *Delian* (Clear) and *Phanaean* (Luminous) for

9

those to whom a part of the truth is already clear and luminous, *Ismenian* (Learned) for those who possess knowledge, and *Leschenorian* (Conversant) for those who are past masters and who wish to profit from dialectics and philosophical conversations."[5]

Oral divination, which partook of absolute knowledge, was far more prestigious than the reading of signs by augurs, because the Delphic oracle was divine whereas the art of deciphering entrails or birds' flights was a human profession. Plato wrote: "You see then what this ancient evidence attests. Corresponding to the superior perfection and value of the prophecy of inspiration over that of omen reading, both in name and in fact, is the superiority of heaven-sent madness over man-made sanity."[6] The craftlike skill of the augur could be learned and passed on—signs were there for anyone to read (and remember that we are here in the heart of the *Phaedrus*); by contrast, the Pythia's voice gave presence to the very thought of the god. When the entranced mantis speaks, it is sonorous Apollo who answers; it is the god who is "patron of the modes and effects of the articulated, signifying, efficacious voice."[7] Nearby, benevolent, and truthful, the god is the author of statements that become intelligible through the lips of his prophetess. No artifice or code intervenes: in a woman's body become a locus, a wall of glass, a blank page, speech does not find a symbolic order; it shines like a beacon. The neoplatonist Iamblichus wrote (my italics):

> Whether the prophetess of Delphi delivers her oracles to men thanks to a subtle, igneous breath exhaled from the abyss through some fissure, or prophesies in the sanctuary while seated on a bronze tripod or on the four-legged throne consecrated to the god, in any case she surrenders to the divine breath and is illuminated by the rays of the divine fire. And when the fire that rises from the pit compact and abundant completely envelops her, it fills her with divine clarity. When she is installed on the god's throne, she is in harmony with his enduring divinatory power. And in consequence of the

two preparations *she becomes entirely the god's possession*. Then the god assists her and illuminates her separately, being other than the fire, the breath, the particular throne, and all the natural or sacred preparations that take place here.[8]

For Iamblichus, the Pythia, whom the Delphic vapors make receptive and whom the god entirely possesses, is the radiant body of truth.[9]

This divination, which required no knowledge of signs and which pagan theology recognized as divine, was given the name *naturalis* in Cicero's dialogue *On Divination*.[10] In Stoic fashion, and in the tradition of firm belief in phenomena and meteors, there was a cleavage between physical forces and *artes*. The Pythia's clairvoyant utterance drew from the body of Earth an energy as spontaneous as it was subject to the vicissitudes of weather and depletion. Thus "it could happen that the force emanating from the earth that affected the Pythia with the divine afflatus [*qui mentem Pythiae divino afflatu concitabat*] would eventually be depleted, much as a spring will dry up and disappear or, as we sometimes see, abandon its bed and follow another course."[11] Whether it was entirely the work of the god or derived its veracity from a telluric source, Delphic soothsaying was characteristically unadorned, pure, and simple. Through it man became Apollo's interlocutor. The man who went to Delphi did not go in search of an ambiguous divinity whose thought issued in brief, brilliant snatches. Whoever came to consult the Pythia in her temple was certain of hearing what he wished to know *spoken* aloud.

> The traditional image of a Pythia in delirium, prophesying in a semiconscious state under the impetus of noxious emanations from the earth, has not stood up well to critical scrutiny based on research carried out over the past forty years into the functioning of the Delphic oracle. The ruins of the Temple of Apollo are in this respect quite disappointing and establish no conclusions that are not open to challenge. When all the

texts are read in light of the context in which they were written, not the existence but the commonly accepted image of the Pythia's "delirium" must be questioned. Yet no clear and uncontestable substitute emerges from the sources.[12]

Today, any study of the Delphic oracle, however modest its purpose, must begin with a statement of caution and acknowledgment of disappointed expectations. Georges Rougemont, quoted above, admirably sums up the current state of the question. For forty years Hellenists—led by Ernest Will with his article "Sur la nature du pneuma delphique" (On the nature of the Delphic *pneuma*)—have had to contend with unkept promises and what is virtually a trap set by tradition.[13] As results from the excavation of the Temple of Apollo have been examined and analyzed, ancient testimony concerning the method of divination has ceased to appear accurate or even plausible. While noting the relatively large amount of literary documentation concerning the temple and the activities conducted there, H. W. Parke and D. E. W. Wormell, the great English historians of Delphi, observed in 1956 that "the procedure of consulting the oracle and delivering the responses at Delphi remains still a very mysterious subject."[14]

The simple, immemorial gestures that were repeated century after century among the laurels of Parnassus probably remained unchanged from Pindar to Plutarch, but, as Marie Delcourt observed, "people formed a new mental image [of those gestures] which was gradually modified until, even before the end of antiquity, a *myth of the Pythia* eclipsed the modest reality."[15] Constant appeals to Apollo through his priestess, as recounted in Herodotus' "fables," were presumably accompanied by a proliferation of images, so that by the fifth century a fictional representation allegedly supplanted faithful chronicles and accurate eyewitness accounts: "Delphi was the only center of divination that enjoyed a literary existence. Indeed, that is one of the reasons why its history is so difficult to write."[16] The seat of a sacerdotal power that took from the Pythia only the alibi of a divine presence, Delphi became, as Delcourt tells us, the most successful fabricator of political myth and religious deception in all of ancient Greece.[17]

In response to much scholarly skepticism about the Pythia's delirium and inspiration, of her hysteria and vapors,[18] Georges Roux took up the issue with a much less hostile attitude toward Greek and Latin sources.[19] Adhering to the principle that we ought to trust the testimony of an ancient author "as long as it is not demonstrated to be false,"[20] Roux attempted to reconcile the traditional images with the archaeological data. The *chasma gēs*, fissure in the earth, that is, the adytum or *manteion* in the strict sense, was, he held, not a fanciful invention but a sort of pit dug in a square of bare earth in the back of the megaron. In a broader sense the adytum was an untiled depression some three feet below the tiled floor of the temple, into which the Pythia "descended" to make her prophecies. There, on the soft ground, in contact with the natural soil of Delphi, stood the tripod, whose supports rose from the edge of the pit, the stomion of the *chasma gēs*. Roux's reconstruction presented the new and by no means unprovable idea that the cavity in the earth was never thought of as a fissure in the rock but rather as a place carved out of a layer of sandy soil by the hand of man and lined with a stone wall. Thus, a gloss by Stephanus of Byzantium that mentions "Delphi, where there is an adytum built with five stones, the work of Agamedes and Trophonius," is alleged to be a reference to the walls of the oracular pit, to the adytum in the sense ascribed to it by Euripides in *Iphigenia in Tauris*.[21]

By preserving the reality of the fissure in the earth, with its delirium-inducing exhalations, and by diligently trying to determine the exact status of such phenomena, Roux opened up the possibility of seeing the Delphic *pneuma* and inspiration in new ways. Setting aside other scholars' demands for positive proof and refusing to reject the testimony of the ancients as a tissue of lies to be exposed and discredited, he stressed the certainty shared by all Greeks as to the existence of the Delphic *mania* and *pneuma*. He rescued the Pythian tradition from the charge of falsity that had reduced it to silence and instead affirmed that it was by nature a phenomenon of the imagination.[22] From Plato to Plutarch and the church fathers the genealogy of a representation takes shape, together with a set of constraints as clear and powerful as physical laws: effects of knowledge that revealed their power in both overt and subterranean fashion. Given that the concepts of enthusiasm and inspiration are indispensable for thinking about divination, the unique sense of Pythian utterance needs to be looked at with alertness to what was always unspoken, and perhaps indecent, in the image of a woman who opened her mouth to speak the truth while her body was penetrated by currents and vapors.

～2～

The Art of Madness

C ONSIDER the Vulci cup and its interpretation. The scene depicted on it—Aegeus before Themis—has enjoyed a singular fate, for it has been widely invoked in support of the most contradictory hypotheses concerning the workings of the oracle.[1] I say singular fate for two reasons. First, in the strict sense, this is the only piece of iconographic evidence used to illustrate consultation with the oracle at Delphi by scholars from F. E. Robbins to Georges Roux. Second, the treatment of that evidence has been singular—in the sense of extraordinary—because it has been presented as one of a series of illustrations, no other example of which is worthy of being reproduced.[2] Like Roux, I believe that the phiale that rests in Themis' open palm probably contains not rattling knuckles but water intended for a libation.[3] The goddess seated on her tripod does not speak. She looks at the two objects she is holding, the phiale and a small branch of laurel, as if posing, striking an attitude rather than performing an act. "Themis is preparing to respond to Aegeus' question," according to Roux.[3] The immobility is plainly total.

In fact we must abandon hope that the cup by the Painter of Codrus will reveal how the Delphic oracle really worked. One might invoke as a general principle of iconographic interpretation the autonomy of pictorial language and the need to

be on one's guard against the temptation of naturalistic interpretation. But in this case there is no need to rely on such a
general principle: the image itself tells us at once that this is no
documentary representation of divinatory technique. The scene
depicted on the bottom of this cup is most definitely an episode
from myth. It is, as Plutarch tells us,[4] the famous oracle an-
nouncing the birth of Theseus: "Do not unbind the foot that
protrudes from the goatskin, O great prince, before arriving in
Athens." In the eyes of Athenians, who held Theseus to be the
founder of their city, the oracle advising Aegeus not to have
sexual relations outside his city represented the first event in
their properly autochthonous history.[5] Plutarch indicates that it
was pronounced by the Pythia, the priestess of Apollo, and not
by Themis. But the painter of the Vulci cup chose to stress the
solemn and legendary side of the story by selecting the archaic
figure of the goddess.[6]

Themis holding a phiale: Roux compares her to the Apollo
copied from a vase in the Hamilton Collection.[7] The god, seated
on a tripod, is holding a bow as well as the libation bowl. A
young woman approaches from the right holding a ewer. To the
left of the tripod a second female figure stares at the god, who
turns to look at her face. It is difficult to believe that she is consulting the oracle, because according to Plutarch women had
no access to the *chrēstērion*.[8] In any case, the small pitcher carried by the figure on the right suggests that Apollo's phiale is an
accessory in a ritual involving water. Furthermore, the creator
of the Themis of Vulci represented a similar "bearing of the
phiale" on another krater preserved in the British Museum.[9]
Five divine couples have gathered for a banquet. Each of the
male gods except Ares carries in one hand a sign of his identity
while holding a phiale in the other. Erika Simon has shown that
the offering of water and the hieratic posture are characteristic
features of the iconography of the gods.[10] It is therefore not implausible to suppose that an artist enthusiastic about the formal
and serious aspects of Greek religious history wished to empha-

size the divinity of Themis by depicting her with a phiale, and that the tripod and laurel are present as symbols of Delphi and divination, just as the column that stands between Themis and Aegeus suggests that the setting is a temple.

Caution is in order whenever one wishes to interpret an isolated image and to compare it with other images by singling out a few distinctive elements. Nevertheless, the analysis given above is useful, for there exists at least one proof that the phiale was not thought of simply as an instrument for use in consulting the oracle and that it did not necessarily indicate a priestess: a Lucanian amphora from the fourth century B.C.,[11] which Jane Harrison reproduced in order to illustrate the relation between Apollo and the omphalos.[12] At the center of the scene is the god, shown in profile, sitting enthroned on an omphalos decorated with ribbons and laurel. Brandishing a branch of laurel and raising his lyre, he looks at the naked youth who stands before him with bent knee. On the right, behind Apollo, another virile figure with prominent muscles is wearing only a short, open himation and carrying a petasos. At opposite edges of the composition are two women: one standing on the left, the other perched on a three-legged apparatus on the right. Any reader of Aeschylus and Euripides will immediately recognize the two youths as Orestes and Pylades, will assume that the woman on the left is Electra, symbolically invited to Delphi, and will be astonished to find, in her customary place, a Pythia. The seat occupied by Themis on the Vulci cup and reserved for Apollo on certain vases is here filled by the priestess. So far as I am aware, this image is unique. To be sure, this Pythia on the tripod is most disappointing for anyone seeking information about how the oracle worked, and perhaps that is why she is not mentioned in any of the works on Delphi that I have cited. This scene of consultation confirms the ambiguity of the Vulci cup, and specifically the purely imaginary mimesis involved in the treatment of the ritual on the surface of painted vases. How can a painting in which Apollo, his prophetess, and characters from a tragic epic are brought together in a single space be treated as if it were direct, positive evidence? What hope is there of discovering the key to the divinatory method in this three-quarter view, in which a delicately embroidered sash is draped languidly between the young woman's two hands?

"Apollo, seated on the omphalos, touches with a laurel branch the blade that Orestes presents to him in its sheath. It may be, however, that the scene takes place prior to the murder, when Apollo orders Orestes to punish his mother and consecrates the weapon of vengeance."[13] With these words L. Séchan rejects a first interpretation that strikes me as indeed quite bold. Séchan then refers to passages in Aeschylus' *Choephoroe* and Euripides' *Orestes* in which Orestes recounts the consultation, the origin of his mission of vengeance. This story, which the hero of the drama tells to his sister (note that the episode is also reported—"cast in words"—on the stage), is interesting in this context because it helps us to understand why the Pythia could be represented simultaneously with her god. The striking thing about Aeschylus' text is the absolutely direct relation between the god and the person questioning him. Orestes tells Electra of his dialogue with Loxias as if no intermediary had conveyed the god's words. Apollo, speaking with his own voice, delivered the commandment of vengeance.[14] This suggests a way of making sense of the simultaneous presence of the god and his priestess on the Naples vase: the Pythia is seated on the tripod, but it is Apollo who is speaking. The prophetess is there, but the god is the protagonist, and he personally instructs Orestes in the law of paternal blood.[15]

At the beginning of the *Eumenides* the Pythia invokes the divinities of Delphi in reciting the succession to the mantic throne: neither Athena Pronaia nor Dionysus is left out. She calls inconclusively upon the waters of the Pleistus, upon Poseidon, and upon Zeus before taking her seat.[16] As she utters the final words of her prayer she moves toward the door of the temple, which according to one scholium was visible on the stage.[17] For a few moments no one remains onstage.[18] Then suddenly the priestess returns, whereupon a repulsive sight drives her out of the *manteion:* "Because she saw Orestes on the altar and the Erinyes asleep, she was overwhelmed and left the temple on all fours."[19] Under the impetus of fright she now describes the dramatic vision that upset her: the prophetess who had been able to list all the Delphic powers does not know the name of the hybrid creatures that surrounded the armed and bloodstained supplicant. Lost, she turns to Loxias, and Apollo appears. At the same time, "a revolving mechanism shows the whole of the *manteion* as it is."[20] The god is there, and henceforth it is he who speaks to Orestes. "No, I will not betray you,"[21] he says; his words are a response to the words of Orestes, who in the *Choephoroe* has declared his full confidence in the oracular god in the presence of his sister.[22] As soon as the god finds his protégé and resumes their dialogue, the priestess disappears: she has become superfluous. An amphora from Ruvo preserved in the Naples Museum depicts the critical moment when the Pythia flees from a horrifying vision while simultaneously the divine archer drives out the Erinyes.[23] In extreme panic the temple guardian rushes with arms raised toward the exit and drops the huge key for which she is responsible. Whereas, in Euripides' *Ion,* the priestess of Delphi admits her ignorance concerning the infant exposed on the doorstep of the sanctuary, here her disorientation is more pronounced: away from the tripod, forced to rely on her intelligence alone, she knows nothing and sinks into confusion.

These ancient images tell us nothing about the Pythia's divinatory service or the details of the ritual. Aeschylus exhibits the grotesqueness of her fear, which exalts the virile power of the young god, the master of her tongue. We are obliged to imagine the Pythia—the woman whose mission is to give voice to past, present, and future—crawling on hands and knees like a child.[24]

Having made this detour through iconography and theater I can now propose the following hypothesis: it is in the form of a story and as the incarnation of a fictional character that the priestess of Pythian Apollo is represented. What is more, she stands apart from and in the shadow of the divine figure who occupies the foreground in both painting and tragedy.

BUT WHERE should we look for her image? Where might we find authentic witnesses of the Pythia's work? To what sources should we turn to reconstruct her acts and the ceremony that accompanied them? Herodotus, to whom I shall turn first, proves more disappointing than the stones of Delphi and more niggardly than tragic theater. Although his histories constantly turn on Pythian oracles, he has only one thing to say about the manner of their utterance. When he refers to the warlike Satrae, the only Thracians never to have been defeated, he slips in an ethnographic detail: "It is in the territory of this people that there is an oracle of Dionysus, situated on the loftiest mountain range. The service of the temple belongs to the Bessi, a branch of the Satrae; and there is a Priestess, as at Delphi, to deliver the oracles—which, by the way, are not more involved than the Delphic."[25] This passage can be read as an indication that all Greeks were familiar with the oracle of Parnassus: "Of all the ministers of the Delphic cult, the Pythia was the most celebrated, and that is why we know so little about her: the Greeks knew her too well."[26] The idea that the ritual was too well known to attract Herodotus' attention is suggested, perhaps, by the brevity of his note. But is it really possible that the only reason for that brevity, which incidentally is shared by Pausanias, was that the nature of the phenomenon was obvious to everyone? Why, then, did Pausanias take such care to depict so many obvious details of Delphi, where he examined every stone and every painting?[27] Herodotus literally says that the oracle of the Thracian Dionysus was no more complicated (*poikiloteros*) than that of the Pythian Apollo. Perhaps this was a way of saying that the oracle of Apollo was as strange as that of Dionysus.

In his tales of consultations at Delphi, Herodotus makes the Pythia into a pure subject of enunciation. In a space without connotations and in accordance with effaced rules, words were exchanged between consultants and priestess.[28] Before the battle of Salamis, the Athenian envoys approach the prophetess and, dismayed by what they hear, come a second time to beg for a less terrible oracle.[29] Herodotus allows us to imagine a scene taking place around the words, but ordinarily the Pythia manifested herself in the form of a voice. And that voice had no body: for the eyes, nothing was there. No behavior was described. When she "functioned," the Pythia was no longer even an instrument: her words came forth in order to be set down on tablets of wax. Like the Sibyl, whose slow metamorphosis is narrated by Ovid, the Pythia lost her body and, "invisible to all," was recognized only by her voice.[30]

From a later, Christian world the physical presence of the Pythia—by this time all that remained of the oracle of Delphi—would be subjected to a scrutiny insensible to what her voice had uttered. For the church fathers the woman who had prophesied in pagan Greece was just that: a female creature, an unsettling body. She was always spoken of as a spectacle for the eyes.

Origen's treatment of Greek prophecy in *Contra Celsum* makes use of these fundamental themes. For Christian writers the problem was to explain an obviously supernatural phenomenon that yielded knowledge of the future but outside the context of scripture and revelation. Faced with an undeniable historical fact, Origen cannot simply dismiss it as pagan imposture. More subtly, he uses the existence and methods of the Delphic oracle as further proofs of the falsity of pagan religion. The Pythia became living proof of the demoniac nature of the pre-Christian gods. By taking the tradition of divination quite seriously and eagerly seizing upon those traits that made her seem a figure of *enthousiasmos*, Origen was able to make an important point: since the prophetess was possessed by Apollo, it is clear that Apollo was not a god. In *mania*, which Plato, Plutarch, and Iamblichus had defined as the presence in one human being of another who speaks through the first person's mouth, Origen saw precious proof that the Greek pantheon was never anything more than a society of demons. Sophisticated argument was unnecessary; it was enough to observe and point out in order to persuade: "Let us grant that the responses of the Pythia and other oracles were not the invention of people feigning divine inspiration. And let us see whether, even in that case, we cannot show that even if we accept these oracles we are not obliged to recognize in them the presence of certain gods. They are rather evil demons and spirits hostile to the human race, which prevent the soul from ascending."[31]

With this challenge to Apollonian theology Origen began his dissection of the talking priestess: while she sits over the mouth of Castalia, a vapor enters her body by way of her genitals. Filled with *pneuma*, she proffers what the Greeks took to be venerable and divine. "In this was there not proof of the impure and vicious nature of this spirit? It insinuated itself into the soul of the prophetess not by way of scattered and imperceptible pores, much purer than the female organs, but because the chaste man was not allowed to look, much less to touch."[32] Under the harsh light of Christian contempt this body took on relief: the relief of that which men were forbidden to see. Utterly without modesty, it exhibited the obscenity of its fleshly speech. "If Apollo of Delphi were the god the Greeks believe him to be, whom would he have chosen as prophet if not a wise man or, lacking such, a man progressing toward knowledge? Why did he not choose a man to prophesy rather than a woman? And assuming he preferred the female sex, perhaps because he had neither power nor pleasure other than in the bosom of women, why did he not choose a virgin rather than another woman as interpreter of his will?"[33] But in fact Pythian Apollo chose neither a philosopher nor a man nor a learned woman but a woman of the most ordinary kind. Of the woman he chose to speak for him he desired neither the wisdom nor the soul but the female nature, the sex. Eloquence falls silent before so sordid a fact. With the Delphic cult reduced to abjection, there is nothing else to do but gaze upon the part of the body from which the utterances of Apollo originated.[34]

John Chrysostom painted a more naturalistic portrait: the Pythia is seated on Apollo's tripod, her legs spread. An evil spirit (*pneuma poneron*) rises from below, enters her vagina, and fills her with madness. Her hair is disheveled, and foam flows from her mouth: she is like a bacchante. And it is in such a state that she speaks.[35] "I know that you were ashamed and blushed to hear this story," the church father apologizes, knowing the effect upon his listeners of visualizing the spread thighs, the open mouth, and the wild hair: the possessed woman accuses her master.

For Origen and John Chrysostom, to describe an oracular session made pornographic by the presence of a body, of sexuality, and of madness was to evoke an apparition. The Greeks believed in what was said by way of such exhibition, and this fact was enough to discredit their false gods as well as their moral depravity.[36] Nevertheless, these vivid depictions of the powerful onslaught of Apollonian *mania* were based on hearsay, on an indirect tradition: *historeitai,* wrote Origen; *legetai,* wrote John Chrysostom. The less likelihood there was that one could view the Pythia directly, the easier it became to imagine her body in detail.

Herodotus and the church fathers represent extreme solutions of an aporia implicit in the very status of prophetic speech. Whether the Pythia was a voice uttering a series of oracles or a woman preyed upon by a demon, although her mouth may have spoken she was not present. Paradoxically, Herodotus, who gives full credence to the oracle of Delphi, cannot help ignoring her female body; he mentions it only for its power to convey a truth. Everything else is superfluous. Nor does Herodotus anywhere imply that the Pythia was visible to those who consulted her. When she answers a question before it has been asked, the suggestion is not that the priestess engaged in face-to-face conversation with visitors to the temple but rather that she possessed clairvoyant powers, which the historian in no way questions.[37] The Apollonian oracle was in a deep sense a phenomenon that cannot be reduced to direct personal communication between human beings. Perhaps the observer-narrator did not paint a portrait of the priestess for the same reason that the church fathers were able, with impunity, to present a "pornographic" version of her image: namely that, as a matter of ritual, the *promantis* was not accessible to view. As Flacelière and Roux have emphasized,[38] even Plutarch—the leading Greek expert on Delphi—when he reports the case of a Pythia forced to give a consultation that will cost her her life, can describe an oracular session only through the sense of hearing. One day, a terrible misfortune befalls a priestess obliged to do her work despite the unpropitious signs given by the sacrificial goat. Her voice is rough, she gives out a frightful cry, and then she rushes out of the adytum and collapses on the doorstep. In Roux's words, "it is as if the witnesses to this scene realized the Pythia's critical condition only because of what they heard, not because of what they saw."[39]

One of the few assertions that can be made with some assurance about the Delphic ceremony is that it actually took place in secret. To be sure, one could argue that the fraud arranged by the redoubtable clergy of Apollo began with the staging of a rite in which the body and actions of the priestess were hidden from view. But beyond that suggestive but ultimately unprovable page of history we shall now explore what was said and thought concerning a double absence: of a subject who was not herself when words were uttered by her mouth, and of a female body that was not present when the god who inhabited it borrowed its voice.

~3~

Lunar Pythia

O NE OF Heraclitus' best-known maxims characterizes the style of the Delphic oracle: "The lord whose oracle is in Delphi neither speaks out nor conceals but gives a sign."[1] J. Bollack and H. Wismann have given a suggestive interpretation of this passage when isolated from its doxographic context and read as an independent statement: "Bearing on the future, stating what does not yet exist, the oracle includes in what it says what cannot yet be said. It does not speak, as people do, about the present; it does not conceal, as people may do, the past. 'Semantic' language itself causes virtual meanings to emerge in what is does not say and what it does not conceal, in a sphere not limited by the double negation."[2] Because it makes present what is not current and because it indicates a behavior, the oracular god can do nothing more than give a sign.[3] If, however, we consider this text as a quotation attributed by Plutarch to a character in the dialogue *On the Oracles of the Pythia,* and if we respect the occasion and the significance of its occurrence and therefore question its value as an argument, then it becomes clear that it alludes to a very specific aspect of the divinatory pronouncement.

The question raised in *On the Oracles of the Pythia* concerns the history—the literary history—of divination. Originally the Pythia recited hexameters bristling with obscure metaphors.

Now (that is, in Plutarch's time) the priestess expresses herself in prose, and her diction is bare, referential, trivial. Theon, to whom Plutarch entrusts the responsibility of explaining this change, attempts to do so by proposing a coherent theory of the prophetic function. Poetry and prose, enigma and information are contrasted in the context of a speech whose intrinsic status is that of being intermediary, a kind of translation, hence subject to constraints imposed by its intended audience. It bears emphasizing, however, that to undertake an analysis of the clarity, transparency, and meaning of the language employed by Apollo's prophetess leads to giving primary consideration to a human voice whose role is not limited to articulating ready-made propositions. Inspired by the god, the Pythia conceives her own answers. Accordingly, Theon states that study of the oracles' "semiology" must begin with an examination of the manner in which they are spoken.

The soul of the priestess, which the god uses as an instrument, is not at all comparable to the wax or metal surfaces upon which fixed and changeless symbols are engraved. Nor is it like a mirror at once flat, concave, and convex, "which bestows upon a single figure thousands of appearances and aspects."[4] Neither malleable matter nor deceptive surface, the Pythia's psyche is as sensitive to Apollo as the moon is to the sun. The moon is neither a star nor an opaque mass but a reflecting body. With respect to the sun, "nothing presents a better likeness, and, further, nothing offers it so docile an instrument."[5] "The brilliance and luminosity that [the moon] receives from the sun are not reflected back to us unchanged but are altered by contact with the moon. They change color and take on a different quality. Their heat disappears completely, since it is too feeble to accompany the light. You are familiar, I think, with these words of Heraclitus . . ."[6] This is the point at which the fragment from Heraclitus becomes pertinent, having been called to mind by the frigid light of the moon. The philosopher's words are the most adequate summary of what Theon has just explained: the god does not *speak;* he does not press his seal into a totally impressionable and malleable substance. Nor does the god *conceal*, as if he wished to deceive in the manner of a distorting mirror. Rather, using the soul as an instrument, Apollo reveals his truth in a "mixed," confused, pallid form. The Pythia's psyche, though not false to the truth, inevitably diminishes its brilliance.

Neither crystalline nor deceptive, her language falls somewhere between the written and the illusory: it is a *sign*, defined by analogy with reflected light. *Semainein* is the precise word for the change in direction of Apollo's light after its encounter with the soul of the moon-priestess.[7]

Instead of alluding to the cryptic nature of the Pythia's responses, Heraclitus' apothegm reveals the hidden law of divinatory pronouncement. The sign produced by the Pythia has a twofold structure, since it is the work of both the god and the woman; it is the effect of possession, *enthousiasmos*, in language. The quotation from Heraclitus leads Theon to conclude his series of images of conjunction: "Thus what is called enthusiasm appears to be the combination of two simultaneous movements of the soul: one stemming from the action to which it is subjected, the other from its natural state."[8]

To designate the relation between the two components of enthusiasm, hence of the act of making signs, Plutarch utilizes the vocabulary of mixture.[9] To define the aptitude of the soul and the moon for capturing light he uses the words "docile to persuasion."[10] Is it surprising, then, that the theory of prophetic inspiration concludes that the priestess is like a young bride obedient to the husband who possesses and guides her? Conjugal supervision—the power, devoid of brutality, that a man exercises over a free but feeble individual whose nature is taken for granted—thus becomes the model for Apollo's authority over the Pythia.

An animal whose nature is to walk cannot be made to fly; one who stammers cannot be made to speak clearly; one with weak vocal organs cannot be given a beautiful voice . . .

Similarly, it is impossible for an illiterate, who has never heard verse, to express himself poetically. Now, this is the case with the Pythia who currently serves the god. She comes from one of the most decent and respectable families around, and she has always led a life beyond reproach; but, having been brought up in the home of poor peasants, when she descends into the place of prophecy she takes with her nothing in the way of art or other knowledge or talent. Since the young bride must, according to Xenophon, have seen and heard almost nothing when she enters her husband's home, so, too, are the inexperience and ignorance of the Pythia almost complete, and it is truly with the soul of a virgin that she approaches the god.[11]

This passage could be read as an apology for the mediocre learning of the person who served as priestess in the time of Hadrian, since Theon discusses the alleged decline in the quality of the oracles in this period. However, the decadence that worries the philosophers in this dialogue is not a phenomenon limited to the immediate presence or to a particular case of poetic incompetence. Delphi's literary impoverishment is not simply a flaw in the most recent Pythia but, far more seriously, a matter of diminished formality in the language of oracular utterance. Furthermore, Theon tries if not to contradict then at least to temper the hasty, superficial view that decline is inevitable by pointing out that in all ages the oracles were couched sometimes in noble, epic, or elegiac form, sometimes in flat prose.[12] The central point is that the language of the oracle can take various forms without altering the essence of the divinatory pronouncement.

Everything in this treatise centers on the notion of an *instrument*. An instrument "must, in keeping with its intrinsic qualities, conform as closely as possible to the agent who uses it, and must accomplish the work of thought that is expressed through it by exhibiting it not as it is found in the artisan, pure, intact, and irreproachable, but mingled with many elements intrinsic to it."[13] Note, in Theon's argument, the phrase "as closely as possible." The use of any organon, and therefore of the soul of the Pythia, involves an approximation to perfection. If the efficacy of the soul in divination is nothing other than transparency, then the psyche and body of the priestess are ideal when unencumbered by a strong character or enriching education that might impede the action of the god. These conditions are the equivalents in the Pythia of ignorance in Xenophon's young bride. What might at first seem to be a decline or impoverishment in the rhetoric of divination should therefore be seen, according to Theon, as progress, willed by Apollo, toward an increasingly authentic nakedness of truth.[14] Purified, "the language of the Pythia is reminiscent of the definition of a straight line in mathematics: the shortest distance between two given points. Ignoring the detours and sinuosities of style, the equivocations and ambiguities, it is directed straight at the truth."[15]

A nearly perfect Pythia would convey the Apollonian truth in a toneless voice and straight as an arrow, but inevitably the interference of the Pythia's own passions gives rise to a hybrid movement. "Incapable of remaining passive and offering herself, still and tranquil, to him who moves her, she roils inwardly like a stormy sea, for within her, movements and passions rage. Think of bodies that rotate as they fall: they do not move in a regular or certain manner but rather, owing to the circular impetus they receive and because of their tendency to fall, exhibit an irregular and disorderly turbulence."[16] Plutarch uses these images of turbulent seas and spiraling dives to link the structure of the sign to the psychology of enthusiasm.[17] The more the priestess interposes her own ego between her receptive faculty and the god's power, the stormier and more violent her *mania* will be. Iamblichus, who thought of divinatory ecstasy as a total loss of self-possession in which the god was wholeheartedly welcomed by the recipient, held that oracles became obscure or erroneous if the human soul took the initiative or if the human body intervened in such a way as to disturb the divine harmony.

"The god uses us as instruments, but by himself he does all the work of divination and, *without mixing*, detached from the rest, without the soul or body moving in the slightest, he acts by himself."[18] By contrast, for Plutarch, the human organon always moved more or less in harmony with Apollo. The difficulty of matching the two movements determined—for each Pythia and for virtually every session—the degree of her delirium as well as the semantic obscurity of her utterance. If the human element opposed and resisted the divine, the result was not error but a disturbance in the apparatus itself.[19] If the equilibrium between god and priestess was transformed into tension, the integrity of the Pythia's utterance was destroyed, and her voice was stifled by congestion in her throat.

The functioning of the Pythia-instrument is most fully elucidated at the end of another of Plutarch's dialogues: *On the Disappearance of Oracles*. In this work Plutarch considers the decline of Delphi from the standpoint not of style but, more seriously, of diminishing numbers of consultations. The speaker is Lamprias, whose philosophical allegiances have been a matter of controversy but who can surely be placed midway between the Academy and the Lyceum as a representative figure of Hellenistic philosophical culture.[20] Accused of primitive materialism for invoking Aristotle's theories about terrestrial emanations.[21] Lamprias "then took refuge behind Plato,"[22] as if he invoked first one, then the other authority as each new turn in the debate required. It was Plato, he tells us, who taught us to think of causality as twofold, at once divine and physical; "and it was also [Plato] who was the first, or at any rate the best, of the philosophers to study these two kinds of causes. While ascribing the origin of everything that proceeds from reason to divinity, he nevertheless did not deprive matter of its necessary effect upon becoming, for he understood that the sensible universe, organized as we see it, is not pure and unadulterated but the result of the union of matter with intelligence."[23]

Like Theon in the dialogue *On the Oracles of the Pythia*, Lamprias expresses himself sagely: being neither a theologian nor a physicist, he assumes the role of the enlightened philosopher who has learned to appreciate the "mixture" of causes and the temperament of the world. Thus, like any other phenomenon that takes place between earth and moon, divination must be thought of in terms of an intersection between rationality and nature. For Theon, however, the system does not involve only two factors. Three elements must be taken into account: god, the soul, and the telluric exhalation. An oracle cannot take shape without an agent (Apollo), matter (the Pythia's psyche), and an instrument (the *anathymia*).[24] For Lamprias, the priestess serves the function of *hylē*, or material support. To the god who fashions his response by means of a physical vapor the woman offers a site and a primary substance. This complication of Theon's simple god/instrument model probably derives from Aristotle's technical and genetic model. Just as the female contributes to procreation by supplying her own blood as raw material, so the Pythia supplies the substrate of her soul. Just as the male imposes a form on the underlying female matter through a foamy sperm that ultimately evaporates, so Apollo acts upon the psyche of the prophetess through a "plectrum," the *pneuma enthousiastikon*.[25]

This paradigm is soon forgotten, however, and Lamprias too sees the Pythia as a kind of musical instrument.[26] Her soul is no longer a piece of wood but already a fragile—and very sensitive—instrument. Discomforts and movements threaten her without her knowledge: through her body they insinuate themselves into her soul. "When she is full, it is better for her not to go down there rather than offer herself to the god when not completely pure, like a well-tuned and harmonious instrument, but rather sick and agitated."[27] A Pythia who approached the god in such a condition, that is, filled to saturation[28] with passions, feeling repugnance and aversion and already quite disturbed, was killed by the session.[29] Attacked, grabbed by the throat, as it were, by an improper, impure, and unsettling enthusiasm,[30] she came to grief like a ship run aground on the doorstep of the *manteion*.[31] The consent of the priestess, her willingness to couple with the god, could not be obtained by violence.[32] Since the woman herself did not know the state of her soul, an omen was sought with the aid of a goat. The animal's consent to its sacrifice meant that the Pythia was truly ready to offer herself to Apollo in a pure and untroubled state.[33]

Here, then, is the mechanism of divinatory *enthousiasmos* as it appears in Plutarch: harmony between a woman's soul and a musician god, lunar attenuation of a searing brilliance, navigation of mountainous seas. The Pythia stands delicately balanced between the impossibility of stifling all her own feelings and the rare conflict that stemmed from her outright refusal to participate in the ceremony—balanced on the ridge where the male god married the female voice, where truth veiled itself in a sign.[34]

~4~

Parthenos Audaessa

T HIS IS PRECISELY the context in which Plutarch introduces the question of virginity. If possession is a *mixis* (mixture); if the Pythia goes to the god, couples with him, offers herself to him; and if "going down into the *chrēstērion*" is for her the equivalent of "entering one's husband's house,"[1] the perfect state in which she is supposed to present herself to Apollo can plausibly be compared with that which is expected of a young bride. Lamprias says so explicitly: in order that she may be pure (*kathara*), like a well-tuned instrument,[2] the prophetess must refrain from all carnal union and remain completely isolated from the world throughout her life.[3] If she is to be available exclusively and unreservedly for one purpose only, her body, indeed her entire existence, must be preserved from all contamination; all contact must be forbidden. Since she must "mix" with Apollo, no alien passion may encumber her soul; no other desire may distract her. If the ultimate perfection for which she must strive is, as Theon says, to have a virgin soul or, as Lamprias indicates, to resemble a tablet on which nothing has been written,[4] her integrity must be flawless: not only must she have absolutely no sexual relations, but also she must have no social ties or elaborate education. Intact, illiterate, and solitary: for the philosopher, the Pythian priestess' supreme fulfillment takes place in a void in which intellectual and aesthetic values have no place.

Sexual virginity is the primordial condition of distance, of detachment from all that is exterior. Hence it represents an essential aspect of Apollonian divination. Ammonius, the theologian in Plutarch's dialogue, in accusing Lamprias of underestimating the god's role in the inspiration, remarks how absurd it would be to prescribe abstinence and purity to a designated female if prophecy were merely a natural phenomenon.[5] Outside the singular and faithful relationship with Apollo, his servant's chastity would make no sense.

On this point Ammonius invokes a tradition known from other contexts: a local tradition concerning the origin of the oracle, which attributes the discovery of the *chasma*, the source of prophetic enthusiasm, to the unwitting sense of smell of a curious goat.[6] Pausanias recounts this story briefly along with others,[7] and Diodorus Siculus gives a very long and detailed version:

> Long ago, it is said, goats discovered the oracle. That is why the Delphians today still chiefly sacrifice goats when they question it. The discovery occurred in the following way. There was a hole in the ground where the adytum of the sanctuary is found today. Goats were grazing in the vicinity, for Delphi at that time was not yet inhabited. Whenever an animal approached the hole and leaned over it, it began to leap about in a strange way and to emit strange bleats. The goatherd, puzzled by this, went up to the hole, peered into it, and experienced the same symptoms as the goats; they behaved as though possessed; the man predicted the future. When the people of the region heard of the effects that the hole produced on whoever came near, they flocked there and, intrigued by the phenomenon, all wished to experience it. Whoever approached the hole fell into a trance. That is why the oracle was revered and considered to be the earth's prophetic sanctuary. For a time, moreover, those who wished to consult it were content to approach the hole and deliver oracles to one another. Since many people in a state of possession leapt into the hole and vanished, the inhabitants of

the area, in order to cope with the danger, chose a single woman to serve as prophetess for all, and subsequently the consultation was carried on through her. They fabricated an object upon which she could sit in complete safety while entering into a trance and delivering oracles to anyone who might consult her. This object had three supports, which is why it was called a tripod. On the whole the device was roughly similar to the bronze tripods that are still being made today. I believe I have said enough about the way in which the oracle was discovered and the reasons for the construction of the tripod.[8]

By dispensing with the traditional genealogy of the oracle in a series of stages from the earth to Apollo,[9] the legend recounted by Diodorus transforms the Pythia into a priestess of the earth or, more precisely, into a person chosen to serve as mediator between a telluric danger and man. She is perched not on the tripod, an object that since Homer had been invested with powerful symbolic significance, but upon a device invented specifically for her, which happens to have had three supports. This high stool was not the throne of a woman who was the spokesperson for a great divinity, but a device designed to protect the woman chosen to represent the goatherds of Delphi by exposing herself to the madness-inducing vapors. What we see, then, is the core of a fable in which the landscape, chance, and man's prudence take the place of the theological and Apollonian scenario. According to Ammonius, this is the view of naive and ignorant people. But the pious philosopher is wrong when he denies that the Pythia's virginity has meaning apart from the solar horizon of the great god of Delphi. It is Diodorus—in the context of this naturalist legend, moreover—who provides the most interesting information concerning the Pythia's sexual status:

> It is said that in ancient times oracles were delivered by virgins because of their physical purity and their resemblance to Artemis. They were in effect well suited to keep the secret of

the oracles they rendered. But a story is told that in recent times Echecrates the Thessalian, having come to consult the oracle, contemplated the virgin who delivered the prophecies, fell in love with her because of her beauty, abducted her, and raped her. Following this scandal the Delphians decreed that henceforth the prophetess would no longer be a virgin but a woman above the age of fifty. Yet she wears the clothing of a young maiden as a reminder of the prophetess of old.[10]

Apollo is here alluded to only indirectly, through his sister. By contrast, the tradition that Diodorus recounts attributes the oracle to the *earth,* as if the power that originally engendered it never lost control. The Pythia, in the service of Gē, must therefore be a virgin (*parthenos*). Here, however, the *parthenos* is not a woman whom no one has touched, a pure creature who offers herself to the god. For the fertile earth she is a woman who is capable of holding her tongue, a woman of silence. In Delphic divination there is an aspect that is mystical—in the Greek sense—but that often goes unnoticed, all attention being focused on the spoken utterance. But the Pythia as outspoken voice hides another Pythia, who divulges nothing of what she is supposed to keep protected within herself, who remains chaste so that her mouth may remain sealed, that is, mute.

Whereas the properly sexual aspect of virginity is most specific and pertinent in the priestess' relations with a male god, the woman who is the earth's spokesperson is virgin with respect to her mouth. Thus, the sexual status of the Pythia is a shifting composite of alternate images, and it is important to attempt to identify, if not the reasons for those images, then at least the models. First, however, I must discuss what is evident, indeed almost embarrassing, in the tradition concerning the "Delphic bee," namely, the pertinence of the body and of sexuality in Delphic divination.

In doing so I am not breaking new ground. Indeed, it is thanks to the work of E. Fehrle and K. Latte[11] that I read Plutarch as defining a sacerdotal role modeled on the role of a wife or at any rate of a woman at once faithful and possessed. His vocabulary is clearly one of legitimate and decent sexual union. The fact that the church fathers transformed the encounter between a god and a virgin, effected by means of a supernatural *pneuma,* into a matter of wicked, sensual possession is almost proof that the ancients associated divinatory enthusiasm with love of a god. If it is true that a prophetess, her soul and body intact, received the light of an infallible word, what the philosophers said took place in the pagan sanctuary was perhaps too much like an immaculate conception. If the virginal Pythia was inspired by a god, there was too much purity in her. Hence she would be disfigured, unmasked as the prey of a brutal and evil eroticism. Neither virginal nor procreative, the Pythia as seen by the Christians would be reduced to a female body with gaping genitals; on her lips the foam of the epileptic would take the place of truth, while a false god would entice her into obscene pleasure.

In pagan mythology desire was in fact a fundamental constant in Apollo's relations with his prophetesses. Who was the Sibyl of Cumae but a mortal woman to whom a god granted divinatory powers in exchange for a promise of love?[12] And was not the poetess who sang her oracles at Delphi on a cliff some distance removed from the sacred path the author of a hymn known and commemorated at Delos in which she called herself Herophila and Artemis and claimed to be either the god's wife or his daughter?[13] She wrote her verses in a state of madness and under the god's power.[14] Her funerary stele bore the following lines: "Here hidden by stone sepulcher I lie, Apollo's fate-pronouncing Sibyl I, a vocal maiden once but now forever dumb."[15]

Tragedy celebrates Cassandra, the young Trojan woman condemned to prophesy unheeded because she once refused Apollo her love.[16] Like the Pythia when she resists the god by refusing to speak the divine speech, the legendary prophetess rejects Apollo's desire; a tragic figure, clairvoyance would for

37

her be tantamount to a "great attack." In Aeschylus' *Agamemnon* the thunderbolt and ocean wave are metaphors for the violence that overwhelms this beleaguered nightingale.[17] Mantic power does not await her consent. Cassandra can only anticipate that the god is about to take her, that truth is about to swoop down upon her, in spite of herself, as if the irruption of prophetic utterance renewed the unequal contest between virgin and god. Prophecy is not only violent and unwanted assault but also a labor (*ponos*), a birth combatted by the bearer.[18] When Cassandra opens herself to the mantic word she "loosens the variegated mouth of the oracles" as one might loosen a belt.[19]

Closer to the Pythia as she performs her duties as priestess, however, is the god's heraldic plant, the perennial *Laurus nobilis* that grows in the Temple of Apollo at Delphi and is the god's insignia, much as ivy and thyrsus are regularly found with Dionysus and his acolytes. Before entering the adytum, the priestess burns its leaves on the altar of Hestia,[20] and according to a fragment of Callimachus she sometimes makes herself a litter of them.[21] These leaves, symbols of Delphic divinity, are used to make crowns for the gods, his servant, and athletes victorious in the games. Originally the evergreen laurel was the hair of a nymph, Daphne. Apollo, shortly after killing the dragon that guarded the oracle, took a fancy to her, but in vain. In fleeing him Daphne abandoned her own body and turned into a plant, which became Apollo's favorite.[22] A tradition reported by Diodorus Siculus depicts Daphne as a daughter of Tiresias.[23] Taken prisoner by the Argive Epigones in the second war against Thebes, she was allegedly offered to the god of Delphi. Already expert in divination, she was said to have acquired there even greater skill in the composition of hexameters. Pursued and captured, Daphne was yet another young woman for whom divination was a passion. An *enthousiastikos* power was ascribed to the laurel; its leaves allegedly trembled nervously, revealing the presence of Apollo.[24] In the trembling of the eternally young plant we recognize the ceaseless struggle of the fleeing nymph.

The Sibyl of Cumae, Cassandra, Daphne: virginity is the emblem of all these very similar mythical lives, but in the form of an Artemis-like aloofness, a ferocity of attitude of which the god himself is victim. It is a rebellious virginity, whose counterpart is devastating prophecy. The god's regular priestess is the repository of another kind of virginity: hers is a pure state connoting self-mastery, which signifies an exclusive and dedicated offering. As we have seen, the Pythia—and it is striking to find Plutarch's theory confirmed by fables—is subjected to an enthusiasm comparable to that typical of the Sibyl precisely when she, too, escapes from the god. Lucan, who was well aware of this, based his account of the crisis fatal to the restive Pythia in his *Pharsalia* on Virgil's portrait of the Sibyl of Cumae.[25] Amorous enthusiasm strikes like a disease or a painful contraction of the uterus when the object of desire is absent; Plato describes the dynamic of the passion.[26] By the same token, every prophetess suffers not from possession as such but from that which impedes and prevents possession.

Herodotus remarks upon an oriental tradition that explicitly acknowledges the hierogamy of Apollo and his priestess. He describes the strange city of Babylon with its tower, at the top of which is the temple of Zeus Bēlos. Inside the sanctuary is a bed on which only the woman chosen by the god may sleep. The Chaldean priests say (but the historian does not believe) that Zeus in person enters the temple and lies on the bed alongside the mortal woman he cherishes. Herodotus glosses this tale with an analogue: "There is a similar story told by the Egyptians at Thebes, where a woman always passes the night in the temple of the Theban Zeus and is forbidden, so they say, like the woman in the temple at Babylon, to have any intercourse with men; and there is yet another instance in the Lycian town of Patara, where the priestess who delivers the oracles when required (for there is not always an oracle there) is shut up in the temple during the night."[27] Nothing so explicit is attested for the oracle of Apollo at Delphi: the tripod was not a bed, and the Pythia was not closeted at night with the god in the adytum.

But we do know that the sexual status of the Pythia was a far from insignificant aspect of her priestly functions and that it was considered to be a fundamental factor either in her enthusiasm or in her discretion. We shall see presently that in Delphi, on a site originally associated with an oracle of the Earth, in a temple where the sacred fire of Hestia burned, the virginity of the woman who held the key was seen as a prerequisite of a recognized procreation rather than of a mystical union. Originally, before the large numbers of people wishing to consult the oracle made monthly sessions necessary, the day devoted to consultation with the Pythia was the seventh of Byzios (February–March), the anniversary of Apollo's birth.[28] Was this mere coincidence? Perhaps it was rather that in the neighborhood of the umbilicus, the center of the Earth's body in Delphi, the woman perched upon a high tripod evoked a scene of birth.

～ 5 ～

Open to the Spirits

HELLENISTS are far from any consensus as to the existence of the spirit (*pneuma*) that was supposed to pass through the body of the Pythia—indeed, farther from consensus than ever since results of archaeological and geological research have dashed hopes that a physical cause of the phenomenon might be found. The notion of an evanescent material spirit, an elusive vapor, has been branded a Stoic fiction by some scholars, who see it as nothing more than a naturalistic theory of divination useful only in that it allowed Plutarch and the philosophers of the Stoa to reason about the crisis of the oracles.[1] A sort of mantic aura in which disillusioned beliefs were made concrete, the *pneuma*, these scholars say, had no reality except as an argument or hypothesis. Using the naturalist fable of an earthly emanation that was somehow depleted over time, Lamprias made plausible not so much the nature of the inspiration as the phenomenon of its eclipse.[2]

In fact, the belief that the priestess of Delphi inhaled a subtle substance that made her clairvoyant has very deep roots. The very vocabulary of enthusiasm speaks of it as "a divine inhalation,"[3] a wind, a breeze, a sigh that wafts about the head and enters the nostrils, instilling an extraordinary power in the soul. Socrates, who in the *Cratylus* is pleased to speak as if he were chanting oracles, explains to his interlocutor that perhaps

41

what has rendered him "enthusiastic" has not only filled his ears with a certain divine wisdom but has also taken hold of his soul.[4] In the *Phaedrus*, moreover, Socrates, astonished by his voluble eloquence, attributes it to the cicadas that have "breathed down" (*epipnein*) on him from a tree.[5] Sometimes divine breath becomes an erotic metaphor: for Io, in Aeschylus' *Suppliants*, the touch and breath of Zeus will bring deliverance and reveal the god's love.[6] In Sparta the pair of compound verbs *eispnein* and *empnein* referred to intellectual and affective exchange between two males.[7]

Thus, a primary pneumatic connotation of enthusiasm can be determined from linguistic usage. An ethereal medium transmits the faculty of knowledge in the manner of a contagion.[8] The *anathymia* (exhalation) at issue in Delphi, however, is something very different from a breeze of this sort, which is described in the texts as a meteoric phenomenon. In contrast to the *epipnoia*, which descends from above and acts between mouth and ear, the exhalation that envelops and penetrates the Pythia rises from the earth. And whereas poetic or divinatory inspiration becomes almost a metaphor, *anathymia* figures in a local and geographic tradition.

The existence not of the natural phenomenon but of the tradition is noted by Strabo: "They say that the seat of the oracle is a cave that is hollowed out deep down in the earth, with a rather narrow mouth, from which arises breath that inspires a divine frenzy; and over that mouth is placed a high tripod, mounting which the Pythian priestess receives the breath and utters oracles in both verse and prose, though the latter too are put into verse by poets who are in the service of the temple."[9] This passage should not be read either as the report of a naturalist or as a meaningless account of hearsay. Strabo is actually informing us of a widely shared opinion, a commonplace in the strict sense of the word, to which he himself gives credence as an ethnographer. To appreciate Strabo's critical attitude toward his sources, one has only to read the

pages following those devoted to Delphi. When he uses Ephorus' testimony, for example, he points out that Ephorus hesi-
tates between rationalism and mythology. But concerning what
is said by many anonymous voices about the Delphic tripod he
registers no disapproval. It may be possible to dismiss Lamprias'
pneuma as a Stoic-Aristotelian ploy in a debate among philosophers, but the *enthousiastikē* vapor in which people around
Delphi believe is more difficult to conjure away. In fact neither
Strabo nor Plutarch denies the alleged existence of the Delphic
pneuma, although neither personally affirms its existence. This
vapor was still on the fringes of current thought, one of those
ideas that a scholar might mention in passing without guaran-
teeing to his readers that it was true. For us, however, it demonstrates that the impersonal image of the Delphic oracle did
indeed include vapors.[10]

It is precisely the "viscosity" of this representation that is
worth paying attention to. Why was it only the Pythia, and only
in Delphi, who took part in this invisible ritual in which a tripod was transformed into a throne as a cloud rose up into the
body of the priestess? And why did the prophetic inspiration
become a *pneuma enthousiastikon*, an *anathymia*, in the sanctuary of the Pythian Apollo?

Let us briefly review the parameters of the question. Prophetic enthusiasm, regardless of whether its source was the
Earth or Apollo, was a form of inspiration that required the
Pythia to be a virgin. The consultation was not visible to all. As
a ritual it was virtually never represented. There is no physical
evidence for the existence of the Delphic *pneuma*. Nevertheless,
a number of important authors give an account of a typical consultation. Faced with these diverse elements, we might dismiss
them as arbitrary and of dubious authority, or we might suspect
an artifice or sham designed to hide an unnatural procedure.[11]
Two questions come to mind. First, is there no other image in
all of Greek literature at least *comparable* to that of the Pythia
seated on a tripod receiving a gaseous exhalation through her

genitals? Second, the actual nature of the consultation was hidden from view, censored, banned from representation in iconography and theater. Can this be interpreted as a genuine and classical instance of censorship, a veil drawn over the spectacle to which it alludes? If these questions are pertinent, the criteria of archaeology cease to be paramount. To answer them, moreover, we must cast our net more broadly and look beyond the literature concerned exclusively with the Delphic oracle as such.

Let us take for our guide Pausanias, who makes an important observation about the oracle, namely, that the center of divination at Delphi was always staffed exclusively by women.[12] Let us also listen carefully to Lamprias, whom Plutarch shows discussing the Pythia as a physician might have done.[13] And let us attend to the church fathers, ever so sensitive to the obscene aspects of the prophetic ceremony. But above all, let us not overlook the assertions of Longinus,[14] who is able to see clearly what the chaste Plutarch obliges us ever so cautiously to infer. Their testimony permits us to turn now, without too abrupt a transition, to a body of knowledge, ancient but of uncertain origin, concerning the female body: the gynecological treatises of the *Corpus Hippocraticum*.

TRADITIONALLY identified as the work of Cnidian physicians,[15] the texts devoted to the nature and diseases of women occupied an important place in the medical library. Interest in the anatomy, physiology, and above all pathology of women derived from the value and purpose ascribed to procreation. Although physicians did not hesitate to suggest various contraceptive techniques and methods of abortion,[16] they were convinced that for a woman health was identical with fertility and maternity. In contrast to Soranus, who would extol the hygienic virtues of permanent virginity,[17] the Hippocratic physicians stressed the limitless benefits of regular intercourse and pregnancy. Normal menstruation, proper moistening of the uterine tissue, correct size of the cervix, and correct position of the uterus in the body were all desirable and probable consequences of a timely and prolific marriage.[18]

In addition to congenital malformations (such as atresia) and accidental injuries, female pathology included maladies caused by prolonged sexual abstinence. These "virgins' ailments" also affected chaste widows, and the proven remedy was productive intercourse. Consider one example: "If the womb moves toward the liver, the woman immediately loses her voice; she gnashes her teeth, and her skin turns black. These changes can attack a previously healthy woman without warning. They occur primarily in spinsters and in young widows with children who resent widowhood."[19] For the widow there is effective medication, but "the best remedy is to become pregnant"; the spinster should be convinced to marry, and in the meantime she should take wine with conyrine and castoreum.[20] Intercourse and pregnancy are proper treatments in other cases too: if a patient suffering from dropsy "gives birth, she will get well," for example.[21] The conception of a viable fetus is the natural and decisive remedy that the physician works to achieve: many of the prescriptions deal with the treatment of sterility. This may be the result of a hidden defect (such as a membrane obstructing the cervix or a cervical opening that is too wide or smooth), which the practitioner must discover by performing various tests, or it may be the painful consequence of serious disease.

To treat the many afflictions of the uterus Greek gynecologists used preparations based on herbal and animal medicines as well as refined products such as honey and wine. These were administered either orally, in vaginal pessaries, or, quite frequently, by a method that Soranus would soon advise against, namely vaginal fumigation.

Dry or moist, warm vapors were used in the treatment of most varieties of uterine disease. Ingredients ranging from cassia to castoreum, from myrtle leaves to powdered horn, were pounded, mixed, and heated, sometimes directly on the coals, at other times in bronze or earthenware vessels. When fumes began to rise, the patient, having carefully insulated herself from the heat, was instructed to seat herself with her legs spread over the mouth of the vessel. Occasionally the procedure was described in detail: "If you wish to administer a fumigation, separate the chaff from the wheat, mill it fine, make a very slow fire of vine shoots, place the mixture in a plate and the plate in a round vessel, place rags all around so that the woman is comfortable, and order her to spread her legs as far apart as possible and to sit on the vessel . . . and forbid her to have sexual relations with her husband as long as she remains in treatment."[22] Or consider this recommendation: "The fumigation should be done over cow dung. The dung should be arranged in the shape of a pitcher of oil. The bottom should be thin. The dung should be dry. The fire should be of vine shoots, and the dung should be placed on it. The woman should sit over a large caldron to receive the fumigation."[23] Or this one: "Administer a fumigation with the aid of a gourd. When the apparatus is set up, pour seawater into the vessel, add some leeks, fit the tube to the gourd, and seal it well so that none of the vapor is lost. Then pass the tube through a square seat of plaited rush so that it protrudes by the width of two fingers. Then heat with coals and take care in placing the seat so that the woman is not burned."[24] Or, for upward displacement of the uterus: "This malady must be treated first with the following vapor bath: take some wild figs and add them to wine, heat the mixture, and place a crab apple over the mouth of the vessel in which the wine is being heated. The core of the apple should be slit and hollowed out, and the small end should be pared away so that it can be fitted over the mouth in the same way that a goatskin is plugged. The odor will pass through this small opening to reach the womb."[25]

Sometimes the method is less elaborate. Instead of arranging vessels, gourds, seats, and the like, the physician simply "digs a hole, roasts grape seeds, throws the ashes in the hole, moistens the seeds with fragrant wine, and, having seated the woman over the hole, administers the fumigation."[26] Frequently the vapor treatment was combined with other therapies, but in difficult cases of sterility it was the principal remedy. In intervals between pessaries and potions "the woman must always be in fumigation, for it is fumigation that softens the parts and causes the humor to flow."[27] It made no difference whether the difficulty in conceiving a child was caused by a cervix that was too narrow or too wide or by a displacement or malformation of the womb: fumigation was invariably the correct treatment.[28] The only side effect to worry about came from abuse of the method: an excess of heat could make the moist cervix so soft that it could no longer retain sperm.[29] In addition, according to the author of the *Aphorisms*, fumigations used to promote menstrual discharge could cause headaches.[30]

Vapors were in fact useful in all phases of a woman's physiological existence. If a young girl's periods did not begin on time, she would experience a syndrome of fever, pain, hunger, vomiting, and *mania*. There might also be a shift in the position of the womb. "In that case warm sheepskins must be applied to the belly and hot fumigations must be applied to the genitals to the greatest possible extent, with the woman seated above the mouth of an amphora."[31] When labor was difficult because, for example, the uterus filled with air, an attempt should be made to deflate it by using a syrup made from goat's or lamb's liver. If the desired degree of distension was not obtained, however, the next thing to try was vaginal inhalation of fumes from resin, cumin, or pine bark.[32] If the womb remained painful and inflamed after childbirth, it could be soothed with smoke from rose leaves, cinnamon, and cassia after the woman had been swaddled in covers and seated over an earthenware vessel.[33]

The mechanism by which this panacea operated was quite simple, because the substances used fell into two categories: those that smelled good and those that smelled bad. The many ingredients mentioned in the fumigation recipes were distinguished only by their odor and by corollary characteristics such as bitterness or sweetness and irritant or emollient qualities.

A. Thivel argues that fumigations and other "invasive" procedures such as bleeding, incision, and cauterization are to be blamed on the primitive state of Cnidian medical knowledge: "Among 'primitives' and even in the magical medicine practiced in higher civilizations, techniques such as incision, bleeding, cauterization, and fumigation with acrid-smelling vapors are used to drive out the evil spirit that is tormenting the sufferer."[34] In fact, in the special case of gynecological fumigation, the treatment is directed not at a spirit or humor but at an organ. Hot, odoriferous vapors are inhaled through the vagina as a means of restoring the womb to its proper place, to its proper orientation, or to its proper degree of moistness. As a general rule, it was essential that the womb be in good condition and the cervix straight and unobstructed.[35] Fumigation with garlic and seal oil, for example, could restore and open up a collapsed uterus.[36] Such an obnoxious concoction, however, would force the cervix upward, and a second fumigation would be necessary, this time with fennel, which "has the effect of drawing the womb downward." If the womb descended too near the vulva, emetics would be administered to trigger renewed retching, and fetid fumes would be directed into the womb "until it regains its proper place."[37]

In a body endangered by a mobile organ subject to many different stimuli,[38] odor acted in a predictable way: it either attracted or repelled a mouth (*stoma*) that desired or rejected the scents that were offered to it. Some vapors were administered from above, others from below: "When the womb is too low, fetid fumigations must be introduced below and aromatic ones under the nostrils."[39] Conversely, if the uterus drifted upward and caused suffocation, "fetid substances should be burned under the nostrils, but slowly (for if they are burned in abundance the womb will move down and cause other troubles), and perfumed substances should be burned below."[40] R. Joly sees fumigation as a striking instance of the tenacity of a particular epistemological obstacle: animism.[41] And Soranus long ago inveighed against misguided physicians who treated the womb as though it were an animal with a keen sense of smell, drawn to fragrant odors and repelled by vile stench.[42] But that is not the whole story: the practice of exposure to vapors implies a conception of the body as a sponge, a soft, porous tissue that vapors could impregnate as they would impregnate a fabric. And this was the Greek view of the texture of the female body.[43]

Clearly, then, there is a body of Greek literature that describes a posture very much like the traditional posture of the Pythia: a woman seated over a caldron with her legs spread, ready to receive the vapors. To be sure, neither the *anathymiasis* of Lamprias nor the *pneuma enthousiastikon* of Strabo was an artificial fumigation, nor were the vessels recommended by the Hippocratic physicians tripods. Nevertheless, so suggestive an analogy between Apollo's priestess and women suffering from diseases of the uterus is worthy of attention. Perhaps it is from the standpoint of healing that we ought to approach a difficult question that arises in all studies of prophetic enthusiasm: namely, was the Pythia a hysteric in the Greek sense? Perhaps we should keep healing fumigation in mind as we seek an answer.

Let us first consider the value of fumigations as therapy. As we have seen, fumigation treatments were various, and the attractive or repellent nature of a substance's odor was what determined its effect on the movement of the uterus. Soranus would give a very precise definition of hysterical suffocation as a syndrome characterized by an upward shift of the uterus toward the respiratory tract, as if the internal migration of the womb caused strangulation and the purpose of vapors was to cause it to descend back to its proper place.[44] Now, the signs of suffocation are not unrelated to the portrait of a possessed and sputtering Pythia as painted by Origen, John Chrysostom, Lucan, and the scholiast of Aristophanes (*Plutus* 39): "When the womb is in the liver and hypocondrium and causing suffocation, the whites of the eyes are visible and the woman turns cold and even livid. She grinds her teeth, saliva flows from her mouth, and she resembles an epileptic."[45] The Pythia is here depicted as a strangling, drooling woman whose body writhes amid rising coils of dark smoke: it is as if a well-known image of a traditional therapy had been distorted for the purpose of representing the disease that it was intended to cure. No truth is spoken here; everything is perverted. But Plutarch's virgin, the *nymphē* who offers herself to the god as an empty vessel and who receives the *pneuma enthousiastikon* as a medication, may perhaps find a balm in the vapor that purifies her and causes her to speak. Plutarch, speaking through Lamprias without contradiction by any of the other participants in the discussion, says that the oracle is believed by priests and consultants to be the effect of a perfume that emanates from the adytum much as water bubbles from a fountain. It is this odor, this *pneuma*, that turns mute (*alalos*) and evil (*kakos*) when an unknown obstruction blocks its path within the body of the priestess.

I do not think that any more can be made of the similarity between the Pythia and the patients of Hippocratic physicians. What we have found so far has enabled us to answer one of the two questions raised earlier about the enigma of Apollo's priestess. The second question remains: Was the shroud thrown over the method of consultation with the oracle a form of censorship? I shall continue to rely on the same analogy in formulating an answer.

As Euripides said, as Plutarch repeated, and as the story of the first midwife shows,[46] the Greeks themselves considered female diseases to be obscene and occult. Hence the treatments for those diseases were also indecent, especially vaginal fumigations. Joly, who stresses the degree to which the paradigm of healing intercourse explains the pharmaceutical uses of testicles and semen, calls attention to the "sexual theme" as unambiguously manifested in one passage of the Hippocratic *Diseases of Women:*

> After [the womb has been drained of pus] and the woman has had time to breathe, take a dry gourd, pierce a hole through both the bottom and the top in the same manner as in the shaft of the injector, except for the small end; it should be slightly smaller in size than the virile member. Place it in a vessel filled with wine. The wine should be very fragrant, very dry, and very old. Place a shiny black rock in the wine as well. On top of this place a piece of white copper that has been fashioned in the shape of a gourd. Have the woman assume the proper position above the gourd that has been made to resemble the virile member, which should extend two fingers' width beyond the outer sheath of copper.[47]

Joly remarks that "commentary would be superfluous." This text states clearly what even a modern interpreter sensitive to the images that have shaped the medical imagination would hesitate to write. With all requisite gravity the gynecologist names the object that is inevitably called to mind by the apparatus required for feminine inhalations, confirming that for the Greeks, the health of the female body was essentially linked to sexual relations.

If the Pythia as portrayed by both anonymous and learned tradition reminded people of such indecent practices, then there was good reason for the silence that surrounded her body and the darkness that hid it from view. More than that, Longinus suggests that the priestess on her tripod carried the god's word within her as an embryo: she was pregnant (*enkumōn*), impregnated by the divine power. Moreover, her seated posture was the same as that assumed by Greek women in childbirth.[48] True, the Christian authors reduced the priestess to a hysteric, concentrating exclusively on her *mania*, her extravagant possession. Nevertheless, the ancient Pythia bore discreet but undeniable signs of obscenity—so discreet that, apart from Plutarch's allusions and Longinus' reference, only silence surrounds the Apollonian mantic at Delphi. The Greeks ask us to view the oracular pronouncement as the effect of impregnation by a god, hence as something akin to giving birth, perhaps an "oral birth" that natural fumigation by the vapors emanating from the earth somehow associated with normal, physical birth, which in pagan Greece was still an indecent occurrence. Among the images that Plato insisted must be conscientiously censured in the theater were those of women ill or mad or in labor.[49] And more specifically, Plato was thinking of a particular portrayal of a woman giving birth in a temple, for he was here criticizing Euripides for depicting Auge, a young priestess of Athena, giving birth in that goddess's temple.

A joyful, positive, creative moment, the birth of an infant was also an occasion for defilement and a time of immodest bodily suffering that had to be kept hidden from view. Hence what scarce information we have about the talking Pythia in a sense justifies its own scarcity. It evokes what ought not to be seen: an inspired pregnant woman in a temple—a woman who simultaneously opens her mouth and her vagina.

~6~

The Tortoise and
the Courtesan

A N ANCIENT TRADITION, coherent in its images but scattered through a variety of disciplines, tends to identify the various orifices of the female body or to characterize them as interchangeable. Physicians, philosophers, zoologists, historians, and mythologists gave varying interpretations of an analogy that seemed rooted in the configuration of the body itself and reflected in the signs and rules of sexuality.

The lexicon of Hippocratic medicine exhibits an early crystallization of this tradition: the upper and lower portions of the female body are shown to be symmetrical through the use of identical terms to describe the parts of both. The mouth (*stoma*) through which food is ingested and from which speech emanates corresponds to the "mouth" (*stoma*) of the uterus.[1] A narrow orifice, the latter is nevertheless equipped with lips that close, just as the lips of the upper mouth are sealed in silence. The image was so apt that it even entered the lexicon of Aristotelian biology, which in other respects was not particularly susceptible to the gastric connotations of the female apparatus.[2]

In the realm of *coniugalia praecepta*, or marital ethics, which formed an integral part of the philosophical literature from Plato's severely "gynoeconomical" chapters[3] to Plutarch's short treatise, the female mouth was an object requiring explicit legislation. A married woman was supposed to speak only to her husband and through her husband. It was he who conversed with her and who spoke to others in her stead, transposing words that were never to be spoken outside the couple's realm into a key better suited to his nobler instrument.[4] A law respecting this principle was established by Numa, Rome's founding monarch, who was greatly concerned with the mores of women. Wiser than Lycurgus, his Spartan counterpart, "Numa showed married women the same consideration and respect as Romulus, who had wanted them to be honored because of their abduction. He insisted on great modesty, forbade all indiscreet activities (*polypragmosynē*), and taught them to be sober, to abstain entirely from wine, and to say nothing even about necessary things when their husbands were not present."[5] Associated with amorous pleasure as well as with unbridled intimacy, wine was banished from the mouth of woman as strictly as she was enjoined to speak only to her husband and no one else, as if discretion in speech and privacy of conversation were the "upper-body" counterparts and guarantors of an absolute fidelity that began with the genitals.

It was unthinkable for a woman to mingle with company except at her husband's side, where she was expected to share his pleasures until, with tactful politeness, she withdrew from the conversation and left a table at which her presence had become superfluous.[6] Plutarch intimates that women were invited to their husbands' banquets so that they would not learn to amuse themselves alone. The proper thing for them to do, however, was to withdraw at the appropriate time, leaving it to the courtesans and (female) musicians to attend to the drunken amusements of a man temporarily given over to pleasures, to a *hēdonē* unworthy of marriage.[7]

Notwithstanding the malicious words of Herodotus, a woman did not remove her modesty along with her chiton. For Plutarch even an unclothed body could be chaste.[8] Chastity was to be maintained even in the marriage bed, which was the only place where the body should ever be naked.[9] With carefully studied gesture and awareness of her vulnerable parts a woman could hide her body without artifice. The two greatest chinks in her natural armor were her two orifices: two mouths, which were supposed to be kept closed at all times except for the purposes of eating, speaking, making love, or giving birth—as well as for laughing, for a woman must be ready to enjoy herself and banter good-naturedly in the company of her husband.[10]

Anything that passed through the mouth of a woman that was not intended for her master and judge was a sign of instability. At once corrupt and vain, women's words were marked by foolish ignorance and bogus knowledge, such as idle incantations and talk of supposed magic potions.[11] A man had to remain always on his guard. He was supposed to pour his philosophical knowledge into all his conversations and discussions. Just as he fertilized his wife's body, so must he deposit in her soul "the seed of the noblest discourses"; for "it is said that no woman can make a child without the participation of a man: the fleshy, amorphous embryonic masses that form by themselves as a result of corruption are called moles [mylai]. Care must be taken to make sure that nothing like this takes place in the soul of a woman." Left to their own devices, women continually conceive deformed and incongruous creatures.[12]

Aristotle, citing Sophocles, is categorical: "Silence is a woman's glory [kosmos]."[13] In an anthropology that accords all privilege to articulate, rational language, this is nothing but pure misogyny. For Aristotle a human being is human not only because he can indicate pleasure and pain with his voice but also because he is capable of discoursing on justice and injustice.[14] An anthrōpos is superior to the animals because he alone can use intelligent and effective speech in place of physical weapons.[15] In the female, however, there is an inversion of values: for her, virtue takes the specific form of silence. The contrast is a systematic one. In a city governed by political speech, woman must wrap herself in discretion: the image of the kosmos once again evokes the idea of an immaterial gown, an elegance of virtue.[16] At the opposite extreme, in a city in the grip of tyranny in which the free men are mute, impotent, and forced into clandestinity, the women become as ignoble as slaves when they avail themselves of their powers of speech for the basest of purposes. Cravenly, servilely, they denounce their husbands.[17] They speak up when political activity is silenced, when the city is subjected to the force of a tyrant and turned into the desert of silence evoked by the sons of Creon in *Antigone*.[18]

Speaking out outside the private setting is one of the forms of *anesis*, the disorder typical of gynocracies. In Sparta, a city that was permanently in a state of war and from which men remained absent for long periods, women were left to their own devices. Their lives were filled with lust in two senses: erotic abandon and avidity for riches.[19] Plutarch does not share Aristotle's view that the women of Sparta were powerful, rich, and lascivious, veritable mistresses of their husbands,[20] but he does criticize them for claiming too much freedom: "They were overly bold and behaved with a very masculine audacity, primarily toward their own husbands. They in fact enjoyed full power to govern their houses and in public affairs gave their opinion on matters of the utmost importance."[21] Such eloquent female counselors were a far cry from the mute, sedentary, tortoiselike women with whom Numa had been shrewd enough to supply Rome by cultivating the femininity and *kosmion* of young girls.[22] For Roman girls speaking in public was such a monstrous thing that it required an explanation from the oracle.[23] Spartan women not only spoke as much as their husbands but as young girls had learned indifference to nudity, "which, being chaste and devoid of any sign of libertine behavior, had nothing indecent about it"[24] but still earned these beautiful athletes a very bad poetic reputation.[25] *Phainomerides* ("showing their thighs") and *andromaneis* ("crazy about men"): such were the images evoked by the *parthenoi* of Sparta, despite Lycurgus' acknowledged pedagogical concerns.[26]

Sparta was thus a city in which women were both too much like men and too remote from them. Equal education and distance meant that women's lives were not under conjugal control. Plato, though interested in Spartan education, remarked that it was insufficiently severe toward certain forms of private behavior. In particular, the lawgiver had been seriously negligent in failing to institute public meals so that "the very half of the race which is generally predisposed by its weakness to undue secrecy and craft" might be compelled to "take their meat and drink in public."[27] A city is half dead and twice threatened if the female sex does not fully abide by the rules that hold society together. Just as men must eat in public, in halls specially set aside for the purpose, girls and their mothers ought to dine with the servants in other nearby halls "under presidents of either sex, whose appointed function is daily to dismiss the tables after review and inspection of the conduct of the company."[28] An absolute symmetry limned in law must be enforced and must regulate every detail of daily behavior and private habit. Nothing is to be exempt from public scrutiny and judgment, and no movement is to be left to chance, arbitrariness, or secrecy. In sum, the legislator's most difficult task will be to draw the female mouth toward the light, woman being a race that loves darkness and falsehood.[29]

Perhaps it is best, however, to leave the utopian city of the *Laws* for the city that was its pretext and object, the familiar Athens of illicit loves and illegitimate children. In a fourth-century trial known to us from Isaeus the issue was a daughter's right to inherit her father's property.[30] The sister of the deceased, represented by one of his sons, challenged the daughter's legitimacy: the mother was allegedly a courtesan and not a duly married wife. The marriage had not been registered in writing, so the evidence in the case consisted of people's memories. Among the points cited to contest the legitimacy of the marriage was the mother's alleged frequentation of banquets, even when it was in the company of her husband, because "a legitimate wife . . . was not seen accompanying her husband to a banquet or feasting with strangers, particularly those who arrived without introductions."[31] In a city where private life attracted public notice only when laws were transgressed and where dining with others was a form not of discipline but of sociability, a woman who shared a table with men could only be assumed to share their beds as well. This woman dined with anyone who happened by, whether or not he had an introduction: she was a courtesan, a *hetaira*, who belonged to any man who desired her.[32] Eating practices were cited as signs of sexual behavior. In addition to the banquets she liked to attend, Neera was also assailed with evidence of ritual meals that never took place: the wedding dinner that a husband would have offered his wife and the feast of Thesmophoria.[33] Unfortunately, in attempting to prove that she was the daughter of a lawfully married citizen of Athens, the child of this immodest hetaera was unable to avail herself of the kind of evidence cited by Kiron's nephew, whose case was also analyzed by Isaeus:[34] "When our father took her in marriage, he gave a wedding dinner to which he invited three of his friends along with his close relatives. He thus staged a solemn banquet for the members of his phratry as befit their status."[35] Moreover, the women of the deme chose her to preside over the Thesmophoria.[36]

A possible objection to this line of argument is that the association of the mouth with the genitals does not apply exclusively to the female body. Modern anthropology has made us aware of the metaphoric link between sexual relations and alimentary ones. In Australia, in the writings of the church fathers, and—as Claude Lévi-Strauss observes—in contemporary French slang, food and sex "are immediately conceived as analogous."[37] The remark is such a commonplace that it needs no illustration. Lévi-Strauss's train of thought is similar to Hippocrates', although his reasoning moves in the opposite direction:

> The most familiar and probably the most commonplace equation represents the male as eater and the female as eaten. In myth, however, the opposite formulation occurs frequently in the theme of the *vagina dentata*, which is significantly "encoded" in alimentary terms, that is, in direct style

(thus confirming the law of mythic thought that the transformation of a metaphor culminates in a metonymy). It is possible, moreover, that the *vagina dentata* theme reflects not an inverted but a direct perspective in Eastern philosophy.[38]

An object of appetite rather than a *vagina dentata,* the female partner can in theory be represented in terms of an alimentary code just as readily as the male. The symbolic relation concerns not bodily images but two forms of interaction, sexual and alimentary. Lévi-Strauss points out that "the least common denominator between sexual coupling and the union of eater and eaten is that both effect a *conjunction through complementarity.*"[39] If sexual difference is seen in light of interaction, of conjunction, it is inevitable that attention will be focused on the active protagonist, the eater, the male. The idea that a lifeless dish can transform itself into a hungry mouth immediately takes on fearsome connotations: the cutting maw.

Were the female mouth and genitals subject to analogous symbolic treatment in Greece? Recent work on Hesiod and Semonides has revealed the archaic image of the *gastēr* woman, whose ravenous appetite and desire make her presence ruinous.[40] This is an image constructed deliberately for polemical purposes. The medical and philosophical literature, whose concern is to reduce the difference rather than magnify it, is sometimes less explicit. Some physicians offered assurances that the uterus was an organ like the rest.[41] Plato offers an even more shining example. The minute detail of legislation concerning marriage and the family in the *Laws* reflects the effort to establish a city in which all that is feminine—falsehood, dissipation, irrationality—is neutralized. In Isaeus the wedding banquet seems to stand for female behavior in opposition to that signified by the social banquet. In the *Laws* the wedding banquet is also discussed, but no attempt is made to show husband and wife at the same time, both sober and sharing an identical awareness of their conjugal mission: "And we may lay down one sole rule for all matches. A man should 'court the tie' which is for the city's good, not that which most takes his own fancy."[42] The Athenian who imagines the laws of the Platonic city has very clear ideas. From the number of guests to invite to a banquet to the number of children a couple ought to have, from the quantity of wine to serve to the size of the dowry, everything must be determined by common public criteria: "Balance and due proportion are out of all comparison more excellent than an undiluted [*akraton*] purity."[43] Moreover, the consecration of the marriage should take place without drunkenness. The spirit should be master of the body, and attention should be focused on the children that the couple are preparing to produce.[44] "For in all the affairs of man's life the first step [*archē*] holds the place of a god and makes all the rest right, if but approached with the proper reverence by all concerned."[45] On that day and night[46] the banquet and the love to which it is a prelude are the mirror of the life that is about to begin. That this moment is the culmination of the great change[47] marked by marriage is a fact whose significance we discover later on, when Plato reminds us that eating, drinking, and depositing semen are the three primary human desires[48]—or at any rate the three primary desires of human beings when conceptualized without regard to their sexual differences. But the marvelous harmony of bride and groom cannot efface memories of the anatomy in the *Timaeus*, in which the uterus alone is portrayed as a mindless animal endlessly seeking to make children.[49]

Concerning the mouth that speaks, I shall cite an example drawn from the same tradition and from the work of the author who was closest to Delphi. Plutarch wrote a series of short moral monographs devoted to the values of silence, discretion, and brevity.[50] In them Apollo is depicted as the model recognized by the ancients:

> In the sanctuary of Pythian Apollo the amphictyons engraved neither the *Iliad* nor the *Odyssey* nor the paeans of Pindar but such sayings as "Know thyself," "Everything in moderation," "Make a commitment," and "Woe is near." They admired the

compactness and simplicity of expression that enclosed in a concise form a thought struck like a medal. Does not the god himself like concision, and is he not brief in his oracles? People call him Loxias because he avoids garrulousness and not because of his vagueness.[51]

For Plutarch it was unthinkable that the utterances of Apollo make use of metaphor or images to veil the truth. The enigmatic expression that had earned the god the epithet *loxos* (oblique) was in fact a kind of verbal mime all the more eloquent the more its *phōnē* was compressed. Figures of speech make things appear without really talking about them. Apollo, however, represented the divine perfection of a wisdom that had to be translated into exempla on a human scale. Further on Plutarch mentions several people memorable for the brevity of their expression. One of them in particular brings us to the crux of the connection between speech and sexuality. No disease is as dangerous, hateful, or ridiculous as garrulousness: "That is why Anacharsis, who had dined with Solon and was resting after dinner, was seen with his left hand on his virility [*meros*] and his right hand on his mouth: he believed that the tongue required a more powerful restraint, and he was right, for it would not be easy to count as many men lost through incontinence in amorous pleasures as cities and empires ruined through reve-lation of a secret."[52] Here, mouth and genitals are closely asso-ciated in the body of a man—closely but asymmetrically, for right and left are always asymmetrical. This circumstance is all the more significant because in this set of monographs garru-lousness is classified as a form of incontinence (*akrasia*).[52] It is a failure of oral self-control whose model is explicitly located in Aphrodite's domain. The semantic relationship becomes clearer if one considers the prelude to this incontinence, its phase of accumulation,[53] namely, *polypragmosynē*, the curiosity that im-pels a person to intrude into other people's affairs in an insistent and active manner. "Being curious is a form of incontinence like being adulterous, which in addition to incontinence reveals an astonishing degree of madness and stupidity." [54] The curious, the garrulous, and the adulterous deserve criticism for the same reason: failure to make proper use of a good tool. Moreover, wine is inevitably associated with this failing, for wine causes garrulousness when it is drunk improperly—that is, when it is drunk in its pure form, undiluted with water (*akratos*). [55]

IS THERE nothing specifically feminine, then, about the association between mouth and genitals? It would be a mistake to draw such a conclusion. To say that feasting, conversation, and pleasure are linked together in a context of feminine social images is possible only if there is assumed to be a more or less hidden opposition between the sexes. That is a simple fact. Yet once one has chosen a question on the basis of which to make a comparison between masculine and feminine—using the ancient method of analogy and thus without being especially zealous to uncover anything specifically feminine—it becomes increasingly exciting to look for differences. True, Plutarch distributes garrulousness and desire on the one hand, discretion, sobriety, and chastity on the other, within the same masculine universe; and Numa was full of esteem and respect for Roman matrons. But why did the king specifically forbid *women* to show garrulous curiosity (*polypragmosynē*), as if this were a risk to which women were invariably exposed? [56]

Despite all philosophical efforts to elaborate a sexually neutral anthropology, two insurmountable obstacles remained. First, there was the legacy of misogyny, a firm belief that the female was somehow flawed and obviously inferior, which was construed to mean that she posed an obscure threat. Second, there was an image that cropped up frequently and seemed to encourage distrust of woman, an image of her body, of Pandora. Thus Plutarch (my italics):

> The Roman Senate behind closed doors held a secret council that lasted several days. Since this affair, shrouded in mystery, gave rise to much speculation, *a woman, modest but still a*

woman, badgered her husband and begged him to reveal the secret. Oaths and imprecations promised her silence. In tears she called the goddesses to witness that she was not trusted. The Roman, seeking to confound her *stupidity*, said: "My wife, you have convinced me! Listen to a terrible, prodigious affair! The priests have told us that a lark has been seen flying with a golden helmet and a lance. We are considering whether this prodigy is good or bad, and we are discussing the problem with the soothsayers. But say nothing about it!" Whereupon he left for the forum. The woman immediately beckoned to the first maid who entered and, while beating her chest and tearing at her hair, said: "What misfortune for my husband and the nation! What will become of us?" She wanted the servant to ask what happened. When the other woman finally did ask, she told her everything, adding the words that always accompany all gossip: "Do not tell anyone else. Keep your mouth shut." The little maid had no sooner left her mistress than she told the story to another maid who seemed not to be busy, and the latter repeated it to her lover, who came to see her. The story thus quickly reached the forum, so quickly that it preceded the arrival of the man who had made it up.[57]

The episode has a happy ending, however, for the senator makes the requisite denials and congratulates himself on having survived his wife's verbal incontinence.[58] "He had taken precautions and protective measures in order to test his wife, as one might test a *cracked vessel* by filling it not with oil or wine but with water."[59]

Let us return to the female *stomata*, that is, to the close association of mouth and genitals expressed in the relatively stable everyday vocabulary yet seriously called into question by Aristotelian biology. The oral anatomy was associated with a coherent functional imagery. Emile Benveniste points out that the classical Greek words for pregnancy were *en gastri lambanein, syllambanein, echein* (to take, embrace, or have in the stomach).[60] This was in fact the syntagm regularly used by physicians, with a subtlety sometimes difficult to follow when they are describing the organs of digestion and childbirth. A passage from the Hippocratic *Nature of Women* will help to give some idea of a contiguity that comes close to confusion without losing its descriptive precision. It has to do with the signs of a false pregnancy: the uterus is displaced and closed up, and menstruation ceases. Under these conditions "the lower stomach [*gastēr*] swells, and inexperienced women think that they are pregnant [*en gastri echein*]. They in fact feel all that pregnant women feel until the seventh or eighth month: the abdomen swells as time goes by, the breasts sag and diminish in volume, the belly [*koiliē*] also sags, and there is no trace of milk. When the time of birth arrives, the abdomen drops and disappears. Then the womb [*hai hysterai*] contracts strongly."[61] Here, the physician has seized the opportunity provided by a false pregnancy to list the signs and symptoms of a real one. The female abdomen, a cavity that obviously is filled with nourishment, can also become full with a fetus.[62]

"To take into the belly" is clearly not a technical expression invented by physicians. It is plausible to think that the common terms for getting pregnant and gaining weight were similar in the everyday spoken language. Herodotus, for example, illustrates the nonspecialist usage when he describes the reproduction of hares and snakes: "Because the hare is hunted by animals, birds, and men, it is extremely prolific: alone among animals the female hare conceives while pregnant. Some of her young are covered with hair while in the belly [*en tēi gastri*]; others are not. Some are growing in the womb even as others are being conceived."[63] Vipers, on the other hand, are prevented from poisoning the entire world by their self-destructive behavior. Their sexual ethology is characterized by an implacable allelophagy: every birth is compensated by the death of the parents. First the male is devoured by the female at the moment he ejaculates his sperm into her. Then the female is punished in the following manner: "Avenging their father, the young, while still in the mother's belly [*en tēi gastri*], devour her, and it is by devouring her entrails that they create an exit for themselves." [64] This tragedy, repeated generation after generation, is according to Herodotus an illustration of divine wisdom,[65] but in fact it exhibits two repulsive fantasies in their most extreme form: the power of female sexuality to devour and the cannibalism of the fetus that grows by eating its mother. The female viper swallows (*diaphagei*) the male whole the instant his semen is deposited in her belly: in this female body the two mouths function in synchrony. Yet she herself becomes fodder for the offspring growing in her belly. As voracious as Hesiod's woman, the viper—her role reduced, like that of the mother in Aristotle's biology, to one of simply providing food—is a condensation of the most frightful confusion of sexuality with alimentation.[66]

P. Chantraine defines the word *gastēr* as follows: "Stomach, belly (Homer, etc.), whence the use of the word to refer to the hungry belly, gluttony, or the belly of a woman insofar as it conceives and carries a child. Finally, the curved portion of a shield, the base of a bottle (Cratinus), or a kind of sausage (*Od.*, Ar.)." [67] The universally accepted etymology is *gas-tēr*, devourer, from *graō*, with dissimilation of the two *r*'s. This etymology remains the semantic core of the term, for Chantraine emphasizes that "*gastēr* and its compounds and derivatives figure in many expressions conveying the idea of a large stomach or of gluttony, and the word does not mean either stomach, *stomachos*, or intestine, *koilia*." [68] Pregnancy concerned the belly because it made people think of the consequences of gluttony. "To take into the belly" may have been a metaphor, but its degree of lexicalization was such that it was a dead metaphor. It may have been a euphemism, but if so it nevertheless possessed the same referential pertinence that turned the adjective *aidoion* (shameful) into *to aidoion* (the shameful part), that is—beyond any doubt—the genitals. Whatever the linguistic status of *gastēr*, the word's polysemy superimposed or at any rate associated two specific images: to ingest and digest through the upper orifice, to be penetrated and caused to conceive a child through the lower.

Greek physicians were fully aware that the stomach and womb were distinct parts of the body and that sperm was not deposited in the same place as ingested food, but they did not dwell on the fact. A body grew fat when one of its mouths closed around the seed that it had swallowed. It was only in images of pregnancy that the *hystera* ("rear") could be confused with a hungry belly. When there was a need to describe the specific pathology of the uterus itself, the physicians wrote *hystera/ai* or *metra/ai*.

For gynecologists there was no need to remark upon a difference with which their hands were perfectly familiar. But when Aristotle undertook to make a systematic study of the animal kingdom and to construct a taxonomy based on the parts and functions of the healthy body, he could not accept such crude ambiguity of language. D. Lanza writes: "It can perhaps be said that the first Greek treatise on anatomy is contained in the first book of Aristotle's *Historia animalium*. Anatomical descriptions, in some cases quite extensive and complex, are not absent from the writings of Hippocrates and other physicians of the *Corpus*, who of course preceded Aristotle. But what made Aristotle's text a treatise was its primarily definitional character."[69] Like the physicians, Aristotle did not invent his terminology; but, rejecting their tolerance for ambiguity and superfluity, he worked to ascribe clear meanings to existing terms.[70] First, without giving a metalinguistic explanation, he eliminated the alimentary image from the notions of conception and pregnancy. Nowhere in his biological treatises is a woman or female animal said to "have" or "take into the belly" the offspring that she is nourishing in her uterus. As an example of Aristotle's deviation from common usage, consider his quotation from Herodotus. The passage I quoted earlier on the hare's extraordinary reproductive capacities occurs in a more austere version in both *Historia animalium* and *De generatione animalium*.[71] That Herodotus was one source for this view is not apparent from the text, but an explicit reference in the same paragraph of the *Historia animalium* suggests that this was the case. Immediately after discussing the hare, Herodotus turns to the lioness, whose offspring are said to tear the womb with their claws in order to make their way out into the light. Aristotle calls this a stupid fable:

> The lioness gives birth in the springtime, and generally she produces two cubs, with six the maximum size of the litter. Sometimes, however, she has only one cub. As for the *fable* concerning the expulsion of the offspring from the uterus during parturition, it is a piece of foolishness: it stems from the scarcity of lions, a fact for which the fable's inventor was able to find no cause. The lion genus is indeed not very common and is not found in many areas.[72]

The naturalist, who is able to identify not only the error but also the reason for it, is well aware of the account of animal procreation given in Herodotus (III.108). He is attentive to the zoological observations recorded there, and where Herodotus uses, as a physician would, the phrase "to have in the belly" to refer to pregnancy, Aristotle paraphrases him without using the word *gastēr*.[73]

For Aristotle *gastēr* denotes a part of the torso apparent to anyone who scans the exterior of the body from head to toe: "After the thorax, still on the front of the body, comes the belly, with its root, the umbilicus."[74] *Gastēr* is therefore the area of the body to which the cord that rooted the viviparous offspring in the uterus of its mother was once attached. At its center is a reminder of fetal life, a fossil of the autotrophic, almost plant-like state in which the most perfect of animals began its existence. The belly is seen from the standpoint of the child, at the other end of the omphalos. It is seen in its convexity, as a vessel that has been filled, that has drawn its *trophē* (nourishment) from the cavity of the *hysterai*. The Aristotelian theory of generation, according to which the role of the female is solely to supply food and shelter (in the form, respectively, of residual blood and uterus) to an embryo whose form is determined by the father, conceives of the child as a tiny belly directly plugged into its source of nourishment. The fetus is lodged not in an abdomen but in a well-furnished house,[75] where it is supplied with the final residue of the feminine *trophē*. The woman is passive toward both the child that feeds on her and the man who heated and congealed her menstrual blood; she eats in order to be eaten. This is no naive fantasy of a tiny creature who sucks with his mouth inside the mother's body as he will do later at her breast.[76] It is rather an account of female metabolism. What the woman swallows is digested, that is, cooked. It is transformed into blood, blood being that which is most assimilated, most essential for the body in which it circulates. Whatever surplus of blood there is has the potential to become the body of an infant. Hence the issue here is not the specialization of one part of the body in the function of oral nutrition but rather an entelechy touching on the principle and structure of the living thing.[77] Images having to do with the representation of the mother-belly remain,[78] but the female body is for Aristotle a storehouse, or, in another image, a piece of wax ready to be shaped. This image of the body is therefore incompatible with the gastric vocabulary of pregnancy. Aristotle retains the verb *syllambanein* and the noun *syllepsis*, but he will not accept the notion that this "congealing" or "conception" takes place inside a *gastēr*.[79]

Rigor does not end with purification of language, for strictly accurate nomenclature depends on a correct anatomy and physiology, carefully observed and correctly interpreted: any judgment of the meaning of a word concerns its correspondence to the thing designated.[80] The ambiguity that Aristotle is eliminating is associated with a whole series of errors, some stemming from mythology, others from incompetence. If physicians saw pregnancy as a change occurring in a belly that became full, there were stories afoot of birds that had intercourse through the mouth, of fish that swallowed semen, and of quadrupeds that gave birth through the mouth: "Hence, not seeing [the coupling] but seeing the swallowing of the milt and the eggs, even the fishermen repeat the same simple tale, so much noised abroad, as Herodotus the storyteller [*mythologos*], as if the fish were conceived by the mother's swallowing the milt."[81] In fact Herodotus gives this account of reproduction not of fish in general but of fish living in the waters of the Nile delta—gregarious fish that cannot give birth in rapidly flowing streams. For them reproduction involves a lengthy journey: "Gregarious fish are not found in large numbers in the rivers; they frequent the lakes, which they leave at the breeding season to swim in shoals to the sea. In front go the males, dropping their milt, which the females, following behind, gulp down. It is this that causes the females to conceive."[82] When the school reaches salt water, it turns around and another chase begins, the reverse of the first: females leave their eggs behind, and the males devour them. The offspring are born from the surviving eggs.[83] Thus, according to Herodotus, these fish do not have intercourse: conception takes place at a distance as the result of a desire that does not drive males toward females or vice versa but that drives all the fish unwittingly toward the sea. The mouth of the male is destructive, like that of the female viper, but the mouth of the female ingests only in order to give birth. Aristotle comments: "People do not see how impossible this is. The passage from the mouth leads to the intestines [*koilia*], not to the uterus [*hystera*]. And what goes into the intestines must be turned into nutriment, for it is concocted; the uterus, however, is plainly full of eggs, and from whence did they enter it?"[84] Such false assertions must be attributed to lack of reflection: because neither the fishermen nor the fabulist "watches . . . for the sake of knowledge,"[85] both are wrong. Fish have intercourse like all large animals not produced by spontaneous generation. Their bodies come into contact, but only for a very short time. That is why their coupling has escaped the notice of all nonphilosophical observers.[86]

"A similar story is told also of the generation of birds. Some say that the raven and the ibis unite at the mouth, and among quadrupeds that the weasel brings forth its young by the mouth; so say Anaxagoras and some of the other naturalists, speaking too superficially and without consideration."[87] As in the case of fish, behavior and anatomy are related. All birds have intercourse, though infrequently, and "these birds have a uterus like others, and their eggs can be seen close to the diaphragm."[88] As for the weasel, the uterus of the female is in much the same position as that of other quadrupeds. How could the embryo exit from the uterus by way of the mouth? "This opinion has arisen because the young of the weasel are very small, like those of the other fissipeds . . . and because they often carry the young about in their mouths."[89]

From the analogy between the mouth and the female genitals to tales of animals that give birth through the mouth, it is clear how the imagination might have confused the two *stomata* of the female body. In this context the utterances of the Pythia become plausible: her knowledge was, in keeping with the Platonic metaphor concerning the generation of speech, engendered or fathered. How was the gaping body of the prophetess, the *enkymōn,* reconciled with the protected body of the discreet *parthenos?* In terms of what concept of virginity did the Greeks think of the body of the Pythia?

II

The Virginal Body

～ 7 ～

Virgin Births

"THE JEWS disdained the beauty of virginity, which is not surprising, since they heaped ignominy upon Christ himself, who was born of a virgin. The Greeks admired and revered the virgin, but only the Church of God adored her with zeal." With these words begins John Chrysostom's *On Virginity,* which recounts the history of the prestige of *parthenia,* fully recognized by Christianity alone.[1] The work was conceived in the fourth century, at a time when the spread of monasticism forced the church fathers to define, or redefine, sexual doctrine to take account of abstinence; it belongs to a rich and polemical literary tradition.[2] Yet there is something unexpected in this text, something implicit in its opening words: it does not inveigh against the pagan gods for being obsessed with sensuality. For Chrysostom, the insidious enemy was not the paganism that had drawn Tertullian's thunder against the female body and its embellishments. Instead the target lay inside the Christian community: the extreme, indeed unhealthy, value that had come to be vested in continence and virginity.

Sectarian rigorism had for some time been practiced and advocated by the followers of Tatian, who stoutly denied the possibility of salvation for the first man. Since then, contempt for matter and repudiation of the body had developed a monstrous and blasphemous counterfeit: *enkrateia,* or continence, the prime Stoic and Christian value, had degenerated into heresy. The encratites, extremist heirs of gnostic asceticism, were guilty of an error that was particularly grave and pernicious because it perverted a fundamental virtue by undermining the dogma of the Creation.[3] "I will not call the encratites virgins," says Chrysostom.[4] "They are girls who indulge in a hirsute, filthy, and repulsive chastity, the only reason for which is misguided judgment. Their excess of asceticism is based on the idea that matter is metaphysically wicked because its creator is not the supreme God but a demiurge who acted without the knowledge of the supreme God and in opposition to him."[5] Hence for them to embrace absolute abstinence meant to take a heterodox position: earthly life was unclean, hence unworthy of reproduction.

In their blind worship of continence, the encratites failed to make the necessary distinction between guilty sexuality and conjugal devotion. Chrysostom levels a reproach at them that has the force of anathema: "You refuse to heed the word of Christ transmitted through the mouth of Paul, namely, that marriage is honored by all and that the marriage bed is free of taint."[6] If *parthenia* is to appear meritorious in the eyes of the church, it must reflect a renunciation. A girl who wishes to remain a virgin must first be persuaded that marriage is meritorious and blessed. Then and only then will she be ennobled and sanctified by her wish to forgo its attractions. Otherwise that wish is heresy of the most sordid kind, which camouflages itself with filthy garments and unkempt hair. It is a theological error of extreme arrogance which assumes the guise of virtue. The virginal encratites are more corrupt than lascivious women.[7]

John Chrysostom's view of virginity might appear to be both old-fashioned and useless for understanding the Greek conception of *parthenia*. Hellenists aware of the dangers of establishing a nonexistent continuity between the pagan *parthenos* and the Christian virgin—a sacrosanct scruple—have preferred other approaches. The great moralist of the East, who averted his eyes in horror from a church in which false virgins sought refuge and looked kindly upon the Greeks, the first exemplars of a pre-Marian form of devotion, was the very model of a bad historian. Note, however, that Chrysostom's treatise is not concerned solely with a virginity (in the sense of purity of soul and integrity of body) of girls in general. The problem with the encratites is that they risk discrediting a very particular virginity, that of Mary, virgin and mother. Her glorious body, in which felicitous chastity found fulfillment in childbirth, was insulted by those who confused voluptuous pleasure with the vocation of motherhood by indiscriminately condemning both. The Jews had demonstrated their disdain for Christ's virgin mother by putting her son to death. To the childless virgins who populated the convents of Cappadocia, the virgin with child was the very model of perfection. And according to Chrysostom the Greeks were the first to recognize the value of that very special *parthenia* that included motherhood.

In the second century Justin proposed a demonology that explained pagan legends in terms of biblical prophecies. The birth of Jesus Christ was prefigured not only by a line in Isaiah ("Behold, a young woman shall conceive and bear a son, and shall call his name Immanuel")[8] but also by any number of Greek legends in which a child is born to a *parthenos*. Since the demons were aware that Christ "would be born of a virgin and ascend to heaven by his own power," they invented the figure of Perseus to confuse people.[9] The son of a virgin seduced and impregnated by the sacred rain, equipped with wings that carried him up to heaven, he was alleged to be a clumsy and diabolical prefiguration of the Savior.

Faced with the mystery of Christ's virgin mother, some Christian exegetes sought help from Greek mythology. Others, such as Basil of Caesarea, turned to ancient natural history. Basil, said to have been the author of an important treatise *On True Virginity,*[10] upon which the doctrine of immaculate conception was based, held that vultures were impregnated by the wind, as zoologists were well aware.[11]

For readers of Isaiah and Paul, Greece was therefore the country in which, even before the birth of Christ, *parthenia* was deemed compatible with childbirth. Paradoxically, Hellenists today, by adopting a wholly modern view of the matter, have come to consider virgin birth in antiquity as proof that the pagan concept of virginity was radically different from ours. The Greek concept of *parthenia* looks different, however, if we adopt the point of view of ancient Christians in search of a tradition within which to situate the birth of the son of God. The Greek concept seems strange to us because it encompassed two possibilities that we regard as contradictory: a child could be born to a *parthenos,* yet penetration of her body by a male member was incompatible with *parthenia.*

Hellenists who have studied the problems of sexuality, age groups, and rites of passage have uncovered an important fact: the Greek word *parthenos* does not unambiguously signify the perfect integrity implicit in our word *virgin.* Claude Calame notes: "This term [virgin], which we use along with the words *maiden* and *adolescent girl,* should not be allowed to mislead. In Greece it conveyed a concept of virginity quite different from the one impressed upon our culture by twenty centuries of Marian piety. It actually referred to the peculiar status of the young women who, though pubescent, was not yet married."[12] Determined by age and marital status, virginity was thus a stage through which every woman passed on her way to full social integration. It coincided with nubility and implied proximity to as well as psychological readiness for marriage. A temporal and teleonomic notion, the word *parthenos,* we are told, simply denoted the expectant hiatus between childhood and *gamos.*

Angelo Brelich, who never pauses in his *Paides e parthenoi* to discuss the definition of *parthenos,* briefly sketches a similar view. His chapter on initiations of women in Athens and Brauron is titled "Le fanciulle ateniesi" (Athenian maidens). The use of a word that vaguely suggests a chaste adolescence allowed Brelich not to choose between *ragazza* (girl) and *vergine* (virgin). Elsewhere the word *parthenos* is ambivalently and ambiguously translated either as *vergine* in quotes or as *giovane donna non sposata* (unmarried young woman), suggesting in a sly but unilluminating way that the different senses of the word are somehow obviously synonymous.[13]

In a chapter devoted to the ritual of *arkteia*, Henri Jeanmaire more or less set the pattern for such equivocation; the young female Athenians who "play the she-bear" are also young virgins whose consecration to Artemis "was understood as expiation for the murder of the sacred animal."[14] Jeanmaire is forced to take note of this additional qualification, omitted from the definition of the *parthenos* simply as a girl of a certain age awaiting marriage, because one of the texts on the Artemisian ritual contains an unambiguous formulation: the *parthenoi* must serve as canephorae before marrying in order to satisfy the goddess, for otherwise Artemis would have been offended by the loss of their virginity.[15] Brelich quotes the same passage, and he, too, is obliged to mention a "perdita della virginità" (loss of virginity).[16]

Whereas the word *parthenos* tends to arouse skepticism in nonreligious interpreters and to call for cautious handling, it is not easy to capture the meaning of the abstract noun *parthenia* with a purely sociological definition. It is something subject to seizure (*lambanein*),[17] a treasure that one guards (*phylassein*),[18] a value that must be respected (*tērein*).[19] A seducer offers gifts in exchange for this prize,[20] which he unwraps (*lyein*) with the first embrace.[21] Pollux singles out those marriages in which the bride is intact and provides this gloss: "People say *diakoreusai* for 'taking the virginity of a virgin,' as Aristophanes does, for example, and *diapartheneuetai*, as Herodotus said."[22] When Pindar in his eighth *Isthmian Ode* attributed to Themis the wish that the daughter of Nereus, the future mother of Achilles, "conquered by love of a hero, loosen the charming tether of her virginity," it is not easy to understand the point of the image if virginity refers to nothing more than an age group. The pertinence of *parthenia* is not limited to any one period of a woman's life but is associated with a very definite attitude toward sexuality: in Euripides' *Trojan Women* Hecuba wins her father's permission to remain where she is, "so much does she flee the bed."[22] Virginity is *asterganōr*—it does not love the male.[24] It can turn from expectation of marriage to repudiation. In any case it is a separate existence, which is ended by contact with the male sex.

This interpretation of *parthenos* deserves a closer look, for it is supposed to rest on an irrefutable argument. The word cannot possibly refer to a woman who shuns all sexual activity, we are told, because its derivative *parthenios* (or *parthenias*) means "child of a *parthenos.*"[25] In literature countless children born to "virgins" bear witness to a conception of virginity that had nothing to do with the body or sex: the Partheniai of Sparta; Parthenopaeus, son of Atalanta; Asclepius, son of Coronis; Evadne, daughter of Pitane, and Iamus, son of Evadne; Ion, son of Creusa; Telephus, son of Augeus—Homeric heroes. The list may be long because, as Pausanias points out, to have a mother and two fathers—a divine seducer and a man who marries the *parthenos* and adopts her offspring—is typical of the hero, in the specific case alluded to by Pausanias of Parnassus, son of Cleodorus, Poseidon, and Cleopompe.[26] If this view is correct, Pindar's imputation to Pitane of a "virgin birth"[27] is not a bold oxymoron, since the words would have been a commonplace reference to the labor of an unwed mother. And Coronis, who offended Apollo by rejecting his caresses in favor of a mortal's, and whose body had experienced not only sex but also pregnancy, nevertheless remains a *parthenos,* a *korē.*[28] Making love outside the marriage bed, before a marriage has taken place in front of witnesses at the "nymphic table," did not result in any change in the name by which a young girl was called. She became a woman (*gynē*) only in matrimony, as the *gynē* of her husband.

Sophocles uses this change of nomenclature to characterize the two female characters who share Heracles' attentions in the *Women of Trachis:* whereas Deianira has crossed the line by taking a new name in that crucial moment when "instead of *parthenos* one is called *gynē*,"[29] the intruder Iole, though seduced and wedded, continues to be called *parthenos.* In the final scene Heracles, devoured by the fire in the magic tunic, confides his last wishes to his son, Hyllus. First he begs Hyllus to end his suffering by burning him, and then he orders him to marry his young mistress out of filial piety: "If you wish to act piously by remembering the oaths you made to your father, take this girl for your wife and do not disobey me. Let no man but you possess the woman who once lay at my side. It is your duty, my son, to marry her."[30] Because Iole was only the lover of the master of the house, she is a *parthenos.*[31] Hyllus will be the man who changes her name by making her his wife.

Of all the unwed mothers in Greek mythology, the most memorable is the fleet huntress who, while continuing to embody the very paradigm of Artemisian solitude, became the eponymous mother of a celebrated but unfortunate hero: namely, Atalanta, mother of Parthenopaeus.[32] Her portrait as an archer hunting the Aetolian boar stood at the center of her son's shield, the arms of her house, in Euripides' words, yet not enough protection to permit the young man to return to the side of his strange mother, the *korē* with the handsome bow.[33] Watching the handsome youth advance full of pride in his escort, Antigone, the virgin in the enemy camp, made a terrible vow: "I hope that Artemis, ranging the hills with his mother, strikes with her shaft and destroys him who comes to plunder my town."[34] As an emblematic figure in Euripides' *Phoenician Women*, this young woman whom motherhood has neither driven off the mountain nor dissuaded from the hunt is referred to as *parthenos* in her son's very name. In Sophocles' *Oedipus at Colonus* we hear of "Parthenopaeus, an Arcadian who roused himself to war—son of that virgin famous in the old time who long years afterward conceived and bore him—Parthenopaeus, Atalanta's son."[35] Pierre Vidal-Naquet characterizes Parthenopaeus as a matrilinear figure.[36] In fact his whole mythological life, concentrated in his birth and in his death at the siege of Thebes, is one great allusion: name, face, and shield simply reiterate his virginal origin.[37] Note, however, that Parthenopaeus is a hero. Euripides has Adrastus, the king of Argos, deliver his eulogy; though a metic, he was accepted by the city as a friend. Being neither ambitious nor lascivious nor quarrelsome, he conducted himself as a soldier should, just like a native Argive.[38] Doubly foreign—as an Arcadian and as the son of his mother—he nevertheless had no difficulty integrating himself into a polis that Ion, the virginal son of Creusa, supposedly feared less than Athens.[39] A character summed up by his name, Parthenopaeus in his sole exploit exhibited extraordinary beauty and virtue. A poetic bastard, he was close to the powerful sons of the gods to whom Pausanias alludes. Apparently no shame attached to the child of a virgin if the father was an immortal or a wild hunter in Artemis' woods. Irregular birth and exposure signify privilege and promise of power.

From the age of historians, however, we know of an entire generation of wartime bastards born of human fathers and destined to blush (*erubescere*)[40] because of it: in Sparta the Partheniai are symbolic of the status of children whose fathers were not known and recognized. Their story is told in many versions, whose sociological significance Vidal-Naquet has investigated.[41] It begins during the war with Messenia. Aristotle alludes briefly to the membership of the Partheniai in the Group of Peers and to the rebellious ambitions that he believed to be the inevitable corollary of so uncertain a status. The sons of *parthenoi* are seditious men.[42] Strabo dwells at length on their misfortunes, comparing two different historical accounts of the foundation of Tarentum, a colony that the *partheniai* were sent to establish in Greater Greece by decision of their mother city. According to

Ephorus, the women of Sparta, concerned about repopulating a city drained by war, begged their husbands to take urgent measures. The men received the women's ambassador at the front and immediately grasped the need for action. But an inviolable oath prevented them from leaving the field of battle before the outcome was certain. Ephorus continues:

> And the Lacedaemonians, both keeping their oath and at the same time bearing in mind the argument of the women, sent the men who were most vigorous and at the same time youngest, for they knew that these had not taken part in the oaths, because they were still children when they went out to war along with the men who were of military age; and they ordered them to cohabit with the maidens [*parthenoi*], every man with every maiden, thinking that thus the maidens would bear many children; and when this was done, the children were named *partheniai*.[43]

As a result of the wise decision of the Peers, an entire generation of "reserve citizens" was born in Sparta. Since the repopulation of the city had been carried out in strict accordance with the wishes of the city and with its statutes, the fruit of that effort ought to have borne no hint of shame or rejection. Years later, however, when the war was over, the soldiers had returned home, and it came time to divide the conquered lands, an objection was raised: the birth of the *partheniai* was irregular. The sons of *parthenoi* were bastards, as one of Euripides' characters puts it.[44] Since they were born out of wedlock, it was impossible for them to share equally in the spoils of Messenia.[45] Unrecognized and disavowed by the very city that had brought them into being, these youths had no personal relations with a father but felt bound to one another by powerful ties of fraternal solidarity. They first joined the helots in an abortive rebellion, but when sedition failed they left Sparta in search of a place to build a city.[46]

In the version of the story ascribed to Antiochus of Syracuse, this pathetic and romantic episode appears in a very different form. There was no indiscriminate impregnation of *parthenoi* by young soldiers. Rather, we are told that the term *partheniai* (sons of virgins) was a pejorative epithet applied to the sons of shirkers and cowards during the same war: "After the Messenian war broke out, those of the Lacedaemonians who did not take part in the expedition were adjudged slaves and were named Helots, and all children who were born in the time of the expedition were called *partheniai* and judicially deprived of the rights of citizenship."[47] The inexpiable dishonor of a father stricken from the roll of citizens as a result of cowardice was reflected in a title of manifestly searing irony: the mother of the child so called was married to a nonexistent individual. The wife of nobody, she was therefore a *parthenos*. In Ion's words, reiterating those of a proverb, a bastard is nobody and the son of nobody.[48] Exile, the only escape from slavery and death, was for a whole generation an amplification of the exposure reserved for the superfluous child. In the city as in the *oikos*, natural children had no place alongside legitimate offspring.[49]

A mountain covered with forests stands on the border between Argolis and Arcadia: it is known as the Parthenion, a place reserved for virgin births. Pausanias tells us that a sanctuary there preserves the cult and memory of Telephus, a child born on its summit to a priestess of Athena raped by Heracles.[50] In Callimachus' *Hymn to Delos* it is invoked by Leto as "Mount Parthenion consecrated to Augeus" in memory of this birth.[51] The breathless search for a place to shelter a different kind of delivery begins here, as if, in the memory of a connoisseur of myths, this no-man's-land were the only possible home for a *parthenios*. Here the childhood of the son of Augeus intersects that of the son of Atalanta, for it was in these forests that Parthenopaeus was born.[52] His mother, reenacting her own exposure as an unwanted daughter, abandoned him in the very same area where she herself had survived and grown.[53] And Servius would later gloss the toponym Parthenion as the first stopping place of the Spartan "sons of virgins" on their way to Italy.[54] Mountain of the illegitimate, a wilderness to which was attached every imaginable connotation of the marginal and savage, the Virginal Mountain was the natural setting for individuals without political roots.[55]

The word *bastard* makes it clear that the Greeks did not expect of their *parthenoi* the absolute, unwavering chastity that defines virginity in the Christian ethos. Everything in the adjective *parthenios* that connotes childbirth out of wedlock takes us a long way from Christ. Still, is it not the birth of a child to the Virgin that gives meaning to chastity in the Christian church? By contrast, the Greek pantheon includes three goddesses proud of their absolute *parthenia*. A text as ancient as the *Homeric Hymn to Aphrodite* tells of the fundamental and unwavering distinction between the domain of the mother of Eros and the respective spheres of action of Artemis, Athena, and Hestia.[56] In Athens, the founding myth, which recounts the birth of Erichthonius, centrally involves a virgin who struggles with all her might against seduction.[57]

The tests for *parthenia* offer a new way of approaching the question. Mentioned in Greek literature (though apparently little used in Greece itself), these tests enable us to grasp an important aspect of the concept of virginity. First, *parthenia* was an invisible condition that could be detected only by mantic vision or ordeal. And second, the specifically Hellenic gods did not insist on probative rituals.

Herodotus recounts that the inhabitants of the shores of Lake Tritonis in Libya celebrated an annual festival in honor of an indigenous goddess equivalent to the Greek Athena. On this occasion young girls (*parthenoi*) formed two groups that fought each other with sticks and stones. "Those who died of their wounds were called false virgins [*pseudoparthenoi*]."[58] In contrast to the notion that age and marital status alone determined who was and who was not a *parthenos*, this text suggests the possibility of dissimulation. Among the nubile girls who participated in the battle, some appeared to be virgins but were not. The hidden truth was supposedly revealed by a wound that caused the body to bleed.

It may be objected that this is an ethnographic account. The depiction of eloquent yet lethal wounds belongs to a survey of African initiation rites.[59] Perhaps Herodotus was merely translating the name of an indigenous god into his own language, along with a strange word that would make no sense in Greece. Yet Herodotus offers no commentary, no elaboration, that might betray genuine astonishment over the idea of a virgin who is not what she seems.

Similarly, Aelian describes a trial to which the sacred virgins of Lanuvium were subjected.[60] This ritual took place far from Greece, but near a sanctuary of Hera of Argos. The sacred virgins were forced to descend blindfolded into a cave hidden in the midst of a forest in order to serve cakes to a serpent. Revealing mantic powers, the wise reptile accepted only those cakes that were offered by the hand of a virgin, while "ants, after reducing to crumbs the cake of any girl who had been deflowered, carried the debris out of the woods so as to purify the place." The procession of cleansing ants alarmed the inhabitants of the area. Upon their return, the girls were subjected to examination, and any who defiled their virginity were punished in accordance with the law.[61]

In central Italy as in Africa it thus appears that a *parthenos* possessed an essential and deeply hidden identity: though young and unmarried she might already have lost her *parthenia*, that is, she might have been deflowered.

In Asia Minor, in Ephesus, another remote territory in which the Greek language and culture encountered local religious practices, we know of two ordeals involving sexuality. Our source is Achilles Tatius, the author of *Leukippe and Clitophon*. The truth about a young girl is revealed by a spring and a cave in a region under the protection first of Pan and later of Artemis. First of all, there is a river called Styx that can detect false swearing.[62] The woman who agrees to be examined swears that she has been chaste, and her words are written on a tablet that is hung around her neck. She then steps into the revelatory liquid, barely wetting her legs up to her calves. If she has told the truth, nothing happens; but if she has dared to lie, her perjury arouses the waters of Styx, which froth and roil, rising to cover the text of the falsehood. In this trial, chastity must be indicated in writing on a tablet attached to the young woman's body. By contrast, the second Ephesian trial is reminiscent of the semiotic powers of the Italian serpent as well as of the combat on the shores of Lake Tritonis. Pan's pipes are kept in a grotto. A girl enters, and the pipes themselves render their judgment in music. Virginity is greeted with a sweet, divine melody; a secret sexual experience is met with a mournful howl. The entrance to the cave itself becomes a sign, opening for the virgin but closing upon the woman who has been deflowered, who is left to perish alone.[63]

Both rituals derive from a story of seduction. Before becoming Styx, Rhodopis was a girl fond of hunting and wild animals. Fleet of foot and skilled with bow and arrow, she dressed and wore her hair like a boy. To seal her Artemisian vocation she one day took a solemn oath "to remain a virgin forever, to shun commerce with men, and to avoid the violent passion of Aphrodite."[64] Thus provoked, Aphrodite punished this challenge to her powers by afflicting Rhodopis with a powerful, and reciprocated, desire. Aphrodite's triumphant laughter at the virgin vanquished by one of Eros' arrows aroused Artemis to wrath and vengeance, and to a sudden interruption of the pleasures of Rhodopis and her lover. On the very spot where her *parthenia* was "undone," the young woman is "dissolved"—turned to water—by Artemis.[65] Since then she has tested the oaths of women. As for Pan's pipe, the nymph Syrinx fleeing the goatlike god was turned into a reed. Her hollow body, never possessed in its human form by a man, sings as if the god were playing it whenever a true virgin appears.[66]

Given these means of testing the *parthenos*, there can be no doubt that virginity was a sexual, not a sociological, matter. The original stories are explicit: whether real or invented, the ceremonies conceal the memory of an encounter, or better still, a desire that has absolutely nothing to do with marriage. In *Leukippe and Clitophon* the trial comes just before, and in anticipation of, the *gamos*, in order to verify that the bride to be is not deceiving her beloved when she assures him that she is still a virgin.[67] In confessing her sexual past a girl might not be truthful.

With Achilles Tatius the objection raised earlier in connection with Herodotus and Aelian reasserts itself even more strongly: these inquisitions take place far from classical Greece in both space and time. The vocabulary of defloration, like the use of the word *parthenia*, shows clearly that transition from one state to the other was marked by a passage through the girl's body. One of Aristophanes' *thesmophorae* tells of having been deflowered at the age of seven and says that her first seducer returned to visit her as a lover without her husband's knowledge.[68] Despite their remoteness, these tests for virginity teach us that the Greeks saw nothing strange in speaking of *parthenia* as a fact to be found out, a mystery to be investigated by means of a divinatory ritual. Without delving very deeply into surviving ordeals, we should be careful to bear in mind a passing observation by Pausanias: a pure *parthenos* can become skilled at diving into the sea, but a deflowered girl will die if she tries it.[69] Even if these texts do not come close to clarifying the essential nature of the *parthenos*, they tell us to be wary of defining the virgin solely in terms of the outward sign of youth: nothing in a girl's appearance reveals the nature of her sexuality. We must go beyond the reticent and ambiguous surface to discover the paternal gaze that determined the strict rules of virgin behavior.

～ 8 ～

Hidden Marriages

THE LEXICAL similarity of *parthenos* and *parthenios* is cited as
evidence that in pre-Christian Greece it was no miracle for
a nubile "virgin" to give birth. Yet the barely noticeable change
in word endings cannot efface memories of the red[1] cheeks of
the children of virgins or of the contempt that obliged them to
uproot themselves from their native cities. Sparta set an example of the proper way to treat children of virgins with its
Partheniai, but in Athens a law promulgated by Solon stipulated that a girl whose father discovered that she was pregnant
or even that she had been seduced ceased to be a member of
the family, indeed ceased to exist as a free woman.[2] The
lawgiver, who was under no illusion about the kinds of treatment to which women were liable, prohibited men from selling
their daughters and sisters unless they were discovered to have
participated in a clandestine sexual liaison. But if the male responsible for a *parthenos* determined[3] that she had lain with a
man, he was authorized to treat her as an amputated member,
a body that had become foreign. Seduction (*phthora*)—the only
grounds upon which Solon would countenance treating a free-
born Athenian citizen like a slave—numbered among the gra-
vest of threats to the kinship structure. The *oikos* must not be
deprived of a right essential to its preservation, namely, the right
to expel a female *soma* that had been irretrievably corrupted

(*diaphtheirein*) and thereby rendered unfit for matrimony. Rape or seduction without paternal consent undermined the father's sovereign authority over his daughter. In such a case, instead of *ekdosis* (the act of *giving* one's daughter to another man), the father could exercise his power by putting the girl up for sale. The child living in the girl's body was treated as though it were a parasite, a metic who had entered the sacrosanct precincts of the home via an unguarded door; such a child had to be sent away, along with the girl who carried it and had allowed it in. As Jean-Pierre Vernant has shown, the emblem of the enduring identity of the *oikos* was female: Hestia stood for a fixed and protected source of heat, a power of generation, as well as for the purity of a *parthenos*.[4] She was an unmarried girl whom no husband removed to another location, to another family in need of reproduction; but she was also a virgin whom no man had touched and made mother of an intruder.

The strictness of Greek morals needs to be stressed, for there is a danger that the work of Jeanmaire, Brelich, Calame, and, most recently, Pierre Grimal—who seek to explain the *parthenos* without invoking virginity—may obscure key issues for the sake of a purely lexical interpretation.[5] These writers adduce a series of examples in order to prove that *parthenos* cannot be translated as "virgin." Hence, we are told, a *parthenos* was not a virgin. It follows, they argue, that two different sexual ethics were in conflict. Two models of the feminine and of a woman's relation to marriage and eroticism supposedly heightened this fundamental conflict. Yet the meaning of the word *parthenos* remains opaque and difficult to translate if the fact that the *possibility* of using it to refer to a girl who has had sexual relations and perhaps children becomes the decisive criterion in its definition.

The passage in Plutarch concerning the law of Solon shows unambiguously that the sexuality of a *parthenos* encountered one unbreachable limit: the discovery of its existence. This is not a minor point. The father's acknowledged right to sell his seduced daughter meant of course that a *parthenos* might well make love, but the moment she was caught in the act by her guardian she suffered a change of status far more drastic than that associated with marriage. Being sold into slavery did more than expose her misdeed: she was irretrievably deprived of those with whom she had lived intimately as a girl and cast out of the place that she had occupied and that had made her a *parthenos*.[6] One archon of Athens whose daughter was "ruined" (*diaphtheirō*) by an unknown male preferred to subject her to an even crueler and more irrevocable punishment: he fed her to a hunger-crazed horse. This, Diodorus comments, was an extraordinary penalty,[7] yet one that revealingly illuminates the spirit of the Athenian law: such extreme punishment was a way of disguising an execution and cleansing away the defilement due to the crime.[8] For an unmarried woman the father was the primary social and legal authority, and in his eyes seduction effaced the image of the *parthenos*. A husband was branded with *atimia*, dishonor, if he kept an adulterous wife in his house,[9] but it was up to the father to eliminate every trace of the girl who, having escaped his surveillance, ceased to be what she had been.

If the girl had no right to remain in her father's home, it was because sexual relations had destroyed her, reduced her to nothing. The verb *diaphtheirein*, which expressed the idea of seduction, actually connotes an action that causes something to fall apart or disintegrate. Aristotle applies the word *phthora* to any process of physical dissolution; it is the exact opposite of *genesis*, generation, change in view of some end.[10] For physicians, moreover, abortion was nothing other than a form of *diaphtheirein*: a halting of growth, a failure and reversal of the embryological process. The adolescent girl—*pais, neanis, korē,* or *parthenos*—is nourished in her father's home, in space that is his, as is the belly of a woman in which a child grows; if she is seduced, the inevitable result is total ruin. Regardless of her subjective state of mind what has happened changes her nature, decomposes her being, for in the male world it diverts her from her telos, her fulfillment as woman.[11] The fetal status of the girl tucked away in the depths of the house explains not only why Solonian law permitted her to be sold into slavery but also the nature of the punishment inflicted on the perpetrator of the act under Athenian law. (The stories that we shall be examining never question the girl's "consent.") The terrible law of *moicheia* (adultery) was without mercy for anyone who insulted a citizen by way of his daughter's body; only the male was held accountable for his action. If, however, he could prove to his judges that his partner was a prostitute, his crime ceased to be a crime.[12]

Although it was in fact possible for a *parthenos* to have a sexual life, it was nevertheless forbidden. Dissimulation, clandestinity, and secrecy were necessary conditions. A girl who engaged in premarital relations did not take on a new name. Her relationship was officially nonexistent; if discovered, it destroyed its victim. This explains the meaning of the word *parthenios* or *parthenias*. The gloss given by Pollux makes it abundantly clear that the essence of virgin birth was falsehood and that a "son-of-a-virgin" was so called because his mother, while seeming to be a virgin, was in fact a *false* virgin. "*Parthenias* is that which someone has made with a seeming *parthenos* outside of legal cohabitation; *skotios*, obscure, one who was engendered clandestinely or delivered by a woman in hiding."[13] The word does not contradict the mother's virginity but means that the newborn is there despite the mother's status and that the child was conceived behind a misleading appearance that deceived society. Sexual relations and motherhood do not alter the appearance of a *parthenos*, and she retains her name only because she wears a mask.[14] The semantic ambiguity of *parthenos*, caught between a *parthenia* that she is losing and a *parthenios* who is being born, in effect rests on an imperative and implicit model of behavior: in principle a nubile young woman does not make love. If she gives birth to a child, that child will be a person whose mother was presumed never to have had relations with a male body. But the child is living proof that its mother's virginity is henceforth merely a sham. By causing the mother's belly to swell[15] or in some cases suddenly emerging from it, [16] the child was sometimes the only sign of a fraud that had otherwise gone unnoticed; without subjecting her body to mantic scrutiny a Greek virgin was sometimes betrayed by the very fruit of her womb. Unexpected and unwanted, the *parthenios* was one whose very name connoted the surprise and displeasure caused by its presence. The texts that tell us about the Spartan *partheniai* clearly indicate, moreover, that the term was intended as an epithet. The word expressed not so much the status of the illegitimate child as the irony and contempt of those who uttered it. Pollux adds that the comic author Eubulus "humorously refers to clandestine offspring as 'a premature lifting of the skirts of a *parthenos.*'"[17] The least mention of virginity seems to elicit cruelly sarcastic winks.

The evidence of lexicographers, Hellenists, and historians of the Greek language is invaluable; it helps prevent us from introducing illegitimate meanings in translating from one language to another. Clearly, it became more difficult to recognize the nature of the ancient *partheniai* after the birth of the only son of a virgin recognized by Christianity. The Greek expression was obviously a kind of euphemism, which carried with it the same sort of stigma that the words *figlio di buona donna* do in southern Italy today.

The hypothesis that sexuality and virginity were compatible only if sexual activity remained secret must now be tested against a series of texts. Herodotus reports that certain Thracians "carry on an export trade in their own children [*tekna*]; they exercise no control over young girls [*parthenous*], allowing them to have connections with any man they please; their wives [*gynaikas*], on the other hand, whom they purchase at high prices from their parents, they watch very strictly."[18] Here, the contrast between *parthenos* and *gynē* turns on the nuptial purpose: it is clear that in Herodotus' mind the girls begin to make love because they are not monitored and are already *women* by the time they are purchased as brides. "Virgin I came and woman I return home," says a Theocritean shepherdess after surrendering to a persuasive lover in a field.[19] A phenomenon worthy of ethnographic attention, deliberate suspension of paternal supervision over a girl is described by Herodotus as senseless negligence that can lead only to repeated debauch. It is of course at the age when a girl becomes a maiden, and desire, brought on by the first menstrual discharge, begins to course through her veins, that educational zeal must be redoubled: "Girls of this age have much need of surveillance," Aristotle points out. "For then in particular they feel a natural impulse to make use of the sexual faculties that are developing in them; so that unless they guard against any further impulse beyond that inevitable one which their bodily development itself supplies, even in the case of those who abstain altogether from passionate indulgence, they contract habits which are apt to continue into later life."[20] In describing the laws of nature, Aristotle teaches that puberty determines the final complexion of both males and females: the imperfection of childhood gives way to the adult form. Breasts swell, hair appears, and the voice changes—all corollaries of a maturation that prepares the individual for procreation. Subsequent to the anesthesia of childhood and prior to the assumption of a regular maternal role, desire surges with elemental, inchoate force. A woman's entire sexual life is determined at this juncture by the adults who supervise the economy of her sensibility. "For girls who give way to wantonness grow more and more wanton."[21]

If a *parthenos* experiences love, it must be hidden from the gaze that channels nature's great aphrodisiac force toward its social purpose. She can know love thanks to secrecy, and only on condition that secrecy is maintained, for if it is sexuality directed toward marriage that turns a girl into a woman, an overly public sensuality condemns the girl who would be called *parthenos* because of her age to be known by a less noble name:

paidiskē.[22] Although Herodotus recognized young Thracian girls not supervised by their parents as *parthenoi,* he bluntly applies the term *paidiskai* to Lydian girls who earn money for their dowries by selling their bodies in exchange for a cash tribute that the society neither ignores nor criticizes.[23] In Lydia prostitution was sponsored and protected by the girl's own family: fathers introduced their daughters to the trade much as they committed them elsewhere to marriage contracts; it was by showing girls how to earn money in this way that their fathers provided them with a patrimony. In Greek eyes, however, not even the nuptial telos could efface the venal and therefore unchaste nature of the practice. Such an initiation into the labors of Aphrodite was a shameless commerce and as such not to be confused with the furtive loves to which a *parthenos* might surrender either willingly or by force.

Euripides refers to these clandestine amorous encounters as hidden marriages.[24] The best gloss is a passage in Sophocles' *Women of Trachis*: "Even a shameful [*aischra*] action does not result in dishonor [*aischynē*] if carried out in obscurity [*skotos*]."[25] Shame is rooted in visibility: as Aelian intimates with respect to the deflowered maidens of Lanuvium,[26] *aischynē* is what the trial reveals. It is the reproving gaze that transforms an invisible occurrence into an insult to virginity.[27] Euripides' words tell us what semantic area to look at in order to detect the difference between the "marriages" of a *parthenos* and ordinary marriages. If the loves of a *parthenos* are a hidden *gamos,* the marriage ritual itself is in all its details a struggle against secrecy.

POLLUX'S dictionary definition of a *gamos* tells us that the symbolism of the ceremony—acts and words—should be interpreted as a discreetly allusive prefiguration of the sexual inauguration, or *archē* as Plato called it,[28] that made the wedding day and night the commencement and mirror of all married life. The day's acts and words, which continued by torchlight into (and in opposition to) the darkness of evening, chastely prefigured the intimacy of the night. Following Pollux, we witness a mimesis of commencement in the form of gift-giving and the lifting of the veil to uncover the face of the *nymphē*: "The gifts given by the groom are called *hedna, optēria, anakalyptēria;* for this last word refers not only to the day when the bride is unveiled (*ekkalyptei*) but also to the gifts that are given to her on that day. The gifts-of-the-lifted-veil are also called gifts-of-greeting."[29] Thus, the presents given by the *nymphios* to the girl he is marrying evoke the gesture that accompanies them: unveiling a face and bestowing a name. According to the cosmology of Pherecydes of Syros, Zeus held up his gift of fine embroidered fabric as he spoke the words of marriage to Chthonia: "Greetings to thee, come with me!"[30] Since then the gods and men of the earth have continued to observe the custom of *anakalyptērion,* or unveiling.[31] Glossing *optēria,* Pollux specifies that the gifts-of-the-glance are those that the *nymphios* offers to the *nymphē* "when he lifts his eyes up to her for the first time."[32] Thus the man who unveils the unknown woman as he greets her also takes her in exchange and by so doing marries her. When Plato recommends that men take care in choosing a mate and marry only women they know, he reveals that the custom was for the groom to approach his bride as a stranger on their wedding day—quite literally a day of epiphany.[33]

In the panoply of female accessories the veil (*kalyptra, krēdemnon*) was not worn exclusively by maidens. Homer, for example, shows Nausicaa removing her veil in order to play ball,[34] while Calypso dons hers when she dresses each morning as though after a night of love.[35] Penelope wears hers when she appears before the suitors.[36] *Parthenos, nymphē*, and bride all wear the veil, which physically embodies the ambiguous difference between chastity and seduction. The first woman amazed the gods by appearing before them in just such a transparent veil, which conceals yet also promises.[37] Though not justified by any function as apparel, the veil takes on its full symbolic value in the *anakalyptērion*. The veil is there for the groom to raise: though functionally superfluous, it is indispensable for marriage, because the man who receives a woman as his bride must discover in the marriage ceremony a previously unseen face. The veil remains permanently on the wife's head and shoulders in commemoration of the step she has taken. Andromache, upon seeing her dead husband's body dragged through the dirt under the ramparts of Troy, falls into a blind rage. The moment she realizes she is a widow, she loses her veil: "She fell backward, and gasped the life breath from her, and far off threw from her head the shining gear that ordered her headdress, the diadem and the cap, and the holding-band woven together, and the circlet [*krēdemnon*], which Aphrodite the golden once had given her on that day when Hektor of the shining helmet led her forth from the house of Eëtion and gave numberless gifts to win her."[38] In Euripides' *Phoenician Women* another kind of despair echoes this mourning of a lost husband. An equally distraught Antigone (a *parthenos*) weeps over the death of her two brothers and her mother: "No veil now covers the curls on my delicate cheek, nor in maiden shame have I hidden the blush on my face, I come as a bacchant, celebrating death. I have thrown the veil from my hair."[39] Driven mad by grief like Andromache,[40] the virgin mourns in her brothers' death a marriage that now can never take place.[41] Deprived of her guardian, the young girl finds herself thrust into a kind of virginal widowhood, which affects her not only as a sister and daughter but also as a future wife. The veil that she rips away from her tearful face is one that no husband will ever raise.[42] Even more explicit is the game with which Euripides ends *Alcestis*. A girl is escorted back to her husband but offered as a new fiancée, a grateful gift from Heracles to his host; the girl appears wrapped in such a way that she cannot be recognized. And Admetus, faithful widower, specifically refuses to make the gesture that would indicate his acceptance of the gift, his willingness to take another wife. He agrees to touch the hand of the unknown woman, but he averts his eyes, as if he were cutting off the head of the Gorgon.[43] The *Unveiled Women* (*Anakalyptomenē*) is the title of a comedy by Evangelus, a passage of which (the only one that we possess) is cited by Athenaeus.[44] It consists of a series of exchanges between the master of the house and the cook in charge of organizing a wedding banquet. To speculate a little, it seems possible that the cook was the central figure in the comedy. The *nymphē* wears a ritual costume that lent itself so well to use as a disguise that Zeus, according to a Plataean tradition, used it to trap his jealous wife.[45] Pausanias reports that the god dressed a *xoanon* as a bride and placed it on a chariot in imitation of a *nymphagōgia*, or wedding procession. An enraged Hera hurled herself upon this supposed rival, whose wooden face caused the wrathful goddess to erupt in laughter.

Whether tragically torn as a tangible metaphor for a marriage that had become impossible or been destroyed, or jestingly employed as a device for comic recognition, the veil was an essential object in the familiar scenario of the *gamos*. More precisely, the *anakalyptērion* represented in chaste, public form the scene that took place in secret at night.

Not only did the veil cover the *nymphē*; the marriage bed was veiled by curtains: Pollux explicitly draws the analogy,[46] Discreetly yet by virtue of a precise correspondence the bridal veil suggested the canopy of the bed. Like the *nymphē's* body, the place where the marriage was consummated was shielded from view. Comic language did away with the circumlocution in the allusive association of face with bed. Pollux, citing Amphis, points out that the gifts of greeting, unveiling and apparition were also referred to as *diaparthenia*, or gifts of the deflowered virgin.[47] This and other synonyms go straight to the significance of ritual; the gift is defined by its quid pro quo without benefit of metaphor. The whole ceremony was epitomized in the discreet itinerary of the gaze, in the unveiling of a face as fresh and unseen as the sex that would later be bared within the bridal chamber.

The idea that the gaze directed at the bride was a very important part of the marriage ceremony does not depend solely on an interpretation of the vocabulary of gifts. Several sources attest to the fact that the *anakalyptērion* took place during the banquet, hence in the presence of witnesses, and for the specific and definite purpose of showing "the brides to the grooms and guests."[48] The first vision is also a spectacle. With his hand the groom lifts the veil that covers the mouth and eyes of the woman he is marrying so that the guests may see not only the bride but also this very gesture of his, this first act of disrobing, which one obscene poet was cruel enough to describe as an equivalent of defloration.[49] The exact place of the *anakalyptērion* in the ceremonial sequence has been a subject of controversy, however. In a 1940 article J. Toutain mentioned two contradictory hypotheses:[50] either the unveiling took place during the wedding banquet,[51] or the nymphē remained veiled until she reached the intimacy of the chamber.[52] Toutain concluded that the difference of opinion stemmed from a change in the custom itself: originally the girl remained veiled and thus protected against the evil eye throughout the banquet and nymphagōgia and removed the protective garb only in her husband's bedroom. Later, however, "such superstitions" allegedly "lost their value in Greek and Roman society."[53] The wearing of the veil is supposed to have lost its religious significance; hence "the place of the *anakalyptērion* in the sequence of the marriage ceremony was ostensibly emptied of its true meaning. Afterward, the reason for the now profane act was supposedly to show the face of the new bride to relatives and friends invited to the wedding.[54] In fact this diachronic solution enabled Toutain to reconcile two interpretations, both of which are based on an assumption that has been shown to be false: that the banquet took place in the girl's home, and that the *nymphagōgia*, the noisy procession that accompanied the bride to her new home, took place after dinner. If events occurred in this order, it is difficult to see how the *anakalyptērion* that is described as taking place during the banquet could be compatible with the image of the *nymphē* riding on a chariot with her veil still in place.[55] As it happens, a comedy by Menander, *The Samian Woman*, suggests that the order in the ceremony was reversed. Beyond a shadow of a doubt this play depicts a procession, accompanied by singing of the nuptial song, conducting the girl to her husband's house prior to the banquet.[56] The meal offered by the father of the groom stands for the solemn reception of a faceless female stranger into the male *oikos*. It was at this table, before an audience gathered to receive her, that the *nymphē* was probably supposed to be introduced. The groom shows his bride and demonstrates that he is seeing her for the first time in order to complete and indicate his approval of her reception. Those sources that set this scene in private, attended by the couple alone, fancifully embellish an allusion contained in the public ritual, indicating that the unveiling begins the undressing of the bride.[57]

The external portion of the ceremony, the *nymphagōgia*, was also a public presentation, and introduction to the city. After sunset, when darkness fell, the procession with its choruses and whirling torches illuminated and proclaimed to all what the night would cover with silence. Just as the *anakalyptērion* evoked the nudity that the veil protected, the torches and nuptial song made visible the darkness they interrupted: "They were leading the brides along the city from their maiden chambers under the flaring of torches, and the loud bride song was arising."[58] The oldest description of a marriage scene, on the Homeric Achilles' shield, portrays the noisy felicity of a city at peace. A veiled girl proceeds from virginal chamber to wedding table followed by many eyes. Later, to cover the cry that she will emit in the midst of her first embrace, the epithalamium will be sung.[59]

Thus, the wedding feast is organized around two gazes: that of the husband who discovers the woman he is marrying, and that of the entourage which noisily inaugurates the couple's married life. The sexuality of the *parthenos* is defined essentially in relation to this wedding ceremony. Linguistic usage confirms that marriage itself was often identified with one of its public manifestations. In a line of the *Odyssey* that did not escape the notice of Pollux,[60] the word *gamos* refers to both the wedding feast and the marriage. Conversely, *anakalyptērion* could refer to the whole ceremony.[61] Above all, however, it was the triumph of the wedding song that was identified with marriage: *hymenaiō* can mean "to wed," and the adjective *anymenaios* is therefore synonymous with *agamos*.[62] A metonymy for nuptials, the hymn, sung beneath the light of torches, that presaged and announced the marriage led to the characterization of the girl as *anymenaios parthenos*.[63] Joined in privation and similarly bemoaning their fate were Antigone, who was escorted to the grave that would be her bridal chamber,[64] and Polyxena,[65] who, having been promised to a shade, was a "husbandless bride, an unvirginal virgin."[66] And Creusa, who became a mother through "virginal labor," would explain to her rediscovered son that all voices remained silent and no light shone on the night she suffered the hidden marriage that was in fact no marriage at all.[67]

THE CASE of Creusa deserves further attention. In a world in which a young girl was as likely to meet a man as she was to be visited by a god, and in which a stranger who courted a mortal might be an immortal in disguise, every father had to learn prudence. To punish a *parthenos* whose virginity had been taken by a god as though it were a matter of mere human seduction would almost inevitably incur the vengeance of the gods.[68] A powerful immunity surrounded and protected the woman singled out by the desire of a god whose sacred sperm her body harbored.[69] The only way to diminish the shame of a furtive marriage was to pretend that it was a *hieros gamos*. A comic theme, the mythologization of a seducer, was used by Euripides, when Ion (suspicious as the father of Tyro) whispered this indiscreet question to his mother: "Might you not have faltered, as *parthenoi* will, and might you not be blaming a hidden love on the god?"[70] Pushed to the limit in a piquant situation, Creusa reacts vigorously: Loxias was the father, and it is the lord of Delphi who watches over the future of his heir. Ion's suspicions cannot possibly be true, she points out, because she herself had concealed her union with the god, going so far as to plot her child's death.[71] True, a clandestine marriage (*kryptos gamos*), an ordinary adventure and one less flattering than love with a god, could be disguised as a sacred union. But Apollo's lovemaking was also shrouded in secrecy. Creusa repeatedly states that everything that happened between her and Apollo took place in darkness. Without her father's knowledge she made love in a dark cave.[72] Without her mother's knowledge she crouched in the same place to give birth, then abandoned her "virgin's labor."[73] Without torchlight, without wedding songs and dances, her *gamos* was furtive. When she gave birth her witnesses were Misfortune and Mystery.[74] Clandestinity is truly the protagonist of this play: at once the spring and motor of the plot, it reveals the contours of virginal sexuality. Upon discovering an unidentified infant at the temple entrance, the Pythia resorts immediately to a formula: "Astonished that a girl of Delphi should have dared to cast the fruit of secret love before Apollo's temple, she would have banned it from the sacred precinct."[75] Later the prophetess sends Creusa's son in search of his unknown mother.[76] Thus Ion's birth points to a coherent model: the loves of an unmarried girl, whether willing or not, are by definition hidden.

Nicole Loraux has pointed out the dramatic importance of the fact that Creusa, though seduced and a mother, has not lost her status as a *parthenos*: "It is not certain that she succeeded in depriving herself of the status of *parthenos*, which for her is at once a fate and a proof of innocence."[77] If we look at some of the passages in *Ion* that Loraux cites, we can grasp the degree to which the character is marked by this persistence. Nevertheless, the continuity of an unalterable name appears to depend on secrecy, on the absence of suspicion in the minds of others, for whom nothing has happened either in or to the girl's body. In the eyes of the world Creusa has never lost her virginity. By calling herself a *parthenos* when she reveals her secret, she retrospectively gives herself a name that was publicly hers already and that she hoped to maintain by eliminating any proof to the contrary. In what is the present time in the play, Creusa is *gynē*. Ion greets her as such when he comes to Delphi for the children of her legitimate marriage with Xuthus. Throughout the play, both her divine son and her human husband refer to her as *woman*.[79]

Let us further consider the Euripidean representation of sexuality in young girls by looking at the treatment of Auge, mother of Telephus. Only fragments survive of two tragedies, *Auge* and *Telephus*, the first of which—probably the story of the loves and motherhood of the daughter of the king of Arcadia—drew angry criticism from Plato after being the target of a fierce satire by Aristophanes.

A scholium to line 1080 of *The Frogs* explains how Euripides, defying both aesthetic and religious convention, wrote that Auge, daughter of Aleus and priestess of Athena, gave birth to Telephus in the temple. In the first place, childbirth was not a subject for the stage. Second, the birth of a child in a holy place was a sacrilege.[80] For a priestess—and worse still, a priestess in the service of Athena—to insult the sanctuary of the Parthenos violated so many taboos that this lost and much-reviled work seemed to epitomize what was blasphemous in Euripides' corrupting works.

Pausanias recounts three versions of the story: two Tegean traditions and one *logos* by Hecataeus.

Auge gave birth to Telephus on her way to the sea, where her father wanted to drown her after discovering her pregnancy. A temple of Ilithyia, built on the agora at the spot where Auge squatted to give birth, is called "Auge-on-her-knees."[81]

Auge gave birth in a bed without her father's knowledge and later exposed the child on Mount Parthenion.[82]

According to Hecataeus, Auge had made love with Heracles. When Aleus realized that his daughter had given birth, he shut her up with her child in a basket, which he gave to one of his servants with orders to dispose of it at sea.[83]

In none of these versions does the birth of Telephus take place in the temple of Athena Alea. It is true that the goddess has a sacred bed in the temple next to a portrait of Auge, and the office of priest is filled by a prepubescent boy.[84] Yet Pausanias makes no reference to anyone's having given birth in the divine bed. Diodorus Siculus includes the story not in the mythology of Arcadian sites but in the peregrinations of the protagonist hero, Heracles: "Heracles returned to Arcadia; and, after staying with King Aleus and secretly [*lathra*] making love with the king's daughter, Auge, and making her pregnant, he returned to Stymphalus. Aleus, who knew nothing [*agnoōn*], learned of the seduction only when the girl's belly began to swell, and he sought to find out the identity of the seducer."[85] Auge accused Heracles but was not believed and, heavy with child, was sent to the sea. When she reached the heights of Mount Parthenion, her pains became so severe that she went into the forest, gave birth, and abandoned the newborn after hiding it in bushes (*krypsasa*).[86] The tradition that seems closest to Euripides' tragedy is recounted by Apollodorus: "While passing through Tegea, Heracles seduced Auge, not knowing [*agnoōn*] that she was the daughter of Aleus. After secretly giving birth, the girl left the child in the temple of Athena. Because the region was ravaged by a famine, Aleus went to the sacred compound and found traces of the birth [*ōdinas*]. He ordered the child exposed on Mount Parthenion."[87]

In this variety of traditions concerning one of Heracles' many adventures, a common core narrative yields several different stories: an unmarried girl, either a priestess of Athena or a princess, must find a hiding place—bushes or temple—to conceal from her father the fact that she has made love. Sooner or later, however, the fact becomes known. Euripides has the unfortunate girl choose to hide the delivery of her child in a sacred place, thus giving clandestinity an extreme form and preparing for the most resounding of failures, because the taboo against staining the *klinē* of Athena is a thousand times more powerful than the impunity provided by an altar. With the same acuity as Iphigenia reminding Artemis of her sanguinary sophisms, Auge points up the inconsistency of Athena, who relishes the blood of war yet is horrified by the blood-tinged effluvia of the woman giving birth.[88]

Girls other than Creusa and Auge share similar biographies, divided in the same way between a clandestine *gamos* and a proper wedding with torchlight and guests. Lovely Polydora, for example, having conceived in the arms of the river Spercheius, gave birth to Menesthius of the shining corselet, but later she publicly married Borus and was showered by him with gifts.[89] Or Polymele, another beauty, furtively (*lathrei*) loved by Hermes and made mother of a *parthenios*, who enjoyed with Echecles[90] a marriage with *nymphagōgia* and thousands of presents. Coronis, who carried in her womb the divine seed of Apollo, would have experienced the same fate if she had not lost her senses and "in her confused heart accepted a second marriage, in secrecy from her father."[91] An audacious and unprofitable impatience impelled her not to wait "for the coming of the bride-feast, not for hymen cry in many voices, such things as the maiden companions of youth are accustomed to sing at nightfall . . . No. She was in love with what was not there; it has happened to so many."[92]

With Pindar we come back to the image of virginal maternity (*parthenia ōdis*) in the sixth *Olympian Ode*. We are in possession of a very simple touchstone: that amorous encounters outside of marriage are condemned to nonexistence. The labor of a *parthenos*, a phenomenon readily expressed in Greek, can now be seen in its proper context. It is mentioned in the middle of a verse: she *hid* her virginal labor in the folds of her robe. Again, fear and the effacing of a sign, between a prohibition and a certainty of punishment. Pitane sends his little daughter Evadne away. Evadne too will be loved by a god, Apollo, who will make her mother of the great Iamus, the first of a dynasty of soothsayers. The destiny of this *parthenios* will be splendid: founder of the oracle of Zeus in Olympia and chosen interpreter of the paternal voice, he and his entire *genos* will be renowned. Yet he, too, must suffer exposure after being born "under the darkness of low trees."[93]

~ 9 ~

Anatomy without Veils

I N VIEW of what has been said thus far, is it not surprising that a girl could lose her *parthenia* and still be called *parthenos*, but that discovery of sexual relations before marriage could result in her repudiation or even death? Penetration by a male organ deflowered a virgin, yet the event existed only if it was found out by family and society or revealed by its consequences: the parthenic state depended on sexuality, hence on the body, yet was also a purely negative fact. Only seduction could be verified.

In fact the crucial question has yet to be posed. It can be formulated as follows: What was the specific physical correlate of maidenhood? Were the Greeks aware of a part of the female genitals whose breaking (*qua rupta*, in the words of Servius[1]) meant that a woman was no longer a virgin? Did the ancient Greeks believe that the anatomy of the female genitals told the truth about a girl's sexual life?

Mantics and ordeals permitted probing a woman's integrity by means of signs that revealed to men's eyes a secret already visible to the clairvoyant gods. The object of oracular inquiry was beyond the competence of medicine, however; tests of virginity were not directed at a particular area of the body. Such signs as the wound, the serpent's appetite, the spontaneous music, and the opening of doors shed light on an episode from the past: the whole being of the *parthenos* was examined, not a part of the body. Her life was judged, and what she said was either confirmed or contradicted. This was neither a physical finding nor a diagnosis. If the status of a *parthenos* was defined by others' belief in her integrity, what was the attitude of the Greeks toward that concrete reality, that anatomical veil that we call by a Greek name and that seems to be evoked if not invoked in the hymn that, from the time of Homer to that of the lexicographers, was sung on the wedding day?

On the one hand, for the Hellenist, the derivation *parthenos-parthenios* evokes girls whose bodies were exempt from the constraints of "Marian piety" and physical virginity.[2] On the other hand, lexical similarity is only too likely to suggest a notion that for us is the result of scientific observation: namely, that the female genitals are initially sealed by a membrane called the *hymen*. In Greek the wedding song was of course the *hymenaios*. Yet as we shall see presently, the seemingly incontrovertible association of hymen with *hymenaios* was not made by the ancient Greeks.

Hymen, hymenaios! These words were shouted by those who accompanied the bride in the procession known as the *nymphagōgia*.[3] Photius collects three eytmological interpretations in the *Chrestomathia of Proclos*:

> He says that the *hymenaios* was sung at marriages to express regret and longing for Hymenaeus, son of Terpsichore, who is said to have disappeared on his wedding day. Others say that it is to honor Hymenaeus of Athens, who one day chased some thieves and rescued the Attic maidens they had abducted. My own opinion is this: ὑμέναιε is an exclamation to herald a happy life, and people join in the prayers of the newlyweds that they may find companionship and affection in their marriage. Since this prayer is couched in Aeolian dialect, when people say ὑμέναιε to them, it is as if they were wishing that the couple might live together [ὑμεναίειν] and in harmony [ὁμονοεῖν] for a long time.

Continuing an ancient tradition, Proclus is supposedly comparing the clamor of marriage to a funeral lamentation, the voice of a *pothos*, nostalgia for one who is absent. Pindar was the author of a threnody of which a scant fragment remains, in which Hymenaeus is cast as a poet as unfortunate as Linus and Orpheus because he died before experiencing the joys of marriage.[5] And the Orphics, according to Apollodorus, credited Asclepius with having resurrected Hymenaeus.[6] The fact that he dies on his wedding day and bears so evocative a name inevitably results in Hymenaeus' being taken for an allegory of defloration. As the god who inhabits the *membrana virginalis*,[7] Hymen is supposed to be the victim of the first night. Taking note of this same tradition, Servius details the circumstances of his death: "Some say that he was a young man who on his wedding day was buried beneath the walls of his house [*oppressus ruina*]. For that reason he is named in weddings by way of expiation."[8] Treatises on dream interpretation are categorical: "For the sick person, to [dream of] marrying a virgin [*parthenos*] signifies death, for all the ceremonies that go with marriage also go with funerals."[9] Artemidorus adds that to dream of marrying a woman who has already been deflowered is reassuring.

Was the wedding therefore a sort of dramatized execution? Did the wedding feast evoke a passion by mourning a torn veil? Following Brelich, who interpreted the ritual of *arkteia* in Brauron as the death of a *parthenos* prior to marriage, that is, prior to becoming another person, a woman,[10] one might conceive of a model of *gamos* as telos, in the sense of ultimate end: destruction of virginity in the body, transposed in myth into a story of a young man named Hymenaeus and his misadventures. The ancient texts, however, lead us in precisely the opposite direction.

The accident that led to the death of a newly married youth did not, in the Greek mind, symbolize rupture of the hymen. I feel warranted in making this assertion because an anatomical exegesis does exist. It appeared quite late and took its place *alongside* the mythological version already mentioned. In speculating on the roots of the word *hymenaios* (in Photius' compilation), Servius, a commentator on Virgil who lived in the fourth century, observed: "There is also another reason for the word, for it is said that the hymen is a certain membrane, the so-called virginal membrane."[11] The grammarian does not regard the factual explanation as the key to deciphering the myth or explaining the origins of an image; he seems to include it only because he wishes to be scrupulously exhaustive. "Quaedam membrana . . . quasi virginalis . . . dicitur": the diction reveals a wary circumspection, as if not only the linguistic relevance but the very existence of hearsay concerning "the so-called virginal membrane" were not truly credible.

Servius makes no bones about the fact that for him the correct etymology points to the history of Hymenaeus of Athens, protagonist in a heroic love and happy marriage. The anatomy of the female organ remains a vague rumor, and the idea that the nuptial invocation commemorates a tragic death is an error (*falsum est*).[12] The same attitude, critical concerning a marriage disturbed by the memory of a dead man and at least hesitant with respect to what one scholium called a "naturalistic" explanation,[13] can also be found in the compilation of the third of the Vatican Mythographers. This scholar of the ninth and tenth centuries, who, as A. Mai points out, calls himself not just Christian but Catholic, limits himself to paraphrasing Servius.[14] On the one hand he borrows the still anonymous explanation of the Greek name for the membrane: "In Greek, moreover, *hymen* is the word for the membrane that is an intrinsic part of the female genitals, in which people say that childbirth takes place. For that reason Hymenaeus is called the god of marriages."[15] On the other hand, he reports Servius' opinion concerning the evocation of death: "The opinion of some people, according to which the adolescent Hymenaeus was crushed on his wedding day by the collapse [of his house], so that his name was invoked at weddings by way of expiation, is said by Servius to be false."[16]

The gynecological derivation did not win the favor of ancient historians of the lyric genres: Photius does not even mention it, and Servius prefers an episode from Athenian history. Hymenaeus was a very handsome youth, an adolescent so graceful that then he wished to keep his eyes fixed on the girl with whom he was in love, he was able to hide among a group of *parthenoi* without being recognized. Though obliged to say nothing about his hopeless love for the daughter of a prominent family in his town, he ultimately managed to display his virility and courage and reap the benefits of his desire. For one day pirates kidnapped the noble virgins of Athens. Among them was Hymenaeus, who was mistaken for a girl and abducted with the others. No sooner had the brigands brought their booty to a deserted place than they were overcome by fatigue and fell asleep. The youth then leapt up and killed them. Before returning the pride and joy of his city's most notable citizens, however, he set his terms: he would turn over the girls in exchange for the hand of the one he loved. The exchange was accepted, and Hymenaeus saw his wish come true: "He obtained in marriage the virgin he desired. And since this union was a happy one, it pleased the Athenians that the name Hymenaeus be present in all marriages."[17]

In fact the etymological question has never been resolved. Already in antiquity the range of conjecture was vast, as P. Muth has observed.[18] Despite the apparent and plausible proximity, the relation between the hymeneal song and the hymen of histology remains "obscure."[19]

IT MAY BE objected that the question of the Greek conception of physical virginity should not be put to experts in literary genres, commentators on Virgil, or writers of myths. Since the question concerns a part of the body, the people competent to answer it ought to be physicians and naturalists, scholars interested in female morphology and diseases. Scientists as well versed in popular beliefs and traditions as the Hippocratics and Aristotle should be sources of useful information. Concerning the *mem-*

brana quasi virginalis mentioned by Servius, we must consult the specialist literature of the ancients. And, surprising as it may seem, neither the eyes nor the hands of Greek practitioners told them that a membrane initially seals a woman's vagina.[20] Anatomy, as it can be reconstructed on the basis of Hippocratic therapies, was unaware of a hymen specific to the *parthenos*. For all the precision of Aristotle's classification and nomenclature, he neither saw nor described a diaphragm closing the mouth of the vagina. No natural barrier was supposed to obstruct that symbol of female health: no one thought of the opening through which the purifying catamenial blood flowed as a stitched wound.

As a particular type of tissue, the membrane (*hymen*) was an important part of the body's structure. Every vital organ and all the bones were wrapped in a light film that was indispensable to their function and conservation. In *Historia animalium* Aristotle examines first the hair and then the hymens of the body, which he describes in terms of their location: "In all sanguineous animals membranes are found. And membrane resembles a thin close-textured skin, but its qualities are different, as it admits neither of cleavage nor of extension. Membrane envelops each one of the bones and each one of the viscera, both in the larger and the smaller animals; though in the smaller animals the membranes are indiscernible from their extreme tenuity and minuteness."[21] Subtle to the point of invisibility yet robust and compact, hymens enveloped the organism's internal parts, just as the skin covers the body's exterior. The largest of these membranes surrounded the brain and heart,[22] because while all the viscera needed protection, the defensive sheath around the most vital parts was most important.[23] This fine tissue exhibited many apparently incompatible qualities, however, and nature did not intend it to serve solely as a transparent shield. For Aristotle, the epiploon, mesentery, and diaphragm were all hymen-organs. The epiploon, we are told, is a membrane of fat and grease "that grows from the middle of the stomach, along a line which is marked on it like a seam. Thus attached, it covers the rest of the stomach and the greater part of the bowels."[24] The mesentery is also a hymen, through which run numerous rootlike vessels that draw nourishment in the form of sap from the entrails.[25] As the name indicates, the diaphragm is a sort of wall or dam: it is located below the heart so that the sensory soul "may be undisturbed, and not be overwhelmed, directly food is taken, by its up-steaming vapor and by the abundance of heat then superinduced."[26] A veritable barrier erected along the frontier between the upper and lower body so as to filter the upward flow of dangerous *anathymiasis* to the *kyrios* organ, the phrenic hymen served a function so similar to what the function of the virginal panniculus might have been that Aristotle's silence on the subject is all the more significant. "If membrane be bared and cut asunder it will not grow together again."[27] The Greek hymen lacked none of the qualities needed to become the impossible-to-mend protective veil over the virgin's *aidoion*—the hymen as we know it. Yet plausible as it may have been, such a role was never assigned to it.

In Rome, between 169 and 195, Galen wrote a manual of dissection titled *Anatomicae administrationes*. Intended to guide the anatomist's blade through the interstices of the body, the book paid careful attention to the membranes enumerated by Aristotle. A skillful technician was one who after peeling away the external derma of each member without removing the membrane that lay beneath, could "uncover" the organs of nutrition without tearing the large hymen adhering to their surface.[28] After detaching and unfolding the peritoneum, the web[29] and *chitōn* of all the entrails, the anatomist turned his attention to the organs of respiration. Once again, his first task was to peel away the outer layer, for the lungs were covered by yet another web, resembling a membrane in consistency and a tunic in function.[30] With masterly patience he then repeated the same delicate procedure in order to lay bare first the heart and finally the brain.[31] For Galen, the hymen was a homogeneous part, that is, a tissue, which was spread throughout the body for the dual purpose of linking and at the same time separating the organs.[32] From head to toe the membrane wrapped and compartmentalized all the parts of the animal's body; its supple yet robust texture tied the organs together and determined their spatial distribution. Deeply influenced by Aristotelian teleonomy, Galen attached great importance to the specific function of each anatomical part. He felt astonishment and admiration for the beauty of nature's works and her infallible wisdom in putting ornament where it was appropriate and protection where it was necessary. The virginal membrane is absent not only from the anatomy of a superficially observed body but also from the best of all possible bodies. In that masterpiece of nature, the human body, the hymen is everywhere except in the virgin's genitals. "This is my final work on the utility of the parts of the human body," Galen wrote in the introduction to book 18 of *De usu partium*. "There remains nothing about which I have not spoken in detail."[33] Later he excuses himself for having dealt with parts of the body with no relevance for therapy simply because he wished to be exhaustive and because, in order to refute the "sophists," he wished, as a philosophical physician, to show nature's rationality in all its manifestations.[34] He declares his encyclopedia of human anatomy and physiology to be a comprehensive work. And we are in fact told about both the major parts and their accessory instruments. Galen explains *per causas* beards, eyelashes, pubic hair, foreskin, and buttocks: all are natural sources of modesty and dignity in human beings.[35] He also offers a far more detailed analysis of the female genitals than does Aristotle: he distinguishes between labia and clitoris but never once alludes to the maidenhead.[36]

Given Galen's strong interest in the medical tradition, manifested in the form of commentary, citation, and polemic, his dogged silence on this point might lead one to think that the question had never been raised. On this point we might well share the view of Ambroise Paré: "Some anatomists have held that virgins have a membrane or panniculus in the cervix known as the virginal panniculus. Said panniculus is broken in the first coitus, in the struggles of Venus. This is implausible, for one finds no such panniculus in the anatomy of virgins, besides which Galen does not mention one."[37]

Galen notwithstanding, however, we have the invaluable and authoritative testimony of Soranus, a physician of the methodist school. A native of Ephesus who taught medicine in Rome in the time of Trajan and Hadrian, hence at the beginning of a century of which Galen saw the end, Soranus wrote a large number of books in which considerable attention is devoted to gynecology. A portion of his treatise *Gynaikeia* survives in Greek, along with two Latin translations of the whole work.[38]

The female genitals, Soranus tells us, were called the female sinus (or gulf). This is a hymen, he says, and nervous. It is located at the place where sexual intercourse takes place. It resembles an intestine with an ample interior but a relatively narrow external opening. Thus, the vagina itself was *defined as a membrane*. This definition is followed by specific comments concerning the genitals of the *parthenos*: "In virgins the vagina is depressed and narrower [than in other women], because it contains ridges that are held down by vessels originating in the uterus; when defloration occurs, these ridges unfold, causing pain: they burst [the vessels], resulting in the excretion of blood that ordinarily flows." Soranus continues: "In fact, the belief that a thin membrane grows in the middle of the vagina, and that it is this membrane that tears in defloration or when menstruation comes on too quickly, and that this same membrane, by persisting and becoming thicker, causes the malady known as 'imperforation,' is an *error*."[39]

So far as I know, this text is the first in Greek medical literature to mention a virginal hymen. The same text reappears in the rhapsodic compilation prepared in the fourth century by the emperor Julian's personal physician, Oribasius.[40] It is valu-

able evidence but unfortunately much too reticent, for it recounts an opinion (*oiesthai*) that remains anonymous. Was this
a disputed medical theory or a popular prejudice? Was it the
view of Christian gynecology, or was it a pagan—but Roman—
conception of the defloration of virgins? Was it perhaps one of
the vague notions common among midwives? These questions
are very difficult to answer. My hypothesis is that Soranus'
summation is directed at relatively competent readers familiar
with medical knowledge or at any rate with medical practice,
because it denies not only that a vaginal hymen exists but also
that it is subject to a particular form of degeneration. Soranus
demonstrates that a certain etiology is incorrect: it is not true
that atresia is caused by the sclerosis of a normally light, thin
membrane that occurs naturally in all girls. "In the first place,"
he argues, this hymen

> does not turn up in dissection. In the second place, if it did
> exist, something would resist the insertion of a probe in vir-
> gins. But until now [*nyni*] the probe penetrates all the way.
> In the third place, if the breaking of the membrane during
> defloration were the cause of pain, there would also have to
> be pain before defloration, at the time of the period. During
> defloration there should no longer be any. Furthermore, if
> the thickening of this membrane were the cause of the mal-
> ady known as imperforation, it should also be found in the
> same place in the same way, just as we always find the other
> parts of the body in their proper place. But in the current
> state of things, the membrane that blocks the passage in im-
> perforated women is found sometimes at the level of the la-
> bia, within our reach, sometimes in the middle of the vagina,
> and still other times in the middle of the uterine orifice. Such
> is the female sinus.[41]

A practitioner who cited evidence from both dissection and
clinical experience, Soranus did not hesitate to refer to the logic
of the body and its parts together with proofs acquired by
means of scalpel and probe. A fundamental distinction is made
between the natural parts of the organism, which are always

found in their proper place, and a pathological phenomenon that appears in various forms and locations. One chapter of the *Gynaikeia*, known only from its Latin version,[42] specifically treats the three different types of imperforation corresponding to the three possible locations of the membrane-diaphragm. This impermeable barrier could interfere with either one, two, or three of the stages of reproduction (coitus, conception, childbirth); hence it was obviously appropriate to treat it as an excrescence. If a girl had the misfortune to be born with a hymen, it was essential to get rid of the anomaly as quickly as possible, to cut it out in order to restore the body's proper female anatomy.

Hippocratic nosography did not neglect this congenital infirmity. The meninx (another name for membranous tissue) was one of the causes of infertility through obstruction of the uterine passageways. In *Diseases of Women* we read that "if the woman does not receive the semen even though menstruation occurs regularly, the problem is that a membrane is in front."[43] After the presence of an obstacle has been determined by manual inspection, a tampon (of resin, copper bloom, and honey wrapped in a rag) should be inserted as deeply as possible. After removing the pessary, the woman was supposed to wash with warm wine in which myrtle had been cooked. The use of emollients suggests that the purpose of the treatment was to soften the obstruction. But the physician goes on to say that the decisive remedy is to excise the "tunic" with a scalpel.[44] At no time, either in this connection or in any other, did the gynecologists of the classical period allude to a normal form of atresia in virgins. Aristotle, so attentive to teratological phenomena, does not mention the membrane itself. He does note the anomaly of a closed uterine orifice as one of a series of related minor deformities, however. The occlusion, he says, may give way when menstruation begins, but if necessary it must be opened with an incision.[45] This congenital obstruction is as abnormal (*paraphysis*) as obstruction of the penis or anus would be; such deformities are rare, but not unknown.[46]

From the *Corpus Hippocraticum* to Soranus' *Gynecology* anatomical-physiological observation perfected the description of the *pathos* that afflicted a few unfortunate *parthenoi*. Moreover, in analyzing the various forms of imperforation in detail, Soranus specifically argued in favor of its pathological nature: an innate deformity so inimical to woman's maternal function must certainly not be thought of as an organ. What is especially noteworthy about this case against the virginal panniculus is that Soranus was also a theorist of *parthenia* who fervently believed that virginity ought to be preserved, cultivated, and respected. As a physician who based his opinion solely on grounds of health, he opposed those who held that permanent virginity was unhealthy. He resolutely maintained that absolute chastity was physically hygienic behavior for both men and women. As proof he pointed to the excellent health of the priestesses, so long as the sedentary and inactive life of the temple did not cause them to gain weight and did not disrupt their menstrual cycle.[47]

Thus, the idea that a hymen was part of the virgin's natural endowment was doubly superfluous. First, it was not needed to explain the bloody trauma of defloration, which was said to be merely the effect of a first, violent penetration to which an organ not yet fully relaxed reacted painfully.[48] Second, as Soranus' text makes quite clear, the notorious panniculus was of no use whatsoever in thinking about or extolling virginity as such.[49] Here we see at work *in vitro*, that is, within the pages of a book, the fundamental compatibility that enables us to understand the Greek conception of female integrity: a woman could lose her *parthenia* yet conceal what was a mere *event*, for nothing irreparable had taken place, that is, a person whose body and genitals were intact (in the sense of never having been touched), yet have no hymen.

The difference between the Greeks and us therefore lies not in the contrast between a social status and a physical state, between an unmarried young woman and the victim of an anatomical assault, but in the value of a body as opposed to that of a sign. Thus by abandoning our suspicion that there is an obvious correlate of virginity of which the "inventors of the word" were profoundly unaware, we can discover both the truth and the simulacrum of the *parthenos*, both the value and the secret of *parthenia*.

LET US LEAVE Rome and the age of Hadrian, by which time the panniculus already loomed on the horizon of medical knowledge. A paradigmatic story such as that of Creusa in Euripides' *Ion* becomes much easier to understand if one accepts that Creusa was a *parthenos* both for her father, who knew nothing of her hidden marriage, and for the man she was marrying, who also knew nothing and who had no way of verifying anything. Creusa had experienced the anguish of violated *parthenia*, and outside paternal authority she paid by becoming sterile. Apollo did not assume the guise of a rainshower in order to seduce Creusa; he did not abandon his male body before deflowering the mortal virgin. The only trace he left was his son, the child whose mother was unable to get rid of it and who came back home, unique and living proof of a well-hidden sin.

Where hierogamy was involved, it might be argued that the impossibility of finding any physical evidence of defloration had to do with the supernatural character of divine love. The Greek gods could indeed miraculously erase the evidence of their entry into the bodies of the women they seduced. It was no doubt within their power to convert their amorous exploits into miracles comparable to that performed by the Christian God who impregnated a virgin and made her a mother while preserving her hymen intact through delivery. But neither Poseidon nor Zeus nor Apollo felt any need to restore an extraordinary and mysterious virginity to their conquests, for the female genitals tended naturally to reseal themselves. The male audience that attended Euripides' *Ion* must not have felt any particular surprise upon witnessing the perfect credulity of Creusa's legitimate husband, in whose eyes nothing had happened. This was an abuse of confidence, not unlike another case involving an Athenian politician, a minor scandal recounted in pseudo-Demosthenes' *Against Neaira*. An Athenian law stipulated that the archon king marry a woman who had not known any man and who married as a *parthenos*, that is, quite unambiguously, a virgin in the sexual sense. But a certain Stephanus, a vile pimp and accomplished blackmailer, induced the king to marry the daughter of a prostitute, the girl herself practicing the same profession as her mother. Thanks solely to an investigation conducted by the Council of the Areopagus into the reputation of this unworthy queen, the sacrilege was uncovered. The king, though required by law to choose an inviolate girl, had been unable to determine her condition by direct and intimate examination.[50] In the *Argonautica* by Apollonius Rhodius, moreover, it seems that a person in authority who wished to determine whether a girl was or was not still a virgin was obliged to determine whether she had engaged in a notorious *gamos* or was in the first stages of pregnancy.[51] Leave aside the outrages committed by fathers who opened their daughters' bellies to see if there was a fetus inside.[52] "Unfortunate girl, who are you? Are you ignorant of man, or have you already given birth?" This is the blunt question with which Deianira welcomes Iole in Sophocles' *Women of Trachis*.[53] *Anandros hē teknoussa:* what phrase could better epitomize, in the Greek tongue, the opposition between virginity preserved and virginity lost? As Poseidon says in bidding farewell to a girl to whom he has just made love, the loves of the immortals are never infertile,[54] and those of men are also often followed by a birth. The lively body of the offspring betrays the sexuality experienced by the mother's body—not in the same way as a torn meninx, to be sure, but just as revealingly.

The existence of a *parthenios* or being caught in the act: let us now confirm that these were the chief if not the only means of verifying virginity in ancient Greece by comparing a Greek story with the African ordeal of combat between young girls and the Italian consultation with the serpent. Pausanias mentions a docimasy involving bull's blood and performed by a priestess; its existence was attested at Aigai.[55] The nature of the beverage used for detecting a woman's sexual status might seem to suggest the symbolism of wounds and defilement. The women being tested here is not a *parthenos*, however, but a *gynē*, a woman who has already been deflowered. Not far from Aigai, Pausanias tells us, was a sanctuary of Broad-breasted Earth containing one of the oldest of wooden idols. The woman who assumes the office of priestess must be chaste from then on, and even beforehand she must not have had experience of more than one man. Candidates are tested by being asked to drink bull's blood, and if anyone lies about her past she is punished on the spot. Given the toxic qualities ascribed to bull's blood, it is legitimate to interpret the penalty for perjury as sudden death, despite the strange interpretation given by Pliny.[56]

This example suggests a need to reflect on the model of the virginity test itself. Gustave Glotz attempted to explain many legends and practices as survivals of judgments by ordeal. In particular he argued that the waters of rivers, wells, and oceans were used to test virginity.[57] To be sure, swimming and bathing are often associated with sexual acts and gestures, but an account such as that in Aeschines' tenth *Letter* cannot be interpreted unequivocally as a probative ceremony. The passage in question concerns a journey in Asia Minor.

> We had already spent several days in Ilium . . . when the day arrived on which most of the inhabitants prepare for marriage those of their daughters of marriageable age. There were many girls to be married, and in the Troad the custom was for them to go to the banks of the Scamander, swim in the river, and pronounce these supposedly sacred words: "Take my virginity, O Scamander." Along with the others a virgin [*parthenos*] named Kallirhoe, a girl of imposing stature

and daughter of a man of modest station, came to the river
to bathe.

It is easy to imagine the sort of comic situation likely to ensue
when a river was invoked as a man. A handsome youth named
Cimon emerged from the bushes along the Scamander and eagerly responded to the girl's exhortations: "With pleasure I,
Scamander, receive and take Kallirhoe! And I shall do you
much good!" He abducts the girl and disappears. To justify his
actions he later claims that there is a tradition of similar exploits. For example, a Magnesian youth disguised himself as the
river Meander and became the father of an athlete. The immersion of the girl's body on the eve of her wedding is in no sense
a judgment, however. Her virginity is simply being placed at the
disposal of Scamander. She makes an offering of her virginity,
as Martin Nilsson put it, though he also sees the prenuptial bath
as a metaphor for perforation of the hymen.[58] Strange as it may
seem to us if we do not give up the idea of a membrane to be
ruptured, the water of a river was one of the possible metamorphoses of the male body. A bath becomes an embrace for Tyro,
whose ghost Ulysses encounters on the banks of the river of
blood that revives the souls of the dead. "She had gone daft for
the river Enipeus, most graceful of all running streams, and
ranged all day by Enipeus' limpid side, whose form the foaming
girdler of the islands, the god who makes earth tremble, took
and so lay down with her where he went flooding seaward,
their bower a purple billow, arching round to hide them in a
sea vale, god and lady."[59] Aquatic lover as in the story of Tyro,[60]
a river could be called quite simply "Male."[61]

The Scamander ritual is not presented as a test, any more
than Auge's father is in doubt about the virginity of a girl who
is already a mother when he orders her tossed into the Aegean
(as Glotz would have it). To take one last example of Greek
indifference to ordeals, let us compare Aelian's description of
the Lanuvium ritual with his treatment of a similar ritual in

Epirus.[62] Initially the setting is almost identical: a temple of Apollo, a sacred wood in which serpents live, a virgin priestess who enters the temple grounds with food for the epigones of the Delphic Python. Here again the reptiles' appetite is a sign of the god. Will he be questioned about the food-bearing *parthenos?* Not at all: the god will reveal whether the coming year will be a good one or disease and disorder will threaten the populace.

Given the value attached to the sexual purity of the Pythia, it is indeed remarkable that it was not tested beforehand or verified during her long tenure. As the story recounted by Diodorus Siculus indicates, the question was settled once and for all when a man was overcome by desire for one of the first priestesses and raped her. Following this incident, the Delphians decided to protect the Pythia from male desire by entrusting the tripod to an older woman who dressed like a girl.[63]

If we forget about the hymen, the picture is clear and relatively simple. Many details become explicable, including the attitude of Greek historians toward tests of virginity. How could they not understand methods for discovering the true *parthenos* and unmasking the false, when for a Greek the loss of *parthenia* was so easily concealed? It comes as no surprise, therefore, to discover medical treatments capable of making a violated woman look like a virgin. Were these operations performed by skilled surgeons, good at mending torn membranes? No. They consisted simply of inserting perfumed pessaries into the vagina to alter and revitalize its appearance.[64]

Another possible objection to the contention that for the Greeks the hymen did not exist is the text of the Hippocratic treatise *Diseases of Women*. But no membrane is mentioned or assumed in this discussion of the pathology of virgins. Indeed, the text becomes more coherent if one stops thinking that the Greeks shared the assumption that the hymen exists. According to this physician, puberty exposes girls to madness because the hermetically sealed body stifles and suffocates. It retains the first menstrual blood, and this imprisoned humor spreads indiscriminately throughout the body, impedes breathing, and makes the girl wish to hang herself. When this occurs, the girl must not be allowed to run off and offer her clothing to Artemis. The best thing is to marry and have children. To be sure, her body needs to be open, and the menstrual *katharsis*, that physiological form of bloodletting, must not be impeded. But was the obstruction a membrane? If so, this would be superb psychosomatic atresia, for the gynecologist is here concerned with a disease. In reality, however, the problem does not lie with either the vagina or the vulva. It is actually the passageways through which blood flows to the uterus that have atrophied and grown tenuous. Coitus and above all maternity have the power to stimulate dilation of these veins, thus preparing them to fulfill their function: "I maintain that a woman who has not had children is affected more quickly and more seriously by menstruation than one who has had children. In fact, childbirth makes the veins of the latter flow more easily for her periods, and the womb opens more."[65] It is the plumbing around the uterus that impedes the circulation and evacuation of the female blood.

This model of the body is identical with the one inferred earlier from the Pythia's virginity. If the hymen is not indispensable for explaining the value of *parthenia* or the pain of defloration, neither is it the only way to account for the closure of the virginal body. The body of a woman who no longer makes love is threatened by the same forms of uterine suffocation as the body of a woman who has never made love.[66] The body clamps down on itself and resumes its infantile state: I say the body because it is not a specific part, a unique opening, but rather all the parts that open downward through a mouth and lips. Defloration is the end of a kind of silence or fast. Better yet, it is the interruption of a continence that, like the marriage veil, is not destroyed by a final laceration but suspended like a raised *kalyptra*. The ritual shows that the *parthenos* and the widow are equivalent if both are chaste. Hera, who at Stymphalus experiences the three stages in the life of a woman, bathes each year at Nauplia in a spring that restores her virginity.[67] Hagne is a maiden as inviolate as a faithful wife.[68] And the idea of a purity that comes with age, even more complete and prized than that of the virgin, underlies Socrates' speech on midwives[69] as well as Diodorus' on the Pythia. If the freshness of youth and beauty marks a temporary time menaced by male desire and the powers of Aphrodite, the older woman, her mission accomplished, is safely distant from sexuality. In the city of the *Laws*, all the priestesses are to be above the age of sixty.[70] True, Parthenia bids a bride farewell as if departing forever,[71] for the destiny of a *nymphē* is of course to fulfill herself entirely and permanently in the married life upon which she is about to embark. Yet we know that return is possible, and that nothing in the body of a woman unveiled and visited by a man's sex is irretrievably lost.

III

Neither Virgins nor Mothers

~ 10 ~

The Danaides'
Endless Chore

V ALERIUS MAXIMUS devotes a chapter of his collection of
facta et dicta memorabilia to certain extraordinary public
judgments. He first discusses accusations stunningly confirmed
by the facts and then turns to individuals unjustly suspected of
crimes who were able to prove their innocence. Among the famous acquittals he cites the case of a sacred virgin, the vestal
Tuccia. Accused of having violated her vow of chastity, she succeeded in dispelling the "cloud of infamy" that blackened her
name by boldly imploring her goddess to render a verdict. Taking up a sieve she cried: "O Vesta, if the hands with which I
have touched your sacred objects have always been chaste, see
to it that with this instrument I fetch water from the Tiber and
carry it all the way to your sanctuary." Nature itself, Valerius
Maximus explains, acceded to the wishes of the priestess.[1]

Historians interested in prodigies frequently mention this
episode. Pliny the Elder reports that the people of his day still
used "the imprecation associated with the incest of the vestal
Tuccia thanks to which she carried water in a sieve in 518 *anno
Urbis.*"[2] Livy and Dionysius of Halicarnassus[3] repeat the story
of this exploit, and even Christian literature perpetuated its
memory. In a short list of pagan miracles Tertullian mentions
"water carried in a sieve and a ship moved with a belt," minor
feats that pale by comparison with the true miracles worked by

the one God.[4] Augustine grudgingly devotes a few lines to pagan miracles because—*historia* obliges—one cannot ignore the power of the pagan gods.[5] This ordeal was an exceptional and memorable event. No regular ritual called for the repetition of an act that was portrayed as a sudden and unique defiance of the impossible. Like the virgin who pulled the ship carrying the Phrygian Mother off a sandbar in the Tiber by attaching her belt to its prow,[6] the vestal Tuccia performed a feat that would ever after be identified with her name. Her decision was especially striking and her success all the more implausible because in both Greece and Rome to carry water in a sieve was a traditional trope for impossibility.

A. B. Cook devoted a very long chapter of his *Zeus* to the symbolism of vessels with holes, cracks, and punctures.[7] Stories, proverbs, comic allusions, and iconography used such vessels to represent an important meteorological phenomenon: rain.[8] The fine spray, the cloud atomized into drops, the humor that flows from the sky would always be symbolized by a vessel with a leaky bottom. When Strepsiades discovers the nature gods who are responsible for downpours and floods, he candidly admits that he had always believed these were the work of Zeus urinating through a sieve.[9] This simple model may well be useful for interpreting the whole rich mythology of leaking waters. Tuccia's exploit might also be interpreted in terms of this river symbolism. If people could imagine the falling rain thanks to the *koskinon* that transformed a powerful jet into a multitude of liquid particles, then for a sieve to hold water was a "typical impossibility" that could provide "the ideal test for a primitive ordeal, since its successful completion manifestly implied the intervention of the gods in favor of the accused."[10] In Cook's view, the particular occasion for the trial and the fact that it allowed a virgin priestess to demonstrate her integrity were mere accidents. Yet the ancient tradition that associated Tuccia's sieve with Claudia's belt suggests that is was through a virginal object that unrecognized chastity manifested itself. Just as the *cingulum* and *zona* announced through their intact strength the purity they protected, an instrument whose very function made it unfit to hold water symbolized the closedness of a body that was accused of being open. Furthermore, the meteorological model led Cook to interpret the use of the sieve for transporting water as a rite rather than as a symbol of the truly disconcerting idea of using a sieve to hold a liquid. If one thinks of falling rain, then passing water through a filter appears to be an evocative gesture, so familiar and natural that Tuccia's performance is merely a disruption of the usual practice of the water nymphs or, as C. Picard would put it, the rainmakers.[11]

THE ROMAN ORDEAL is particularly revealing when viewed against a certain mythological background: the well-known tradition that encompasses both those guilty of neglecting the Eleusinian mysteries[12] and certain young women who, shortly after marrying in Argos, slit their new husbands' throats.[13] In the underworld both the uninitiated and the murderous brides are condemned forever to fill a bottomless jar with water carried in a sieve or broken pitcher. Like Sisyphus and Tantalus, these damned souls endlessly repeat a futile task; they are trapped in unfulfillment. According to what has become a traditional exegesis, the fact that the punishment meted out to the uninitiated and the murderesses is the same can easily be interpreted in terms of "the mystical equivalence between *amyētoi* and *agamoi.*"[14] All who refuse the telos of initiation or marriage and who therefore remain in a permanent state of incompleteness are said to share the same punishment, perpetually rebeginning the same task.

In the second edition of *Psyche*, E. Rohde proposed a hypothesis to which subsequent interpreters of the Danaides long remained faithful.[15] Using a sieve to pour water into a bottomless pithos was explained in terms of a funeral ritual, namely, the custom of placing a loutrophoros—said to be a perforate pitcher—on the tombs of *agamoi*. Rohde put this interpretation in the form of a question: "Did this mean that *agamoi* were condemned after death to suffer the same torture as the one reserved for the Danaides because the Danaides' crime made them the mythical prototype of the *agamoi?* And were the Danaides, like the *agamoi,* obliged eternally and futilely to carry water from the nuptial bath to the *loutron?*"[16]

The idea is as appealing as its formulation is discreet, and subsequent interpreters have built solid analyses on Rohde's suggestion. The Danaides have been treated both as well-nymphs and as water-bearing deities.[17] If Rohde introduced the funeral loutrophoros to explain the powerlessness of the unmarried and the meaninglessness of their chore, the ritual naturalism of the act of pouring water from a sieve into a bottomless jar lent it a fundamental and novel efficacy. The author of *Psyche* recognized the sign of the impossible in both the funerary monument and the eschatological scene.[18] By contrast, both Cook and Harrison argued that *agamoi* were equipped, in their sepulchers as well as in the underworld, with the instrument they needed to *complete* the marriage ceremony. "Probably these vases, as Dr. Frazer suggests, were at first placed on the graves of the unmarried with the kindly intent of helping the desolate unmarried ghost to accomplish his wedding in the world below. But once the custom fixed, it might easily be interpreted as the symbol of an underworld punishment."[19] The meaning of the punishment—for these authors recognize that it was a true torture[20]—therefore lies in the perpetual *repetition* of certain actions by a *nymphē* who ensures that her marriage will be fertile by causing water to flow. Alluding to the generalized sympathy between the earth, the dead, and marriage that Eleusinism "is said to have fostered in Greece," Picard broadens the interpretation of the bottomless loutrophoros that was allegedly placed on the graves of *agamoi*. It "recalled not so much the nuptial bath—an evocation that would have been rather surprising— as the invigorating hope of life after death that perhaps lay in store even for those who unfortunately had known neither the family *telos* nor the redeeming, mystical sacrament of the Teles-terion."[21] A watering instrument, the perforated vessel found in cemeteries and wedding processions kept alive the memory of the sacred plant cult.[22]

The activity of the uninitiated and of the Danaides in the underworld—whether it evokes wells, nuptial baths, or pious gardens along with libations to the dead—poses a problem, however. Are we to assume that a hopeless, sempiternal chore is the survival of one of the most venerable and ancestral of rituals? If so, it is essential to explain why that ritual was de-formed. It is not enough to assume that the damned are *imitating* a ceremony; one must explain why and when the Greeks began to imagine that ceremony in the form of a punishment.

Cook sees the event that transformed the meaning of the Danaides' behavior in their very crime, that is, within the story itself. Their marriage was supposed to act as a fertility charm and slake the thirst of parched Argolis, but killing their husbands supposedly negated the magic. Because they caused this important operation to fail, the Danaides, we are told, deserved to be punished by performing the same act over and over again.[23] Harrison and Picard, however, look to Greek religious history for a deeper explanation of the ceremony: whether after the establishment of a patriarchal order,[24] or following the over-throw of Achaean domination,[25] these benevolent female ge-niuses, who had power over well water, allegedly became baf-fling figures totally alien to the new divine order, which was divorced from the symbols of the earth. Irrigation, once a val-ued and constant activity, supposedly became meaningless and unintelligible, a senseless occupation. The same Danaides said to have been the founders of the Thesmophoria devolved from positive marriage deities to hapless shades.[26] The first initiators, they allegedly became so alien as to pass for uninitiated.[27]

I will not take time to comment on the theory of a cata-strophic loss of memory due to major historical and religious upheavals, which allegedly made it impossible for any Greek to decipher the nonetheless quite simple gestures involved in watering. If the Eleusinian cult has any essential and enduring feature, surely it is the power of Demeter over agriculture, and the Eleusinian mysteries did not belong to a forgotten religion of another age. How can one make the *loss of meaning* of a fundamental agricultural practice coincide with an allegory about neglect of Eleusis? Let us accept the fact that the primary significance of the leaky pithos was to distribute water in order to make plants grow. Does it make any sense to conjecture that such watering became an enigma *within the cult of Demeter?*

The assumptions on which the interpretations mentioned above are based involve two misunderstandings: first, that the daughters of Danaus are unmarried;[28] and second, that the loutrophoroi placed on the tombs of the unmarried were perforated.

CONSIDER FIRST the question of the funerary vessels. Rohde bases his analogy between the Danaides' jar and the hydria of the unmarried on an archaeological finding.[29] As long ago as 1902 Bonner pointed out that the vessels carried by underworld figures are not loutrophoroi any more than a pithos is shaped like a bathtub.[30] More than that, one should not underestimate the extent to which Rohde's tone is dubious in his discussion of the discovery in the Dipylon of "certain bottomless vessels" used for funerary purposes.[31] In a note Harrison makes it clear that this type of vessel cannot be exclusively or significantly attributed to the unmarried.[32] And that is not all. None of the ancient texts (of Demosthenes, Pollux, Hesychius, and Eustathius) cited as proof of this practice mentions a perforated bottom.[33] Now, if the loutrophoros was a distinctive monument to *agamoi* because water passed through it, it is surprising that the lexicographers failed to note or were unaware of so essential a fact. Demosthenes is categorical in asserting that a loutrophoros on a tomb means one thing and one thing only: it is a sign (*sēmeion*) that the deceased person (in this case a male) was unmarried at the time of death. Furthermore, the glosses ascribe to this sign the power to evoke the water of the nuptial ablutions as though it were an *effective* instrument for that purpose, thus implying that its bottom did not leak.

As for the unmarried state of the Danaides, once again the texts are unambiguous. The Danaides are not maidens: not only did they cut off their husbands' heads after celebration of a lawful *gamos*, but their wedding night was more than just the occasion of a murderous ambush. Another violent act had already been committed, an act seemingly made legitimate by the agreement between Danaus and the suitors. The crime of the rebel *nymphai* was merely a response. Why should they have waited until that night to kill? Why did the murder have to take place in the marriage bed after the husband had fallen asleep? The story's horror as well as its power resides in the tension between an imperious desire and a no less irresistible hatred. Furthermore, as Apollodorus' version proves,[34] the only condition under which any of the women could refuse to go through with the prearranged murder plans (as one of them in fact did refuse) was if her adversary for some reason gave up his own plan. Lynceus respected the virginity of Hypermestra; he did not avail himself of his legitimate right to commit rape, and Hypermestra therefore did not slit his throat. No blood stained this couple's sheets: neither the blood of defloration transformed into a wound by an arrogant virility, nor the blood from wounds inflicted by women out of hatred for the male sex. In the *Suppliants* Aeschylus alludes to marriage between cousins only by way of hostile metaphors: the suppliants are fugitives, of course, doves harassed and attacked by a flock of crows.[35] Yet they make themselves wolves in order to drive off the pursuing hounds,[36] and they invoke *kratos*, victory, for women.[37] Determined to make a weapon of their weakness, they warn the king of Argos that they will hang themselves from the gods' statues with their belts if their request for aid is not granted.[38] The army of fifty Danaides claims symmetry with the fifty Egyptiades; determined not to endure male hubris,[39] the Danaides resolve to act in common. Since the *genos* of cousins is "insatiable for combat,"[40] they will satisfy the desire. We do not know what form Aeschylus gave to the events of the night of massacre. But Prometheus' words set the stage for a bloody exchange:

> A generation of fifty virgins shall come again to Argos, not of their own accord, fleeing from incestuous wedlock with their cousins; and these with fluttering hearts, like falcons left not far behind by doves, shall come pursuing marriage such as should not be pursued, but heaven shall be jealous over their persons, and Pelasgia shall receive them after being crushed by a deed of night-fenced daring wrought by woman's hand; for each bride shall bereave her respective husband of life, having dyed in their throats a sword of twin sharp edge. Would that in guise like this Venus might visit my foes! But tenderness shall soften one of the maidens, so that she shall not slay the partner of her couch, but shall be blunt in her resolve, and of the two alternatives she shall choose the former, to be called a coward rather than a murderess. She in Argos shall give birth to a race of kings.[41]

In this singular struggle the courage of a female Ares plays an important part,[42] and the doves display the cruelty of carnivores: the sword that is plunged into a male neck evokes an aggression that, though unspoken, is nevertheless the object of the desire that brought the sons of Egypt as far as Argos.[43] Prometheus intimates that it was after making love that Hypermestra was seized by pity for her spouse. She suddenly hopes that a fruitful marriage will succeed this first embrace. Feeling tender and weak, she is all but disarmed, according to one scholiast.[44] Apollodorus says that Hypermestra is the only virgin; Aeschylus, that she is the only Danaid to fall in love. Thanks to her we understand that none of her sisters arose an *agamos* on her wedding night.[45] It is for this reason, as Jane Harrison observed, that for them the trial of carrying water in a sieve had to end in a lamentable and irremediable discharge.[46]

~ 11 ~

The Matter of Despair

I N ORDER to understand the values attached to the image of the leaky jar let us turn now to ancient tradition. From the time such an object is first mentioned, pouring water into a leaky vessel signifies a definite sort of behavior: a futile task or an insatiable desire, neglect of Eleusis, indiscretion, forgetfulness. The Danaides introduce a variation on this multiplicity of already established meanings but without contradicting them; on the contrary, they personify in strikingly symbolic form the type of behavior already implicit in the image.

In Ischomachus' "maieutic" dialogue with his young wife,[1] the leaky vessel is invoked to explain the division of labor in the household. The husband instructs his wife as to their respective tasks: for one, to accumulate; for the other, to conserve (*phylassein, sōzein*).[2] This strict division allows the domestic community to survive by dint of both nature and custom.[3] If the work of one partner is not to be ridiculous, the other must do his or her part. It would be ridiculous to conserve, the young homemaker says, if no one brought things into the home from outside. And the husband, eager to show how their respective duties complement each other, admits that "from my point of view, I would look very ridiculous indeed accumulating these things if there were no one to conserve what I brought home. Do you not see how people pity those who, as they say, pour water into a bottomless jar, because they think their labor is futile?"[4]

Let us first consider the question of "ridiculousness." In a discussion of *oikonomia*, of efficient and therefore thrifty household management, a leaky jar is the first image that comes to the husband's mind to express foolishness: a stupidity so silly that laughter is sufficient punishment. Xenophon's wise householder's concern that he not become the laughingstock of the neighborhood on account of a woman is reminiscent of Hesiod's counsel to the shrewd peasant to remain on his guard.[5] A well-bred woman such as the one Ischomachus has chosen for his wife was above all a woman who would take good care of the household stores. To live with such a woman was not to fill a jar even as it was being emptied. In the *Oeconomicus* attributed to Aristotle the simile is less extended. The author gives this summary: "The economist ought to possess four qualities in relation to wealth. He ought to be able to acquire, and to guard it; otherwise there is no advantage in acquiring it, but it is a case of drawing water with a sieve, or the proverbial jar with a hole in it."[6] And Aristotle himself, referring not to household economy but to the policy of poor relief dear to Athenian democrats, remarks that the system is really quite futile. The poor, the *aporoi*, continue despite the distributions to have the same insatiable needs. Hence relief is like pouring water into a leaky jar.[7]

This is a revealing form of the metaphor, an attested proverbial use. Here we are concerned not with the punishment of the uninitiated or the Danaides but rather with an anonymous action having no religious connotations. The *tetrēmenos pithos* is a jar with holes in its bottom, hence useless.

Now, a pithos was preeminently a storage container. It was a large earthenware vessel that the Greeks used for storing wine, oil, and grain. Note, moreover, that these economic treatises (concerning both public and private economies) do not mention transferring water.[8] On the contrary, the image is used in a way that closely mirrors the writers' concerns: to bring supplies to an unguarded house or to feed the penniless is like storing vital necessities in a leaky container.

The countless texts cited by Mau in his article "Dolium" in the *Realencyclopädie* make it quite clear that a jar was quite distinct from a well.[9] In the tradition of Hellenic and Latin agronomy from Hesiod to the *Geoponica* and from Cato to Pliny, the pithos or dolium is described as an essential piece of equipment for any family farm.[10] Already in the world of the *Odyssey* and the *Iliad* we find jars used for storing food and wine. In Ithaca the storehouse of the king's manor holds pithoi filled with old and very sweet wine, an exquisite drink that waits for Ulysses to return to a home protected by sturdy gates and a female steward.[11] The suitors will drain much wine from the jars,[12] but the *thalamos* guarded by Euryclea will remain inviolate. Even Zeus possesses two of these household receptacles, solidly rooted in the ground and filled with gifts for mortals: one holds goods, the other evils: "If Zeus who delights in thunder mingles these and bestows them on man, he shifts, and moves now in evil, again in good fortune. But when Zeus bestows from the urn of sorrows, he makes a failure of man, and the evil hunger drives him over the shining earth, and he wanders respected neither of gods nor mortals."[13]

The significance of the divine jars derives from the symbolism of repletion and insatiable hunger. They represent the fortunes and misfortunes of mortals in terms of the most elementary and archaic forms of wealth, the *trophē*. If the image of the leaky pithos appears with the frequency of a familiar commonplace,[14] it is because a whole tradition of practical wisdom emphasized the symbolic value of the jar—not only in the commonsensical form of the maxims but also in esteemed and venerable literature. The economic discipline taught by Hesiod envisioned a goal that was not easily achieved: namely, to make sure that one's pithoi were carefully sealed to protect the commodities they stored.[15] Works and days—the peasant's patient daily toil—became tangible when stored in the *bios*, safe above all from bad weather but also from greedy appetites. Jean-Pierre Vernant writes: "Since wheat does not grow by itself, man cannot live without working, certain that he will find each day what he needs for his revels without worrying about the days to come. Just as he must bend his back over the soil to make sure that the kernels of wheat grow to maturity, so after the harvest must he store the grain in pithoi in the storeroom, to be opened on appointed days (not all were good for the purpose) and in full awareness of how much substance he had been able to secure."[16] In other words, the pithos symbolized domestic abundance, just as its outdoor counterpart, the tilled field, symbolized finite resources and the ever-present threat of shortage. The jar is mentioned five times in *Works and Days*, "all three times in connection with opening (*oigō* in line 819, *archomai* in lines 815 and 368)."[17] This is because the pleasure of the first taste is diminished by the shortage it risks causing. To eat, to fill one's own belly, is to empty the belly of the jar, and unless one eats sparingly the bottom of the pithos becomes visible all too soon. In order to guarantee his own source of food and a rough household autarchy, the man who lives apart from the gods is obliged to create, between the earth and his own *gastēr*, a "domestic belly"[18] in the form of large amphora. It is intact, however, and equipped with neck and mouth. If Hesiod does not raise the specter of the leaky pithos, it is because the gluttony of people who daily help themselves to all they need is enough to consume all reserves.

The use of jars for storing food products is confirmed in treatises on farming and agronomy. *Dolia picata*, or casks sealed with pitch, are especially recommended for wine,[19] whereas unbaked jars whose pores still breathe can be used for oil, grain, marc, and lupines.[20] And, continuing with the *realia*, Cato says that when a container is cracked, a rainy day should be used to repair it with a *medicamentum*, a packing made of pitch, resin, and gypsum,[21] or with metal strapping. The person in charge of a farm should not permit a moment to go by that is not employed in some useful way.[22]

The sieve was also part of a household's equipment. Jane Harrison, in an early article titled *"Mystica Vannus Iacchi,"* gave a historical interpretation of the use of the sieve, normally intended for separating grain from chaff, for drawing a liquid.[23] How and why was the winnowing basket, which numbered among the instruments of Demeter-Ceres, transferred to the service of Iacchus? After identifying the *liknon* as an accessory of mystical purification and fertility magic, Harrison argued that the presence of the sieve in association with Dionysus was a memory of the fermented beverage that preceded wine in Thrace, a grain-based liquor supposedly invented by the god himself: namely, beer. The old sieve, essential for purifying barley, was ostensibly converted into a basket for carrying Greek grapes, so that besides its original cathartic function it also served as a horn of plenty. The sieve, carried in processions and filled with what was most precious—from the grains of Sabazius to the fruits and phalli of Dionysus—apparently remained a central element of mystical practice.[24]

Notwithstanding the inevitable difficulties of chronological reconstruction, Harrison's analysis draws our attention to the agricultural context in which the sieve was used and reminds us that it served not only in the baking of breads and cakes but also in the processing of wine. Just as the pithos-dolium was used to hold wine as well as other liquids and small food items, so the sieve was used both for separating grains and for skimming wine. Cato prescribes a *cribrum* for seeds, another for kernels,[25] and three "filters" (*cola*) for removing the surface scum from wine.[26]

There are rewards to be gleaned from delving into the technical details of agricultural literature: jar and sieve are part of the indispensable equipment of civilized life, forever used for storing what is necessary and for getting rid of what is unnecessary. The twin expressions *tetrēmenos pithos* (leaky jar) and *koskinōi antlein* (to draw [liquid] with a sieve) literally invert these fundamental actions of storing and separating. A jar that allows its contents to leak out, a sieve[27] used as a container: what better way to suggest improvidence in the head of a family?

Ischomachus calls riddled with holes or "rotten"[28] a jar that is supposed to be used for storing food items, *eisphero-mena*[29] that must be properly measured out and distributed over time. Nothing in this economic context suggests a water ritual. Yet nearly all the classical and recent interpretations of the per-forated pithos, from Rohde to Eva Keuls, have been concerned exclusively with the hydraulic phenomena—rain, bath, liba-tion, or *katharsis*—that scholars have assumed to underlie every occurrence of the leaky container image. It is true that if we take the first certain literary appearance of the punishment of the Danaides in the underworld (namely, the pseudo-Platonic *Axiochus*) as our point of departure, we find "the Danaides end-lessly drawing water."[30] As I hope to show in a moment, how-ever, the water is a variant specifically associated with the un-derworld. In Hesiod pithoi are not used to hold water. If there is one good thing in Boeotia that the gods have not hidden, it is this fruit of the earth that springs up spontaneously and inex-haustibly in the middle of a drought. Abundant and cool, it can be mixed with wine and eaten along with meat or buckwheat cakes as the one element that man neither produces nor con-sumes: it is perhaps the only vital resource that Hesiod does not recommend saving or storing inside the house.[31]

Here it is important to consider the precise meaning of the verb *antlein*. Does it always mean "to draw water," or can some-thing else be "drawn"? A proverb is useful: *ek pithō antlein*, "to draw from the jar," means to slake one's thirst at the source, to go straight to the place where Dionysus' beverage is most re-fined and most abundant.[32] Furthermore, *metantlein* is a tech-nical compound that means to transfer wine from a pithos into smaller containers.[33] Under Demeter's patronage, moreover, the *antlētriai* are women who, in the secrecy of the Thesmophoria, go down into adyta in the earth to bring back the remains of sows that have been tossed into them.[34] According to Picard, this ritual (performed during the Thesmophoria) revealed the latent dowsing abilities in all women, but there is no reason to think automatically of water-carrying just because we find derivative forms of a verb that originally meant "to bail" but was often used to mean "to draw."[35]

If THE JAR is understood as the epitome of agricultural prosperity and the sieve viewed as a symbol of the care taken of the jar's contents, it becomes easier to understand why neglect of Eleusis was punished by the obligation to pour *water* into a *perforated* jar after *carrying* it in a *sieve*. Reading the *Gorgias* and imagining the *Nekyia* (The Underworld) painted by Polygnotus at Delphi and described by Pausanias suggests that the substitution of water for wine and wheat was a significant change that reinforced the already noteworthy substitution of a defective container for a usable one.

Consider first this passage from the *Gorgias:*

And perhaps we are actually dead, for I once heard one of our wise men say that we are now dead, and that our body is a tomb, and that that part of the soul in which dwell the desires is of a nature to be swayed and to shift to and fro. And so some clever fellow, a Sicilian perhaps or Italian, writing in allegory, by a slight perversion of language named this part of the soul a jar [*pithos,* making a pun on *pithanon* and *peistikon*], because it can be swayed and easily persuaded, and the foolish he called the uninitiated, and that part of the soul in foolish people where the desires reside—the uncontrolled and nonretentive part—he likened to a leaky jar, because it can never be filled [*aplēstia*]. And in opposition to you, Callicles, he shows that of those in Hades—the unseen world he means—these uninitiated must be the most unhappy, for they will carry water to pour into a perforated jar

in a similarly perforated sieve. And by the sieve, my informant told me, he means the soul, and the soul of the foolish
[*anoētoi*] he compared to a sieve, because it is perforated and
through lack of belief and forgetfulness unable to hold anything . . . Come then, let me offer you another image from
the same school as the last. Consider whether you would say
this of each type of life, the temperate and the undisciplined.
Imagine that each of the two men has several jars, in the one
case in sound condition and filled, one with wine, another
with honey, another with milk, and many others with a variety of liquids, but that the sources of these liquids are scanty
and hard to come by, procured only with much hard labor.
Imagine then that the one after filling his vessels does not
trouble himself to draw in further supplies but as far as the
jars are concerned is free from worry; in the case of the other
man the sources, as in the first instance, are procurable but
difficult to come by, but his vessels are perforated and un-
sound and he is ever compelled to spend day and night in
replenishing them, if he is not to suffer the greatest agony. If
this is the character of each of the lives, do you still insist that
the life of the uncontrolled man is happier than that of the
orderly?[36]

Plato's two analogies are closely related.[37] In fact the second is present only to shift the locus of the first from the afterlife
to life on this earth, since Socrates is unable to persuade Callicles—who is compared to a plover[38]—by describing the punishments of the damned. If we read the two arguments as re-
inforcing a single point, we can see the differences between
them. The second version is surely the one that comes closer to
the proverb concerning the perforated jar. The improvident
man who accumulates essential supplies but fails to store them
properly and who therefore wastes his energies day and night
is someone we recognize at once: the ridiculous master, or the
demagogue who depletes the public patrimony. Before trivial-
izing his argument by comparing such a man to a bird, the
plover, who eliminates what he eats,[39] Socrates chooses a more

familiar image, perhaps in order to emphasize this familiarity: the storeroom with its jars of wine and honey belongs to the realm of the visible, as opposed to the initial allegory of water-bearing shades with its undefined setting. The other allegory was immediately troubling: Callicles had protested that happiness identified with control of the passions is the happiness of stones and corpses.[40] Perhaps we are all dead, Socrates retorts. We live in tombs, it seems, and in this invisible world the saddest of us are the "unclosed," those whose souls are like sieves and who are incapable of filling the perforated jar of their desires. In this Hades to which we are confined, to be insatiable is to toil endlessly in order to sustain a flow. But Callicles is not convinced, and Socrates then speaks to him of men of flesh and blood, which we certainly are, and of great outflows of honey and wine.

Thus, the perforated pithos in a poorly run household is not the same thing as a similar object amid the flames of the underworld: Plato shows us the metamorphosis. In Plato's time, however, a large painting by Polygnotus of Thasos had covered the walls of the Lesche at Delphi for a century.[41] Pausanias describes and interprets it. The underworld is depicted along with its mythical inhabitants. The virgin who introduced the "orgies" of Demeter to Thasos is shown seated and carrying a closed cist on her knees;[42] she is happy. Next to Penthesileus, however, are melancholy women identified by an inscription "the uninitiated." They carry water in leaky vessels.[43] Along with Sisyphus and Callisto in the same part of the fresco is a group consisting of an old man, a child, and two women carrying water to a jar. It is conjectured (*eikaseis*), says Pausanias, that the older woman's hydria is broken. She tries again to pour the water that remains in the pitcher in the jar. "One is inclined to conjecture that they are people making a mock of the Eleusinian rites. But the older Greeks considered the Eleusinian mysteries as much above all other religious services as the gods are superior to heroes."[44] For the souls of those who had forgotten Demeter, it was more than a question of poor house-keeping: for them the jar became a noncontainer, a vessel from which water leaked. This image is the antithesis of Demetrian values. Before substantiating this assertion, however, I want to explain how a punishment involving water could have become an integral part of the morphology of the underworld.

Plato's *Republic* will be our guide.[45] Plato evokes the parched Plain of Oblivion, through which flows a river that does not irrigate the earth but whose only quality is to flow. No vessel can hold its water,[46] and the soul that drinks from this river is drained of all memory, stricken by oblivion. (The foolish souls in the *Gorgias* who poured water into a perforated jar from a similarly perforated sieve also suffered from forgetfulness.[47]) A stream flows indefatigably through a torrid desert. But there are also cold and stagnant waters. To those friends who are with him as he waits to die Socrates says that "anyone who reaches Hades incomplete and unfulfilled will have his place in the mire, while he who has been purified and initiated will reside in the society of the gods."[48] According to telestic tradition, it is into a lake of mud, a bottomless swamp, that the souls of the uninitiated are thrown. Aristophanes portrays initiates (*memyē-menoi*) who, after enjoying a sumptuous feast, march in procession invoking Iacchus and Demeter.[49] The condition of the wicked is contrasted with their full stomachs, with their lives free of fatigue in reward for unremitting piety,[50] and with the springtime sun that warms them gently.[51] Those who were not worthy of initiation lie sunk in a huge swamp of endless muck.[52]

One of Plato's characters, Adimantus, speaks for the unjust and atheistic; he says that the stories told by poets and theologians about the justice of the gods are naive illusions. Homer and Hesiod hold that among the blessings awarded to righteous men is that of witnessing the growth of abundant and nutritious plants. But "Musaeus and his son have a more excellent song than these of the blessings that the gods bestow on the righteous. For they conduct them to the house of Hades in their tale and arrange a symposium of the saints, where, reclining on couches and crowned with wreaths, they entertain the time henceforth with wine, as if the fairest meed of virtue were an everlasting drunk."[53] Adimantus then mentions the punishment of the unjust and impious as though he were merely repeating the most obvious of contrasts: "*But* the impious and the unjust they bury in mud in the house of Hades and compel them to fetch water in a sieve."[54]

Thus both swamp and sieve indicate similar punishments: an excess of moistness, in the form of either eternal soaking or interminable and exhausting dripping, is the best-known form of punishment in the Greek underworld. The muck belongs to an anonymous eschatology,[55] but the motif of the perforated vessel derives from Empedoclean fantasy (according to Olympiodorus and a scholium to *Gorgias* 483a5).[56] In fact, none of the existing fragments of Empedocles alludes to either the perforated pithos or the sieve.[57] By contrast, the *katharmoi* speak of an unhealthy place in which disease feeds on miasmata emanating from muddy ponds.[58] In this meadow of Ate lives murder (*phonos*).[59]

Plato is in fact effecting a syncretism: in a tradition centered on *teletē* and *katharsis*, the mysterious "Sicilian or Italian" of the *Gorgias*[60] is crossed with Eumolpus, founder of the Eleusinian mysteries,[61] and the other famous initiator, Orpheus.[62] What is constant in this mythology, which the philosopher borrows in order to speak of thought[63] and continence,[64] is the presence of a corrosive substance, either flowing or sticky, which moistens without quenching thirst, which sullies and fatigues. Plato's underworld geography is little more than a maze of rivers, which in view of the omnipresent mud and fire are like lava endlessly spiraling around the belly of the earth. Tartarus, the cavern that pierces the globe, is a cavity (*chasma*) that can hold an undulating fluid only because it is in motion, for it has no bottom or support.[65] The underworld is a perforated jar, said one proverb;[66] and Plato's Tartarus, which resembles Empedocles' clepsydra with its pulsating masses of liquid, is physically perhaps a gigantic bottomless vessel. The other world in the *Phaedo* is a watery abyss, and the floating Islands of the Blessed bathe in an aerial ocean.[67] In Polygnotus' fresco at Delphi the uninitiated, forced to carry water, do so beside the lake in which Tantalus is immersed: the man who had wanted to bring the food of the gods to man is immersed in a water that does not slake his thirst, while his hands cannot grasp the fruit suspended above his head.[68]

Thus, the element indispensable to the earth's fertility is transformed in the underworld into a monstrous power.[69] Its movement, which man prides himself on having mastered, is out of control; its transparency is sullied; its power to slake thirst is eliminated. And the water of the river Ameles, which brings neither leaf nor plant to the Plain of Oblivion, destroys memory. It wipes out all remembrance in souls about to be reborn.[70]

～ 12 ～

The Jar

⁜

I N THE DIDACTIC LITERATURE of agriculture, to fill a perforated jar or extract with a sieve was to economize in a manner doomed to failure. In eschatological literature the same actions punished the uninitiated by requiring them eternally to repeat an act of negligence that transformed the whole of life. To praise thrift, the ridiculous image of a container that could not contain was sufficient; but to describe the punishment incurred for neglecting Eleusis something stronger was needed. Food was no longer at issue; what flowed through the sieve was that subtlest of substances, water. The damned were obliged to separate water from water or to store water in a leaky vessel. A diaphanous leak stood for lack of wheat or wine; it also symbolized the desire that remained when the contents of the container were gone. An essential prerequisite for cultivating the earth symbolized an even more intense absence: the uninitiated had not water but only lack of water.[1]

In order to appreciate the crime of ingratitude punished and cast as allegory in the suffering of the *amyētoi*, who lived foolishly without learning the rules of due proportion and who ate Demeter's fruits without thanking her, we must remember the words of Isocrates and the function officially ascribed to the cult of Demeter at Eleusis. The goddess's arrival in Attic territory coincided with her first response to man's needs: harvests and the rituals of the mysteries, *karpoi* and *teletē*, were the two gifts (*dōra*) granted to mortals, yielding a double benefit: providing food during life and purification before death.[2] Those who allowed their lives to slip away, carelessly living off the fruits of the earth, paid in Hades by being required to fill bottomless jars from leaky sieves. Having lived at the whim of desire, working to fill their pithos-souls without noticing the holes that made them insatiable, they were doomed in the afterlife to hopeless toil. Just as Erysichthon in his own lifetime was punished for attacking Demeter's sacred wood by being forced to devour meal after meal without ever satisfying his hunger, so were the *amyētoi* condemned to pour water endlessly after death.[3]

Gratitude is an essential part of the Eleusinian *teletē* and the key to understanding the whole notion of *accomplishment*. The *teletai* (initiations) were of course a gift to mankind, but they also provided an occasion for securing a happy sojourn in the afterlife by allowing people to discharge their debt to the powers of Eleusis. Athenaeus is very clear on this point: "We still use the word *teletai* for more elaborate feasts associated with some mystical tradition because of the expenditures associated with them, for *telein* means 'to spend.' *Polyteleis* are those who spend a great deal, and *euteleis* are those who spend little."[4] We cannot (Athenaeus continues in a gloss on a fragment from Alexis) hide our wealth from the gods and skimp on rituals. Prosperity is a gift,[5] and the author of an act of generosity expects some gratitude (*charis*) in return. As G. E. Mylonas has shown, initiation involved costs.[6] From the religious standpoint, moreover, the Eleusinian "accomplishment" was a proof of liberality, even payment of an actual debt, as the word *telos* suggests.[7]

D. Sabbatucci attaches so much importance to initiation as a self-imposed loss of self that the obligation involved is obscured to the point where the uninitiated are deprived of their punishment in the afterlife: nothing distinguishes them from the other souls apart from their ignorance of the idea that "dying is a good thing.'"[8] But this very blindness is a mark of their ingratitude, their crime against the goddess who issued a solemn promise when she established the secret rituals at Eleusis: since human stupidity interrupted the immortalization of a small child, mortals will have in the mysteries their only chance to honor the goddess. Through participation in these rites the man who lives on earth will be able to win if not eternal life then at least a privileged death.[9] The death of the blessed is to be contrasted with the anguish and incompleteness of the *amyē-toi*, of those who failed to give the nourishing goddess her due, thereby showing themselves to be as incapable of gratitude as children who refuse to perform their duty of honoring the old. Those who do not pay their debt to the Eleusinian goddess will enjoy neither rest nor satisfaction.

The strictly "economic" content of Eleusinian values is also not to be overlooked. The powers that gave food to man were concerned with teaching not only the art of the harvest but also that of handling and preserving food. Demeter taught us how to take care (*phylakē*) of grains,[10] while Dionysus taught us how to store up autumn fruits for use over a long period.[11] As for Pluto, son of Demeter, he was the first to instill in men a sense of property as something to be accumulated and jealously protected.[12] In other words, the gods of the mysteries were the inventors and masters of conscientious thrift: "Hesiodic" gods, they punished—with the jar and the sieve—those who "took no account" of initiation at Eleusis.

The establishment of a connection between proper proportion and gratitude (as if the wise man were one who not only does not waste his life but who also is satisfied, hence grateful for what he has) allows us to understand why Lucretius called *ingrata* the soul of the man who lived like the maidens with perforated jars. Outside the Eleusinian context the model of desire remains the same:

> Then to be ever feeding the thankless nature of the mind, and never to fill it full and sate it with good things, as the seasons of the year do for us, when they come round and bring their

fruits and varied delights, though after all we are never filled with the enjoyments of life, this methinks is to do what is told of the maidens in the flower of their age, to keep pouring water into a perforated vessel which in spite of all can never be filled full.[13]

From the *puellae* who carry water in the underworld to the guest who, having eaten his fill, is obliged to quit life's banquet,[14] from Plato to Lucretius, the water of the legendary damned reflects a boundless and blind desire.

THIS LATENT MEANING made the semantic space of the perforated jar available to characters with names and histories. The pallid *amyētoi* were joined by the pitiless daughters of Danaus, marked for life by an unexpiated murder.

The Danaides, eternal water-bearers, first appear in literature in a pseudo-Platonic dialogue, the *Axiochus*.[15] A fourth-century vessel, the Apulian hydria of Policoro, which depicts the betrothal of Poseidon and Amymone, offers a picture of life in the underworld.[16] A pithos is partially buried in the ground among tufts of grass. Women are carrying hydrias identical to the one that bears their image. From left to right: a woman moves toward the jar with a hydria upright on her head; a second woman is moving away from the pithos carrying a hydria on her head but lying on its side and therefore empty. A third woman stands close to the edge of the large vessel and appears to be pouring something into it. On the other side, facing her, a fourth woman is standing. She holds her hydria upright by the handles. A fifth woman is turning back, looking behind her and carrying a vessel that is tilted and apparently light in weight. A sixth woman stands beside her hydria, which is resting on the ground; she holds a small phiale in her right hand. Owing to the presence of Amymone and Poseidon in the upper register and the sequence showing the various stages in bearing water from source to receptacle, this representation of the punishment of the pithos is perhaps the clearest we have.[17] M. Schmidt sees in it a moment in one of Lucian's *Marine Dialogues;* the two images superimposed offer an illustration, he argues, of the god's crucial judgment: you will be happy, and, after death, you alone among your sisters will not have to carry water.[18] In fact, this vessel raises more questions than it answers. If it is true that as early as the fourth century the endless pouring of water was already the task of the Danaides, why was this depicted on an Apulian hydria and nowhere else? Picard's interpretation, that the identification of the Danaides with water bearers considerably predates the *Axiochus* and Roman neo-Pythagoreanism, appears to be confirmed.[19]

Since Rohde, the sharing of the perforated pithos between *amyētoi* and daughters of Danaus has been challenged on diachronic grounds. Which was the original tradition, when was the other grafted onto it, and why? Did the jar of the women resistant to marriage precede that of the uninitiated, and how did one give rise to the other? In this conversion of the myth, one had to find, always, the moment of oblivion, the instant of decadence in which benevolent powers were precipitated into the hell of unfulfillment. But the Policoro vessel compels us to take into consideration the coexistence of two versions since at least the fourth century. Just as Pausanias was able to choose between the Danaides and those who neglected Eleusis, the painter depicted the water carriers as women and suggested their identity: at issue are different interpretations of a single, plainly quite evocative image.

If we set the perforated jar and the sieve back in the various contexts to which they relate, their polyvalence will not seem surprising. We saw earlier that the household storage jar, receptacle for the flux of food supplies, was not the same jar found in the underworld. And in the underworld we found both the jar of the uninitiated and the jar of the Danaides.[20] Since the underlying meaning of the metaphor is not apparent, collectors of proverbs, allegories, and images were free to prefer one variant or another, and in all the traditions one figure established itself as most emblematic: the Danaides. Their association with the pithos was furthered both by abridgments (Lucian, Apollo-dorus) and by catalogues of proverb and allegory (Lucretius, Horace, Plutarch). The testimony of epic and tragedy being un-available,[21] we are forced to rely on secondary sources that re-duce the most terrifying and incredible of all Greek murders to familiar stereotype.[22] Witness Zenobius' gloss:

> Unfillable jar: said of those who eat a great deal and are glut-tons. The metaphor derives from the myth surrounding the Danaides and the jar to which they carry water drawn from a well. People say that this jar in Hades is never full. Subject to this ordeal are the souls of the *amyētoi* and of the maidens known as Danaides. They fill leaky vessels with water and carry it to this perforated [jar]. The proverb may also apply to Hades, for no matter how numerous are the dead, it is never full.[23]

Zenobius explicitly states what we can infer from ancient sources, namely, that both the uninitiated and the Danaides carry water. We also learn about the meaning of the proverb, that is, the pertinence of its use: to eat too much, to experience boundless hunger. The eschatological myth is not necessarily implicit in every mention of the perforated jar, nor is it true that the appetite of the glutton is the only reason for mentioning such a jar. For this compiler of proverbs, however, leaking water unambiguously points to a greedy belly. This means that neither the mysteries nor the murder eclipse the primordial image of a storehouse threatened by dearth, the symbol of hunger. What is repeated is not the act of watering, not the bucolic chore of the well-nymphs: there is no question of gardening or rites of purification (in the underworld?). What these damned souls dramatize is far more serious: the anguish of desire, initially desire for food but ultimately desire in general.

Notwithstanding the views of Keuls and other scholars who favor a ritualistic interpretation, the ancient texts all allude to a symbolic punishment in which we read the failure of the most elementary of mankind's communal efforts. As on the black-figured amphora in Munich,[24] the water-bearing souls have as their companion either Sisyphus (who surely does not engage in a ceremony of pushing a rock up to the heights) or, as in Polygnotus' *Nekyia*, Tantalus.[25]

Why the Danaides? Why are they the ones who join those who neglected Eleusis around the water jar? In order to understand their fate we must first ask about the reason for their punishment. One answer is not hard to find, because it is repeated: after the crime, because of the crime.[26] These women were sullied by the murder of their husbands. The *Bibliotheca* of Apollodorus states that Athena and Hermes purified them and that their father cooperated by giving them in marriage to new suitors.[27] This ending is like one that Aeschylus might have chosen or invented. The bloodstains are cleansed, and a regular marriage makes benevolent spouses of murderesses obedient to the authority of their father. In fact, the two longest fragments of the *Danaides*, the final play in the trilogy that began with the *Suppliants*, speak of marriage. In one fragment, Aphrodite in person praises the union of the sexes and procreation.[28] Rain from the sky fertilizes the earth; Gaia gives birth to fodder for the flocks and, for bread-eaters, to the food of Demeter. In the other fragment, an anonymous subject prepares to awaken the kind husbands.[29] Pindar also prefers the version in which the crime is effaced by a second marriage.[30] But Euripides describes the murderesses caught in the *phonos* in which they drowned their wedding night: in *Hecuba* and *Heracles* the daughters of Danaus are exemplary throat-slitters.[31]

These two versions are mutually exclusive. Either the women survive their crime and accept marriage, or they end in Hades, as if their taint exiled them from human society.[32] According to a scholiast of Aristides,[33] the perforated jar signifies that they will never again experience pleasure (*charis*) with any male, so odious have they become because of their taint. The spilt blood thus establishes a primary defining characteristic: if initiation at Eleusis was not possible for foreigners with unclean hands,[34] these suppliants, born in Libya and proud of having killed the men they were supposed to love, typify the kind of person excluded from the mysteries. Before being noninitiates, they were uninitiable. In the selection process conducted by the *hierokeryx* (sacred herald) when he proclaimed the *prorrhesis* at the beginning of the celebration, women in their condition were supposed to withdraw immediately.[35] Yet the fact that the Danaides were murderesses, hence outcasts from Eleusis, does not account for the particular form of their punishment.

Note that in the ancient texts the Danaides are not portrayed as persons not initiated into the mysteries of Eleusis. They carry water like *amyētoi*, yet no specifically *Eleusinian* Demeter is implicated in their story. That story unfolds in the dry plain of Argolis, in the domain of Hera; yet Herodotus writes that the daughters of Danaus imported from Egypt the *teletē* of Demeter that the Greeks called Thesmophoria: the daughters taught these mysteries to the wives of the Pelasgian.[36] Does this mean that the institution of this feast, reserved in many Greek cities exclusively for married women,[37] was a version with a happy ending of the Danaides' blood wedding? After finally becoming wives, did they also embody the very model of the mother? In any case, Herodotus' information points us toward the Demeter of married women, that is, toward a specifically female and pan-Hellenic ritual.

I therefore propose not to forget the uninitiated of Polygnotus and Plato but to relegate them for the time being to the background. Without neglecting the fate that the Danaides shared with other murderesses, I shall examine their punishment as if it were the culmination of their own story and aimed at their own crime.

Think for a moment about the all-too-well-known first act ever committed by a Greek woman: was it not the unfortunate opening of a jar?[38] A pithos is filled with evils (perhaps the one that Zeus guarded beside the one filled with goods[39]), and a woman by the name of Pandora removes its cover to the great detriment of humanity. What do this woman's freshly made

154

hands touch but a jar? The two are so closely associated that a Campanian-style amphora preserved in London depicts a Pandora standing not alongside a jar but in the form of a jar, observed with satisfaction by a club-footed artisan.[40] A body fashioned out of water and earth, the work of Hephaestus, the divine potter, is the source of all the characteristic weaknesses that define the mortal condition and the difficulty of a life in which henceforth nothing can be taken for granted.[41] Hesiod does not say that Pandora was a jar, that the first woman was a vessel filled with scourges. He does, however, establish a connection between the woman who is a ceramic object and the vessel that comes into being with her and almost for her. It is to spread the evils stored "below the lips" of the pithos that Zeus asks the skilled artisan to mold a handsome evil. And then, no sooner is the woman there than she opens, like an automaton or like Heracles in the house of Pholus, the mouth of the container that resembles her. (Interestingly, in the *Theogony,* a genealogical work, the first woman is not called Pandora but remains anonymous. Furthermore, she has no jar. She creates the world's evils all by herself.[42])

A jar with the face of a woman and a woman with the curves of an amphora: with this hybrid the almost comical image on the London vessel condenses an analogy that is suggested and elaborated in *Works and Days.* The pithos regarded as a household implement never loses its female connotations. Its ambiguity as a hollow object divided between fullness and emptiness, its deceptive gaping in which may lurk good as well as evil, reflects the dangerous ambivalence that Hesiod ascribes to the female. A wife may be a sober and fertile belly in which a man deposits his seed as though placing it in long-term storage (with the purpose of ensuring the continuity of his patrimony).[43] Yet at any time a woman in the home may reveal her cavernous nature: a starving belly, a womb burning with desire, this hollow and useless object can sap a man's strength by devouring his seed and drying up his sperm.[44] "No prize is better than a worthy wife; a bad one makes you shiver with the cold. The greedy wife will roast her man alive without the aid of fire, and though he is quite tough, she'll bring him to a raw old age."[45] Fire cooks, but it also burns; and woman gives birth, but she is also starving. Hence in Pandora's story there are not two pithoi, one good, the other bad. There is only one jar, and it is closed, as innocent-looking as the object made by Hephaestus, like a *parthenos*. To open it is to spread woe. Empty it, and its gaping belly will still be filled with hope of a new plenitude.[46] Pandora: a jar. If the first woman in the *Theogony* does not tend to a pithos, if she represents the place from which a race flows, it is because the proper place of the jar (in the referential and symbolic sense) is in the context of an *oikonomia*—hence in *Works and Days*, where the poet teaches the proper use of earth and time, the value of storehouses, and the functions of a wife and an ox.[47] As though sapping a philosophical project from within, woman lusts after the contents of goatskins filled with precious nourishment.[48]

Once one recognizes that an elementary and fundamental opposition is implicit in the distinction between accumulation and conservation, in the division of labor between men and women,[49] it is easy to see the analogy between a jar and a faithful and fertile wife. For a man to marry a creature with boundless appetites[50] and incapable of taking care of what he gives her is to choose a defective container. Is this not the implication of Ischomachus' speech to his steward-wife? Thus, the pithos becomes the focus of representations of both masculine wisdom (correct choice, proper maintenance, supervision) and the possible, indeed all too probable, incontinence of woman (the hidden flaw or, for Hesiod, the frenzy to open). And when Plutarch wished to indicate that it is necessary to test a woman's reliability by confiding in her information of no importance, did he not use the image of a vessel that needed to be tested with water before being filled with wine or oil?[51]

~ 13 ~

Unconsummated

C ONSIDER once again the *amyētoi*, not in order to reconstruct forgotten rituals but in order to understand the uses of the word and its power to evoke images.

In interpreting *Gorgias* 493cff., Linforth argues that there is no reason whatsoever to "construe *amyētoi* as a forced and unnatural derivative of *myō* [to close]." The play on words is unnecessary, Linforth maintains, because it adds nothing to the thought.[1] In a study intended to be attentive to the text and context of every sentence, such an assertion seems surprising, for if one rejects the semantic shift suggested by Socrates, the choice of the word *amyētos* becomes incomprehensible. Plato explicitly states that the soul of *epithymiai* (desires) is a pithos because it is *pithanos* (easy to persuade) and that a perforated jar illustrates the condition of the *amyētos* because it cannot hold anything. Moreover, if the metaphor is justified regardless of the word's ambiguity, why (as E. Des Places observes) did Plato not choose the word *atelestos*, which is synonymous with *amyētos* and which he uses in the *Republic* and *Phaedo?*[2]

The semantic relation between *myein* (to initiate) and *myein* (to close) in the *Gorgias* is not the result of gratuitous humor. The link between the two words, allegedly invented in Sicily or Italy, was in fact recognized by lexicographers. A scholiast on Aristophanes' *Frogs* explains: "We were led by the myst-agogue. The word *mystēria* derives from the fact that partici-pants in the mysteries shut their mouths and repeated what they saw to no one. *Myein* means to close the mouth."[3] This very simple definition is also given by the *Suda,* which defines *myēsis* as initiation in the *mystēria.*[4] It is as if *myēsis* meant com-mitment to silence within the *teletē*[5] and referred to the process of learning how to keep one's mouth shut, a prerequisite of any kind of mystical experience.[6]

What the *amyētoi* lacked was nothing other than a closed mouth. Not that they were indiscreet, profaners of secret cere-monies: their ignorance of *myēsis* was absolute.[7] Moreover, it is in terms of this ignorance that Plato interprets the image of the bottomless jar and the sieve in the *Gorgias.*

If we follow Plato's lead and do not exclude the literal meaning of the very *myein* from the image of the leaky jar and the sieve, a similar yet autonomous interpretation of the Dan-aides becomes possible. What the uninitiated person shares with the woman who has murdered her husband is a space without a bottom. Hence this figure must occur in the story of the nuptial crime.

Let us view the punished Danaides not as *amyētoi* of Eleusis but as women whose behavior has left them in a state of non-closure. Let us assume that the acts and implements involved in their punishment tell us not about a ritual but about them-selves. Let us look at them with the eyes of Plato and Artemi-dorus.[8]

We know that the female body is characterized by a specific form of closure, which defines its principal function. The body of a *parthenos* is a silent body, whose uterine *stoma* and genital passages are in a sense stopped up and whose mouth is capable of keeping a secret.[9] Since no hymen exists, the oral represen-tation of virginity is perfect and complete. But a woman recov-ers or discovers a truly perfect seal, a flawless "occlusion" (*sym-mysis*), when her maternal vocation is realized. Complementary to the fertile body whose plenitude is yet to come and which demonstrates its potential to receive by being hollow and open, a woman possesses another body that makes actual what is only virtual in the first: "In women who are pregnant, the mouth of the uterus closes."[10] This Hippocratic aphorism un-ambiguously states that the crucial point in conception is the moment when the semen is swallowed by the uterus, which instantly seals its contents inside. Subsequent to this reflex action, a new life can begin inside the woman's belly.

"If, after coitus, a woman is not to conceive, usually the sperm coming from the two partners exits when the woman wishes; if she is to conceive, the seed does not exit but remains in the womb. In fact the womb, after receiving the sperm and closing [*myein*], retains it because its mouth contracts in response to the humor, and what comes from the man mixes with what comes from the woman. If the woman is experienced in childbirth and notices at what point the sperm did not exit but remained within, she will know the day on which she conceived."[11] For the Hippocratic physicians as for Aristotle and Galen, the sign was the same: if nothing leaked out, a pregnancy had begun.[12] If all the liquid was retained, it was because the uterus was now hermetically sealed. As Galen points out, this organ could not only dilate to the point of allowing a child to exit but could also contract until its orifice was so small that not even the finest probe could penetrate it. Suddenly this reservoir, in which the residual blood secreted by the female body was stored while awaiting its monthly evacuation, stopped leaking. Whatever nourishing fluid it received was now stored for the purpose of feeding the fetus. "When a woman is pregnant, she does not suffer from the cessation of menstrual flow, because the blood, which no longer gushes out every month, is not disturbed. Instead it flows daily into the womb in a gentle fashion, little by little and without pain. And the contents of the womb grow."[13] In a period of nonpregnancy, retention of blood in the womb would be pathological, for the uterus would choke if it could not relieve the pressure by evacuating un-needed blood.[14] In order to conceive, the body must be empty, unoccupied: it is immediately after the *katharsis* of menstruation that the uterus is ready to receive the semen,[15] but if it is filled with blood it cannot receive the sperm and moves rapidly from place to place.[16] Nasal hemorrhages, varicose veins, vomiting, and diarrhea may develop as a result of the imperious need to rid the body of this superfluous humor, a sort of natural malady.[17] In time of pregnancy, however, the flowing blood finally achieves its end: it becomes the food without which the embryo cannot live. Its diverse flows and movements are arrested. "The blood, descending from the woman's entire body, forms a circle around the membrane (which envelops the coagulated sperm) on the outside. With inhalation, however, it is drawn toward the membrane at the perforated [*tetrēmenos*] and prominent place, where it coagulates and causes the future living being to grow."[18] A small hole remains in the hymen which contains the kernel of the embryo, which serves to fill and feed the fetus. Once the mouth of the uterus closes, nothing escapes: sperm and blood are immobilized as the infant takes shape.[19]

In the Hippocratic treatise *On Generation* this process served to illustrate the way in which nature makes good use of the uterine container and the liquids that pass through it. It was Aristotle, however, who recognized this series of anatomical-physiological states as a logical sequence organized by Nature in view of a telos.[20] Menstrual blood is in fact only a residue (*perittōma*). Though different from waste residues, that is, excrement and urine, it is nevertheless a surplus product. The reason for its existence is feminine weakness:

> But since it is necessary (1) that the weaker animal also should have a secretion greater in quantity and less concocted, and (2) that being of such a nature it should be a mass of sanguineous liquid, and (3) since that which Nature endows with a smaller portion of heat is weaker, and (4) since it has already been stated that such is the character of the female [*De partibus animalium* II.2, 648a12]—putting all

these considerations together we see that the sanguineous matter discharged by the female is also a secretion. And such is the discharge of the so-called catamenia.[21]

A liquid to be evacuated (and defined by that evacuation), the menstrual blood is a consequence of female inferiority and deficiency. These factors are reinforced by others, however:

> This secretion then is necessarily discharged by females for the reasons given; for, the female nature being unable to concoct the nourishment thoroughly, there must not only be left a residue of the useless nutriment, but also there must be a residue in the blood vessels, and this filling the channels of the finest vessels must overflow. Then Nature, aiming at the best and the end, uses it up in this place for the sake of generation, that another creature may come into being of the same kind as the former was going to be, for the menstrual blood is already potentially such as the body from which it is discharged.[22]

The telos, the final cause that is the primary reason for the existence of a being or object, thus ensures that a faulty leak becomes the substance of a future individual. Nature resembles a good *oikonomos*, says Aristotle.[23] It wisely distributes the maternal blood to the various parts of the growing fetus. Beyond that, however, a positive action must stimulate the hidden potential in the flowing blood. At a specific moment this *dynamis*, which remains latent and is wasted in the monthly efflux, must be roused from its inert cycle and given animation. Just as a woman's soul lacks the power to decide,[24] her body is also obedient to a rhythm not under her control. Only the male can transmit a kinetic impulse to matter that is otherwise subject to perpetual loss.[25] When the passive flow of female blood is subjected to the action of the male, it immediately begins to coagulate into a small curd: the outflow is halted.[26] It is already shaped by a project, whose various phases will automatically unfold; they are implicit in the initial genetic impression, which triggers the movement of the entelechy.[27] Aristotle explains that females exist for only one reason: so that someday they may contain and nourish a tiny member of the species that will resemble its father.[28] Furthermore, this teleonomy, which is stated with the authority of the philosopher, is implicitly an evaluation of maternity, which in medical literature already had the force of a hygienic precept. The conception of marriage as telos,[29] when translated into the realm of the body and founded on a metaphysics of matter and form, indicates its fundamental importance. Plato recommended that bride and groom while seated at the wedding table concentrate their thoughts on the children they were about to conceive.[30] The formula of the matrimonial *ekdosis* alludes to nothing other than the fruit of the *gamos*.[31] "We have wives in order to reproduce ourselves." This spokesman for right-thinking Athenians was not mistaken.[32] The end, the fulfillment, of the *gamos* is in its fruit, in the occurrence of a pregnancy that gives meaning to the union of the sexes and to the very existence of sexual difference.

Let us now return to the Danaides, and in particular to the one who breaks ranks with her sisters because she remains a *parthenos*. In Aeschylus' *Prometheus*, Hypermestra decides to spare Lynceus because she wishes to prolong a wedding night in which she experienced intimacy in love. What she really wants, though, is not pleasure. Specifically, she refuses to carry out the murder because of her "desire for children."[33] Thus, there are two variants: the gratitude of the respected virgin and the intention to have children. The telos of gratitude encounters that of womanly fulfillment; the exchange of benevolence comes in response to the completed marriage. And the closed body of the maiden corresponds to the body of the mother who, surfeited with children, has experienced the *symmysis* of her womb.

In the middle are the murderous *nymphai* with useless wombs who, despite having lost their virginity, cruelly prevent consummation of their marriages. Their bodies are partly open, fissured, frozen in the void that has opened up inside them: they are unfillable vessels, incapable of retaining anything fertile.[34] Afflicted with a leak that no one can stop, the Danaides of the underworld are specifically paying for their crime against *gamos*. A perpetual current of water flows through the old food container planted in the soil. And are not the wild grasses that grow around the pithos on the Policoro vase a sign of the steady leakage of water from the cracks in the vessel?

The Danaides' bodies harbor no fruit. The medical tradition conceptualized the development of the embryo within the womb in terms of plant metaphors. Empedocles' analogy between the growth of plants due to heat of the earth and the development of the viviparous fetus was perpetuated in the language of the naturalists.[35] If, as M. Lonie argues, the botanical excursus in *De natura pueri* is merely a not particularly original summary of accepted fifth-century opinion, it must nevertheless be conceded that the model at that time had as yet lost none of its force.[36] Anyone who reflects on plant physiology, writes the author of the Cnidian treatise, "will find that from beginning to end the natural growth of plants is entirely similar to that of men."[37] And Aristotle would later argue that all animals equipped with an umbilical cord (*omphalos*) absorb maternal nourishment through it. Like a root (*rhiza*), this bundle of veins sheathed in skin constitutes the alimentary connection between the embryo and the blood that feeds it.[38]

A belly sealed over a creature that grows within it like a plant; a belly that eats in order to nourish the son of a husband. Plenitude and fulfillment, closure and growth: are not the Danaides endlessly repeating the failure of their sterile bodies? On the surface of the earth they consent to be married off in order to kill, remarry, and found the Thesmophoria. According to one tradition, the hymeneal was sung for the first time on their second wedding day.[39] In the underworld their unforgettable crime condemns them to enact the *contrappasso* of conjugal consummation.

It was necessary to set aside the *amyētoi* of Eleusis in order to see these women as symbols of their own bodies—they who became emblems of our souls in the eyes of the philosophers.

In effect, the presence of the uninitiated faded over the centuries. Of the two interchangeable images, one became predominant: for Plutarch, Lucretius, and Porphyry, as on the hydria of Policoro and in the basilica of Porta Maggiore, the lost water is in the feminine.[40] Is this because carrying water is woman's work? Because a myth impressed itself more forcefully upon literary and artistic memory? Or is it not a consequence of the same basic fact of the imagination—that which associates the exemplary form of the jar with the foolishness of the first woman, scourge of an *oikonomia*—that the perforated pithos of these deflowered and widowed brides offers the best allegory of the vanity of insatiable desire?[41]

It is *women* who will play out the scene, endlessly repeated, of the lack that engenders desire, of the desire that nourishes lack—anxious women diverted from their vocation of transmitting, reproducing, concluding.

Conclusion

Toward a Sealed Fountain

COULD A MODEL of the body about which we learn from medical literature have shaped practices and images outside the realm of anatomy and pathology? The path traced in the previous chapters, involving two representations of the female body in ritual and imagination, seems to prove that it could indeed. From Plato to Plutarch, the Greek philosophers, and Aristotle in particular, were quick to see in the human (and sometimes animal) body an inexhaustible paradigm of everything structured and alive: of the city in the first place but also of the cosmos and meteors and even the well-crafted text.[1] Closer to the body, however, where postures and gestures combine to constitute meaningful behavior, a simpler question arises: are the form of the body and the nature of its parts simply left out? Does it not matter, in particular, whether a body is male or female, fecund or fertile?

Anthropology's answer is unequivocal: evidence of sexual dimorphism cannot be dismissed as insignificant.[2] If the male body is taken to be the model of the human body in general, then the female body with its nonphallic morphology becomes an immobile landscape molded and shaped by the growth of an alien seed. Ancient science attached extraordinary importance to humors, fluids that flowed through the organism and nourished it. The physics of liquids is particularly well suited to a body that produces surpluses of menstrual blood, milk, and a kind of seminal liquid, a body traversed by multiple pathways—mouth being connected to womb and breasts, uterus to eyes and nostrils. But this plethora of flows and leaks is directed toward a goal: maternity. It is all designed to meet the needs of the child, without which it makes no sense. When we reflect upon the available pathways through the female body and attempt to understand the changes it undergoes, we invariably arrive at the same point, the womb, and at the same fundamental mechanism, namely, the opening and closing of a mouth. To my second question, the one concerning the relevance of the female model in ancient Greece, I therefore offer the following answer: no Greek model of sexual difference succeeded in minimizing the specific nature of the *gynē*.

As for the legitimacy of an interpretation that gives priority to the body where complex characters are involved, I know that it cannot be justified a priori. My research is not intended to inaugurate a spate of gynecological speculation on Greek religion. Yet where the Pythia and the Danaides are concerned, the texts themselves invite us to explore femininity and therefore female bodies. Only the cogency of the solution and the ability to unravel two problems with respect for the sources can determine whether or not the method is valid.

The demonstrated interaction between the two orifices of the female body rests on a physiology that is not entirely positive: it is based on a linguistic fact, the double meaning of the Greek words for *mouth* and *lips,* and on all the resonances it had in the imagination. The testimony of medical science, which offers an especially clear view of the subject, also provided a means of uncovering the logic of this portrait. One figure stood out more and more clearly, as though on an ideal dissecting table: a hollow body whose genitals were formed by a pair of lips. And those lips protected a hidden mouth. The utterances of the Pythia, emanating from a possessed body open to certain vapors, appeared to be intimately associated with a contradictory sexual state: though a virgin, the priestess opened herself wide in order to prophesy. What notion of virginity made this body thinkable? What sort of virginity did this woman possess? When I wrote the chapter on Apollonian soothsaying, I did not know that Greek virginity had nothing to do with the presence of a hymen. I discovered this fact via a totally independent route. Yet the moment the body of the Greek *parthenos* took shape before my eyes, I saw that her integrity and silence were qualities well suited to the prophetess of Pythian Apollo. For her this was the only appropriate form of physical virginity. Was it not wonderfully natural and convincing that no barrier membrane should exist between two lips capable of closing upon themselves? The absence of this veil-like accouterment of virginity was a simple, logical complement to the mouthlike image of the female genitals.

Think of the lascivious Congo whose *mirabilia* Diderot described in *Les Bijoux indiscrets*. When asked about the strangely loquacious and truthful genitals of the sultan's ladies, what diagnosis did the illustrious Orcotome suggest? "Yes, gentlemen, the jewel is both a stringed and a wind instrument, but much more string than wind. The internal air impinging upon it acts exactly like a bow on the tendonlike fibers of wings that one might call vocal ribbons or cords. The gentle collision of this air with the vocal cords causes them to tremble, and their more or less rapid vibrations produce various sounds."[3] It was among the authors of the *Encyclopédie,* in the wake of Buffon's natural history, that the debate over—or, rather, against—the existence of the hymen became most earnest and vehement. Like Soranus, yet more indignant about false beliefs, the naturalists of the Age of Enlightenment argued that the panniculus was a fraud, a phantom created by the male desire to possess. This was the context in which Diderot created his courtesans and sensual ventriloquists. And he was of course thinking of Greece, since Orcotome refers to the womb as *delphys.* He was aware, moreover, that "no man ever sat on the divine tripod in Delphi;

the role of the Pythia could be filled only by a woman."[4] In fact the description of the female genital apparatus as an oral cavity is a point of similarity between Diderot and Galen, who compared the clitoris to the uvula and assigned it the function of protecting the uterus from the cold, just as the uvula protects the trachea.[5] Thus, if there was a guardian organ analogous to the veil of the palate, it was the clitoris. Galen had absolutely no idea that another "gate" was even thinkable.

Because of the hymenless representation of virginity, the analogy between mouth and genitals, between sexuality and speech, could be deployed without limit. The "lips" of the inviolate maiden were not marked by what today's forensic physician regards as an "obvious" and unmistakable trait. Since the labia were not sewn together but simply in contact, they were truly lips. Closed but not sealed, vapor could penetrate the Pythia and she could open herself to speak without destroying anything—and without benefit of any miracle. The Pythia as men saw her did not sacrifice her integrity to the body of a mortal male, yet in the obscurity of the adytum she approached the god like a true *parthenos*. A ritual of clandestinity helped her to express herself. She emerged from an invisible place to meet those who came to consult her.[6] A residue, a product of an encounter with the god that had to remain almost secret, the words spoken by this possessed woman elicited images of genuine truth. Although it took the form of speech, the hierogamy of Apollo's prophetess was no less furtive that the loves of other *parthenoi*, of Greek virgins. Thus, historians who believed in the oracles of the Pythia, or who took an interest in them as political phenomena, discussed oracular pronouncements as though they knew nothing about its forms, as if it did not involve *enthousiasmos*. Conversely, incredulous Christians would later endeavor to reveal the frenzy, to unmask the passion.

In the eyes of the ancients, presence of the body and validity of prophesy seem to have been mutually exclusive. Thus the scene of delirium was most vivid and most flagrantly pornographic in the eyes of those whose purpose was to show the demoniac falsity of pagan prophesy. For the church fathers, the Pythia was nothing but a foaming mouth and genitals opened to the spirit of evil. The god of Delphi was a demon who desired and an evil *pneuma* that penetrated. His priestess was a *gynē* whose soul had not been cultivated by philosophy, a woman determined by her sexual type—and her sexuality. Christian literature neglected precisely that which in the pagan mind identified the Pythia's ignorance not with emptiness but with perfection. When Origen scornfully proclaimed that Apollo's prophetess was not even a virgin, he destroyed in one stroke the scholarly understanding of Greek enthusiasm. Since there was a ritual of possession, virginity was irrevocably lost in the relations between woman and demon. How could anyone suppose that an inspiration introduced via the female parts (*gynaikeia*) could be compatible with the *parthenos* mentioned by Plutarch? To be sure, in the third century of the Christian era, it was difficult for a church father engaged in an anti-Hellenic counteroffensive to conceive of a *parthenia* that was not irreparably destroyed in the *katochē* (divine possession). In the first place, he must have believed, and wished to make others believe, that underlying the whole obscene oracular session was a disgusting embrace. But then it would have been difficult to imagine the Pythia accepting the love of the demon, even in pneumatic form, without tearing some part of the *parthenos'* body.

Virginity of soul, life, and body were required of the Pythian priestess, however, as conditions of her divinatory pronouncements. Plutarch in the *Pythian Dialogues* offers a theory of enthusiasm that enables us to understand the role of the prophetess—her body, soul, and language—in terms of a model that is at once theological, psychological, and linguistic. An instrument that interprets the Apollonian truth as the moon reflects the light of the sun, the Pythia must offer herself to the god in the emptiest, most available, most passive state that a human being can attain. Every obstacle and every encumbrance must be abolished in order to prevent enthusiasm from turning into struggle or strangulation and in order to keep the signs in which the truth is embodied from losing their luster. Hence the ideal state of reception verges on naïveté: the Pythia must have neither culture nor feelings nor social nor sexual relations of her own.

The Pythia's virginity connotes a total and exclusive offering to the god, much as the virginity of an adolescent connotes unhesitating docility to the wisdom of a husband. The prophetess remains intact, untouchable, and illiterate for no other reason than to offer Apollo a more perfect welcome. Hers is most definitely not a purity analogous to the "supernatural respect of the body consecrated by its having been inhabited by the Holy Spirit and by reception of the divine eucharist."[7] The god illuminated the Pythia every time she mounted the tripod and opened herself to the foul-smelling vapors and to the speech that manifested itself through her. Restored to her senses outside the temple adytum, she resumed the ignorance of perfect *parthenia*.

What made this representation possible? How could the Pythia undergo a ritual that opened her body up to inspiration yet left her an ignorant *parthenos*? The answer, it bears repeating, is that the Greek idea of *parthenia* did not require the presence of a seal over the genitals. If the oracular scene was like a delivery in that the body of the Pythia was opened wide, it was also true that she, like any other woman, could at any time recover her virginal closure.

Because virginity did not depend on the presence of a hymen, the Pythia's utterance fell between silence and fluency, between purity and enthusiasm. This fact turns out to be invaluable for understanding the history of the representation of the female body in antiquity, even apart from the specific question that led me to discover it. In particular, it was essential to test it by examining the question of reversibility, of alternation between closed and open. And what better way to do this than by considering the image, so vivid in ancient tradition, of the perforated jar, which figured in the punishment of those not initiated in the mysteries of Eleusis as well as of the Danaides?

The Danaides: women tortured by an endless leak, ingrates who sustained the emptiness of an unfillable belly, they embodied the utmost possible incompleteness of the female body. The water that steadily leaked through the crack in the pithos buried in the earth stood as a reminder of their unconsummated marriage; an excess of moisture evoked their sterile bodies. Wives who had cut their husbands' throats on their wedding night were forever prisoners of the crime that had deprived them of husbands and children. It was as if an unstanchable flow kept the mouths of their wombs open and the lips of their genitals apart. Having prevented the consummation of the marriage in impregnation, they were trapped in an intermediate state: no longer virgins, they would never be mothers. The temporality of their bodies was arrested at the moment of the crime, when, fully open, they should have discovered a new and more complete closure.

Undoubtedly it would be most interesting to compare the punishment of the Danaides in the underworld with the fate awaiting them on earth in those versions of the story in which, despite their crime, they are readmitted into human society. The interpretation would have to take account of the Thesmophoria, which according to Herodotus the Danaides themselves revealed to the Greeks. For now, it is enough to note that fecundity here plays an essential role, together with a kind of virginity regained in isolation from males in a mystery in which married women lay on beds of agnus castus. Purity and fertile marriage were celebrated simultaneously in this ritual, whereas the infernal punishment sanctioned the hybris of a sterile crime.

In the Danaides' story the body is neither a container nor a conduit of speech. But do not forget the other aspect of the same punishment: the figure of the *amyētos*, who has not

171

learned to cultivate Eleusinian silence. Flowing water evokes sometimes speech, sometimes food; in conjunction with the female body it describes the failure of a kind of sexuality. Above all, however, this inexhaustible substance interrupts the alternation of closure and openness that defines female physiology. This alternation, first revealed to us by the Delphic priestess of Apollo, is thus confirmed by a negative image.

IN ANY CASE, the debate over the existence of the hymen deserves independent study. Outside of ancient Greece, historical reconstruction could shed light on its treatment in both the medical and Christian traditions. There is no incontrovertible reason why a condition defined by morality (whether religious or secular) should be concretely represented by a sign that is not merely visible but tangible. On the contrary, the hymen is both a crude and contestable sign. It seems to promise a semiotics of chastity, yet no serious gynecologist would write today, as physicians did in the time of Ambroise Paré, that the hymen constitutes credible medical and legal *proof* of either virginity or childbirth.[8] It gives a substantial reality to absolute purity, but since it confines purity to a single location it becomes in effect a camouflage for the most perverse forms of erotic behavior. No theologian would be very enthusiastic about identifying physical virginity with so paltry a sign.

The position of the church fathers is very curious. As late as the fourth century, St. Ambrose dispatched an indignant epistle to the bishop of Verona, whom he blamed for having permitted manual examination of a Christian virgin by a midwife.[9] It was not proper, he said, for a man of the church to approve of midwives' insulting the intimacy of a virgin through profane inspection and exploration. The suspicion was offensive, while the manual contact might not only lead to temptation but, horrible to say, provoke the very catastrophe whose occurrence it pretended to ascertain. Ambrose also cast doubt on the infallibility of such a method of verification, and he cited medical opinion in support of his view. The most venerable of physicians, he noted, maintained that such inspection was not entirely reliable. Even among midwives the subject was controversial. Why look for dubious indications when much clearer signs existed that posed no threat to modesty? Was anything more public than outraged virtue and lost virginity? Nothing was more visible than an offense against chastity: the belly swelled, and the weight of the fetus rendered walking difficult, to say nothing of the fact that conscience betrayed itself through embarrassment and shame. Such wariness of anatomy might seem surprising in one of Christianity's most fervent apologists for virginity. Ambrose devotes much of his work to reflection on continence and in particular to the mystery of Christ's birth. In *De institutione virginis* he comments extensively on Ezekiel 44:2: "And he said to me, 'This gate shall remain shut; it shall not be opened, and no one shall enter by it'" ("Porta haec clausa erit et non aperietur"). What was this gate, if not Mary? It was closed because she was a virgin. Mary was the gate through which Christ came into the world, born in a virginal delivery that left the genital locks firmly shut. Modesty remained intact, and the seals of integrity were preserved.[10] *Porta clausa, claustra, septum, signaculum*: metaphor upon metaphor evokes an enclosure protected by locks, walls, and seals. "Et hortus clausus virginitas et fons signatus virginitas": virginity is a secret garden, a sealed fountain. Ambrose recommended that maidens open their minds while forever preserving the seal that God gave them at birth: "aperi mentem, serva signaculum."

The virginity that one could touch was therefore vulgar, because it justified disturbing manipulations without offering reliable proof. Ambrose did not believe in it at all. Nevertheless, in this Mariological context, the genitals of the Virgin, hence of all virgins, are sealed; the hymen exists. Henceforth this was considered an assumption essential for any interpretation of scripture: it was the physical detail that made the birth of the son of a virgin miraculous, inherently mysterious, and perforce unique. A barrier crossed but not pierced made the birth of Christ a miracle far greater than the birth of Perseus. And suspicious Salome, who, according to the *Apocryphal Gospels,* placed her finger in the cleft between the Virginal Lips on Christmas night, touched the truth of an unprecedented event.[11]

Like Ambrose, Augustine and Cyprian were most contemptuous of vaginal inspection. This was a practice fit only for midwives and unworthy of sacred virgins.[12] Beyond indignation and in spite of suspicion, however, a belief is evident: virginity is marked in the female genitals by a sign distinct from the narrow form of the vagina described by Soranus. What is more, Augustine adds an invaluable detail, which he says he learned from Varro and which therefore tells us something about pagan Rome. The Romans, he says, venerated a host of temporary deities responsible for particular events. In particular the different stages of marriage had their own protectors. Augustine is ironic:

> The god Jugatinus is brought in when a man and a woman are united in the yoke [*iugum*] of marriage. So far, so good. But the bride has to be escorted home. The god Domiducus is employed to lead her home [*domum ducere*]. To install her in the house, the god Domitius sees to her going home [*domum ire*]. The goddess Manturna is called in as well, to see that she will remain [*manere*] with her husband. What else is needed? Should we not show consideration for human modesty, and let the sexual desire of flesh and blood achieve the rest, without violation of the secrets of modesty? Why fill the bridal chamber with a mob of divinities, when even the bridal escort retires? And what is the purpose of crowding it? That the thought of the presence of the gods should make the couple more concerned to preserve decency? Not at all. It is to ensure that with their cooperation, there shall be no difficulty in ravishing the virginity of a girl who feels the weakness of her sex and is terrified by the strangeness of her situation. For here are the goddess Virginensis, and Father

Subigus [to subdue: *subigere*] and Mother Prema [to press: *premere*] and the goddess Pertunda [to pierce: *pertundere*] as well as Venus and Priapus. What does all this mean . . . ? Do you mean to tell me that Venus alone would not be adequate? She is, they say, so called (among other reasons) because not without violence [*vi non sine*] can a woman be robbed of her virginity! . . . And then, if Virginensis is among those present, to see to the untying of the virgin girdle, and Subigus, to see that the bride is subdued to her husband, and Prema, to make sure that, when subdued, she is pressed tight, to prevent her moving—if they are there, what is the function of the goddess Pertunda? She should blush for shame and take herself off! Let the bridegroom have something to do for himself! It would be most improper for anyone but the husband to do what her name implies.[13]

Pertunda is therefore the divine personification of a task, a precious operation: *pertundere* means to perforate, pierce, push through. "After lunch I lie down and I pierce my tunic and my coat," laments an impatient lover languishing after a lady.[14] This eloquent text suggests that in Rome virginity evoked the image of a veil, a fabric curtain, which would explain the polemic of Soranus, a Greek who taught medicine in Rome, against the existence of the hymen. It would also explain why the "anatomical" etymology for the Greek marriage song, the *hymenaios,* is mentioned by Servius, a commentator on Virgil, but not by Proclus.

Nevertheless, although the church fathers protested against a corporeal semiotics of virginity, they did not go so far as to question empirically its legitimacy and foundations. It was left to the physicians and naturalists of the Enlightenment to challenge on empirical grounds the reality of the *signaculum* that God supposedly had given to women. Dissection contradicted the existence of the hymen; observation dispelled the fantasy. Practitioners turned to ethnography and psychology to explain why such an idea had proved so persuasive to men and women the world over.

Midwives claim this to be true, that they can tell a virgin girl from one who has been deflowered by finding a break in a casing [*taye*] that is ruptured in the first coitus, and upon report of such evidence judges often render judgment, and in doing so commit great abuses through the aforesaid midwives. In order to find out the truth, I questioned several of them about where they find the aforesaid slip. One said right at the entrance of the shameful part, another in the middle, and still others deep inside, just in front of the mouth of the womb. Yet others say that it cannot be seen until after the first childbirth. That is how the opinions of the midwives agree. One rarely finds this hymen panniculus. And when one does find it, one can say that it is against nature, in that it cannot be made a certain and universal rule. The blood that flows out is not a result of the rupture of the hymen but comes from the rough surface of the cervix.[15]

These remarks, so close in spirit to Soranus' critique, were made by a late sixteenth-century Parisian physician, Ambroise Paré. Having dissected innumerable young girls, this attentive reader of Galen, Avicenna, and Almensor and curious student of sexual mores took a firm position against a common error: "The vulgar (and even some learned men) believe that there is no virgin who does not have this hymen, which is the virginal gate. But they are mistaken, because one finds it only very rarely, and I maintain that (in composing my Anatomy) I looked for it in several girls aged three, four, five, and up to twelve years, who died at the Hôtel-Dieu in Paris, and I was never able to perceive it."[16] Those ignorant on this score included not only mistaken "colleagues" (such as that "great and excellent anatomist" Realdus Columbus) and the Africans of Mauritania (who displayed the bloody bedsheets after defloration on the wedding night) but especially midwives and the judges who interrogated them: the mistake was widely shared, the prejudice deeply rooted. Clear medical thinking was threatened by the conventional wisdom of midwives. Though not an atheist, Paré did not hesitate to reject as false a "certainty" based on an unfortunate confusion of virtue with atresia.

Two centuries later, the *Encyclopédie* of Diderot and d'Alembert threw itself into a similar struggle against the fantastic, pseudoscientific, oppressive belief in the existence of the hymen, which it was said was worthy of savages and barbarians. To conclude my book I defer to Buffon, that "physician full of wit and enlightenment," whose views are here summarized by the Chevalier de Jaucourt in his article "Virginité" in the *Encyclopédie:*

> Men, says M. de Buffon, jealous of privacies in every sphere, have always made much of whatever they believed they possessed exclusively and before anyone else. It is this kind of madness that has made a real entity of the *virginity* of maidens. *Virginity,* which is a moral fact, a virtue that consists solely in the purity of the heart, has become a physical object with which all men are concerned. Upon this object they have established opinions, customs, ceremonies, superstitions, and even judgments and punishments. Illicit abuses and the most dishonest of customs have been authorized. People have subjected to the scrutiny of ignorant midwives and exposed to the eyes of prejudiced physicians nature's most secret parts, without realizing that such indecency is an offense against *virginity;* that to seek to know it is to violate it; that every shameful situation, every indecent state for which a girl is obliged to blush within is a veritable defloration . . . Anatomy itself leaves the existence of the membrane known as the *hymen* totally in doubt, as well as the myrtiform caruncles whose presence or absence has long been regarded as indicating the certainty of defloration or *virginity.* Anatomy, I say, permits us to reject these two signs not simply as inconclusive but as downright fantastic.

NOTES

INDEX

ABBREVIATIONS

BCH *Bulletin de correspondance hellénique*
JHS *Journal of Hellenic Studies*
REA *Revue des études anciennes*
REG *Revue des études grecques*

NOTES

INTRODUCTION

1. E. Littré, *Dictionnaire de la langue française* (Paris, 1869), gives, under *hymen*, the following definition: "A membranous fold that in virgins is usually found at the entry of the vagina." Since Littré knew ancient medicine well and was also well aware of the misunderstandings that could be caused by the word "membrane," he was careful to say "membranous fold" rather than "membrane" in order to exclude the idea of occlusion. M. Guntz, *Nomenclature anatomique illustrée* (Paris, 1975), p. 188, writes: "Membrane formed in the virgin by a crease in the vaginal mucosa at the edge of the vaginal orifice." A. Buchet and J. Cuilleret, *Anatomie*, vol. 4: *L'abdomen* (Lyons and Paris, 1983), p. 2397, refer to an "incomplete membranous barrier" and note that the "crease called hymen" partially obstructs the vaginal opening near the entrance "in most virgins." It will be seen that anatomists in the classical age took a far more radical view.

2. Sigmund Freud, *The Taboo of Virginity* (1917). D. Grisoni goes so far as to say that for a boy, to deflower is to perforate, whereas for a girl it is an ablation: "a removal of flesh, an irreversible excision"; *La première fois ou le roman de la virginité perdue à travers les siècles et les continents* (1981), p. 37. Philippe Sollers has usefully called attention to the imaginary nature of the hymen: "The membrane, like the censor's white tape, indicates an indefinite reserve of frigidity. Not to have had a hand in its destruction is therefore a precaution to be taken if one wants to receive an echo of a woman's orgasm. That, at any rate, is what clans have always believed"; La Sangsure, *Théorie des exceptions* (Paris, 1986), p. 253.

3. Diodorus Siculus XVI. 27.

4. Marie Delcourt, *L'oracle de Delphes* (Paris, 1955), p. 15.

5. Plutarch, *On the Delays of Divine Justice*, 29.

1. A LUMINOUS PIT

1. Strabo, XVII.1.43.
2. Plutarch, *On Garrulousness* 17 (*Mor.* 511B6 ff.).
3. Ibid. (*Mor.* 511A9–B6).
4. Ibid., 20 (*Mor.* 512E).
5. Plutarch, *On the E at Delphi* 2 (*Mor.* 385B5—C1); cf. 6 (*Mor.* 387D). These etymologies transform Apollo's geographical epithets into allusions to his knowledge.
6. Plato, *Phaedrus* 244d.
7. Georges Dumézil, *Apollon sonore* (Paris, 1982), p. 107.
8. Iamblichus, *De mysteriis* III.11.
9. Ibid., III.7.
10. Cicero, *De divinatione* I.18.
11. Ibid., I.19.
12. G. Rougemont, "Techniques divinatoires à Delphes. Etat présent sur le fonctionnement de l'oracle (résumé)," in *Recherche sur les "Artes" à Rome* (Paris, 1978), pp. 152–154, esp. 152.
13. Ernest Will, "Sur la nature du pneuma delphique," *BCH,* 47 (1942–43), pp. 161–175.
14. H. W. Parke and D. E. W. Wormell, *The Delphic Oracle,* vol. 1: *The History* (Oxford, 1956), p. 17.
15. Marie Delcourt, *L'Oracle de Delphes* (Paris, 1955), p. 16.
16. Ibid.
17. Marie Delcourt, *Les Grands Sanctuaires de la Grèce* (Paris, 1947), pp. 76–92.
18. See A. P. Oppé, "The Chasm at Delphi," *JHS,* 24 (1904), 214–240; and Will, "Sur la nature du pneuma delphique," pp. 161–175.
19. G. Roux, *Delphes, son oracle et ses dieux* (Paris, 1976).
20. Ibid., p. 94.
21. Euripides, *Iphigenia in Tauris* 1257: *adytōn hyper.* This is the lesson taught by the Codex Laurentianus XXXII. 2. H. Grégoire's Budé edition (Paris, 1925) retains Neidler's correction: *adytōn hypo,* which Grégoire translates as "du fond du prophétique sanctuaire" (in the back of the prophetic temple). See Roux, *Delphes,* pp. 91–117.
22. Roux, *Delphes* pp. 147–157.

2. THE ART OF MADNESS

1. See F. E. Robbins, "The Lot Oracle," *Classical Philology,* 11 (1916), 278–285; P. Amandry, *La Mantique apollinienne à Delphes. Essai sur le fonctionnement de l'oracle* (Paris, 1950), p. 226; G. Roux, *Delphes, son oracle et ses dieux,* p. 226 n. 22; cf. ibid., p. 142 n. 1.

2. R. Flacelière, "Le Fonctionnement de l'oracle de Delphes au temps de Plutarque," *Annales de l'Ecole des Hautes Etudes de Gand,* 2 (1938), 83, asserts that analogous images are "innumerable." Amandry, *La Mantique apollinienne,* p. 66, says that they are "rare." Roux, *Delphes,* p. 142, still refers to them in the plural.

3. Roux, *Delphes,* p. 142 and n. 1. On the preliminary use of laurel and water, our informant is Lucian, *Bis accusatus* 1–2.

4. Plutarch, *Theseus* 3.5.

5. See scholium to Euripides, *Medea,* 679–681.

6. The painter of the bowl elsewhere exhibited a pronounced interest in figures of origin: besides the "portrait" of King Codrus, he did a very beautiful birth of Erichthonius—"a paradigmatic figuration of the scene," as Nicole Loraux put it in *Les Enfants d'Athéna* (Paris, 1981), p. 277 n. 5.

7. Roux, *Delphes,* p. 142 n. 1. The drawing is reproduced in ibid., p. 120.

8. Plutarch, *On the E at Delphi* 2 (*Mor.* 385C–D).

9. M. E. Simon, *Die Götter des Griechen* (Munich, 1969), pp. 266–267.

10. M. E. Simon, *Opfernde Götter* (Berlin, 1953), p. 23. The chapter on Apollo's offerings includes numerous images of the god holding a *phiale.*

11. R. Rochette, *Monuments inédits d'antiquité* (Paris, 1833), pl. 37. Cf. A. Trendall, *Vases of Lucania, Campania, Sicily* (Oxford, 1967), p. 113 n. 588.

12. Jane E. Harrison, *Themis: A Study of the Social Origins of Greek Religion* (Cambridge, 1912), p. 411; eadem, *Prolegomena to the Study of Greek Religion,* 3d ed. (1922; reprint, New York, 1955), p. 319.

13. L. Séchan, *Etudes sur la tragédie grecque dans ses rapports avec la céramique,* 2d ed. (Paris, 1967), pp. 97–98 n. 6.

14. Aeschylus, *Choephoroe* 272 (*exaudōmenos*), 283 (*phōnēi*).

Cf. Euripides, *Orestes* 591–594: "You see: Apollo who, from his sojourn upon the world's umbilicus, dispenses to mortals his truthful decrees and finds us docile to all his words; it was to obey him that I killed my mother." The god appears in person at the end of the play to confirm his oracles. At 1668–69 Orestes alludes to the divine voice and words.

15. On Apollo as an expert on sexual procreation see A. Peretti, "La teoria della generazione patrilinea in Eschilo," *La parola del passato,* 1956, pp. 241–262.

16. Aeschylus, *Eumenides* 1–29.

17. Scholium to Aeschylus, *Eumenides* 47.

18. Ibid. at 33.

19. Ibid. at 34.

20. Ibid. at 64.

21. Aeschylus, *Eumenides* 64.

22. Aeschylus, *Choephoroe* 268.

23. Séchan, *Etudes sur la tragédie,* pp. 95–96, fig. 31.

24. For various possible interpretations of this posture, see G. Devereux, "Locomotion tétrapodale dans la tragédie grecque," in *Tragédie et poésie grecque* (Paris, 1975), pp. 197ff.

25. Herodotus VII.111, trans. Aubrey de Sélincourt (New York: Penguin, 1972), p. 479.

26. Roux, *Delphes,* p. 64.

27. G. Daux, *Pausanias à Delphes* (Paris, 1936).

28. See P. -E. Legrand, "Index analytique," in Herodotus, *Histoires* (Paris: Belles Lettres, 1954), s.v. "Pythiē."

29. Herodotus VII.141.

30. Ovid, *Metamorphoses* XIV.152.

31. Origen, *Contra Celsum* VII.3.

32. Ibid.

33. Ibid., 4.

34. Think, in this connection, of the way in which Catholic theologians discredited Lutheran thought, allegedly born in the "monks' secret room." See Lucien Febvre, *Un destin. Martin Luther* (Paris, 1952), p. 40 n. 1.

35. John Chrysostom, *In epistulam I ad Corinthios Homilia XIX* 260B–C.

36. Justin, *Apologies* I.18.4–5, cites the Pythian oracle as proof of the survival of the soul after death: "Look at these men, who are

gripped and shaken by the souls of the dead, whom everyone calls demoniac and raging; look at the oracles of Amphilochus, Dodona, Pytho." And Clement of Alexandria, *Stromateis* I.135.2–3, contrasts the Hebrew prophets, who spoke because of divine inspiration, with those who "were driven by demons or put in a trance by waters, fumes, or a special kind of air." More vehemently, Tertullian, *Apologeticus* XIII.5, exclaims: "Let them bring forth one of those people who pass for being deranged by a god, who with mouths gaping over the altars breathe in divinity with odor, who heal through gasps, who prophesy with breathless voices."

37. Herodotus I.65; II.92.

38. Flacelière, "Le Fonctionnement," p. 99; Roux, *Delphes,* pp. 132–136.

39. Plutarch, *On the Disappearance of Oracles* 51 (*Mor.* 438B); Roux, *Delphes,* p. 149.

3. LUNAR PYTHIA

1. H. Diels and W. Kranz, *Die Fragmente der Vorsokratiker* (Berlin, 1954), fr. 93, p. 172. The translation given here is that of G. S. Kirk and J. E. Raven, *The Presocratic Philosophers* (Cambridge: Cambridge University Press, 1957), p. 211.

2. J. Bollack and H. Wismann, *Héraclite ou la séparation* (Paris, 1972), p. 274.

3. For various interpretations of this celebrated fragment, see F. Calabi, "Il signore il cui oracolo è a Delfi non dice né nasconde bensì indica," *Bollettino del Istituto di Filologia Classica,* 4 (1977–78).

4. Plutarch, *On the Oracles of the Pythia* 21 (*Mor.* 404D).

5. Ibid.

6. Ibid. Since the sunlight, in all its force and splendor, strikes the surface of the moon, it is plausible that its reflection should reach as far as the earth. But owing to the force of the impact and the greatness of the distance, it is not surprising that the nocturnal rays are weak, thin, and cold. Cf. Plutarch, *On the Face That Appears in the Moon* (*Mor.* 926E–937B).

7. Cf. *On the Oracles of the Pythia* 21 (*Mor.* 405C). On the mixed, median nature of the moon between heaven and earth, analogous to the position of the soul between body and thought, see *On the Face That Appears in the Moon* (*Mor.* 945C–D). In regard

to the similarity between the role of the shining moon and that of the Pythia's psyche, note the belief that the moon has the face of the Sibyl (*On the Oracles of the Pythia* 9 [*Mor.* 398C–D]; cf. *On Delays in Divine Justice* [*Mor.* 566D]).

8. *On the Oracles of the Pythia* (*Mor.* 404E–F). Note the theme of mixture, which dominates Theon's argument. Flacelière, in his interpretation of the passage, suggests that it be read as a series of arguments for a theology of illumination. Contrasting the dialogue *On the Disappearance of Oracles* with the one that interests us here, he sees a clear evolution in Plutarch's theory: abandoning the naturalism expressed by Lamprias (*On the Disappearance of Oracles*), the philosopher allegedly moved here to the mature idea of immediate and direct possession of the Pythia by Apollo. See R. Flacelière, "Plutarque et la Pythie," *REG* 56 (1943), 72–111, esp. 87–88; and G. Soury, "Plutarque, prêtre de Delphes: L'inspiration prophétique," *REG*, 55 (1942), 50–69. Without getting into the debate over the respective dates of the two works, I believe that Theon, although he says nothing about the role of a *pneuma* in the inspiration, is describing the mantic phenomenon as a result of the combination of *two* autonomous forces and not in terms of a god's seizing control of a soul that is always completely passive.

9. *On the Oracles of the Pythia* 21 (*Mor.* 404D–E10; 404C1, E1).

10. Ibid. (*Mor.* 404D1).

11. Ibid. 22 (*Mor.* 405 C3–11); the reference is to Xenophon, *Oeconomicus* VII.5.

12. Plutarch, *On the Oracles of the Pythia* 22–23 (*Mor.* 405D–E).

13. Ibid., 21 (*Mor.* 404C).

14. Ibid., 24 (*Mor.* 406B,F): "Furthermore, from the standpoint of the god and his clairvoyance, we see that the change that has occurred has been an improvement . . . By stripping the oracles of verse, big words, periphrases, and obscurity, he inclined the Pythia to speak to consultants in a language similar to that in which the laws speak to cities, sovereigns to their peoples, or masters to their disciples. In the end his only purpose was to be understood and believed."

15. Ibid., 29 (*Mor.* 408F). Although the wise man has always known how to listen to oracular messages, looking beyond meta-

phors (*Mor.* 460F), figurative language itself is well suited to the image-loving children we are (30): those who deplore the Pythia's current prose without understanding its value are the same people who in the past would have reproached the priestess and the god for enigmatic expression.

16. Ibid., 21 (*Mor.* 404E2–6). In *On the Disappearance of Oracles* 51 the Pythia forced to give a consultation against her will is compared with a ship in distress (*Mor.* 438B5). The image of a storm at sea (waves, winds, foam) epitomizes the symptoms of the sacred malady: Hippocrates, *On Winds,* 14 (Emile Littré, ed., *Oeuvres complètes d'Hippocrate,* 10 vols. [Paris, 1839–1861], 6:111; hereafter cited as Littré).

17. *On the Oracles of the Pythia* 21 (*Mor.* 404E5–9). The closeness and equivalence of these two images is surely of significance in the work of Michel Serres, *La Naissance de la physique dans le texte de Lucrèce* (Paris, 1977).

18. Iamblichus, *De mysteriis* III.7 (my italics). Iamblichus sees the Pythia-organon as being subject to an absolute and overwhelming power. This minor but crucial alteration in the role of the instrument anticipates a certain "theologizing" interpretation of Plutarch. Cf. note 8 above.

19. In the classical tradition from Herodotus to Plutarch, the Delphic god's answer was always true; only man's exegesis could be mistaken.

20. G. Soury, *La Démonologie de Plutarque* (Paris, 1942), p. 104: "As for Lamprias' conception of divination, surely it is that of his master," namely, Plato. R. Flacelière, in the "Notice" preceding *La Disparition des oracles* (On the Disappearance of Oracles), in his edition of Plutarch, *Dialogues pythiques* (Paris, 1974), p. 87: "This 'naturalistic' theory [of Lamprias] is inspired primarily by Aristotelian ideas." V. Goldschmidt, "Les Thèmes du *De defectu oraculorum,*" *REG* 61 (1948), 298ff., reprinted in *Questions platoniciennes* (Paris, 1970), pp. 223–229; "Moreover, it seems to me that Lamprias, from his first intervention, professes a perfectly coherent doctrine, which, it should be noted, is that of Plato" (p. 226).

21. In chaps. 44–46 Lamprias explicitly invokes *hoi peri Aristotelēn.*

22. According to Soury, "Plutarque, prêtre de Delphes," p. 56.

23. Plutarch, *On the Disappearance of Oracles* 47 (*Mor.* 435F–436A).

24. Ibid., 48 (*Mor.* 436E–F).

25. Aristotle, *De generatione animalium* I.22: the technical paradigm of conception. On the pneumatic nature and function of the sperm, see II.2 and 3. Consider, for example, this description of the elimination of the male matter: "The seminal matter dissolves and evaporates because it possesses a humid and aqueous nature" (737a7–12).

26. Plutarch, *On the Disappearance of Oracles* 50 (*Mor.* 437D). A musical instrument is a special kind of organon, and the ambiguity of the Pythia—instrument or matter—is clear from the fact that even when she is considered *hylē,* the god acts upon her with a plectrum.

27. Ibid.

28. On the sense of the verb *anapimplēmi* see the semantic analysis by J.Pigeaud, *La Maladie de l'âme* (Paris, 1981), pp. 218–223.

29. Plutarch, *On the Disappearance of Oracles* 47 (*Mor.* 436B).

30. Ibid., 51 (*Mor.* 438A). This passage shows clearly that enthusiasm was not identical with being unsettled, but that there was an *evil* enthusiasm that stemmed from compulsion.

31. Ibid. (*Mor.* 438B). The signs of disturbance in the Pythia can of course be compared with the symptoms of epilepsy, which the physician detects solely with his ears. Concerning abnormal phenomena caused by the sacred malady, see F. Ferrini, "Tragedia e patologia: Lessico ippocratico in Euripide," *Quaderni Urbinati,* 29 (1978), 49–62.

32. As in an episode recounted by Lucan, *Pharsalia* V. 120–224; cf. J. Bayet, "La Mort de la Pythie: Lucain, Plutarque et la chronique delphique," in *Mélanges dédiés à la mémoire de Félix Grat* (Paris, 1946), pp. 53–76. The Pythia whose inspiration is an agony attracted the attention of Roland Barthes, "Une Leçon de sincérité," *Poétique,* 47 (Sept. 1981), 259–267; see esp. 265: "A wrenching sight: the virgin resists entering into a state of hysteria, and it is the fat Roman general who forces her to do so." In a "chronicle" context Diodorus Siculus recounts the story of a Pythia who was compelled to mount the tripod but survived the ordeal (XVI.25).

33. According to Walter Burkert, *Homo Necans: The Anthropology of Ancient Greek Sacrificial Ritual and Myth* (Berkeley, Calif., 1983), "there is a clear parallel between the goat and the Pythia herself. When the Pythia goes toward the tripod, she consents to her death, and that is frightening." It is risky, however, to suggest that *every* consultation with the Delphic oracle was tantamount to a simulated execution of the Pythia. To say more about the relation between the goat and the possessed priestess one would have to study the goat's susceptibility to the sacred disease.

34. Thus Plutarch could have resolved the dilemma of the Hellenists: the conception of enthusiasm as combat between a god and a soul explains both the calm (she is quite docile) and the storm (she struggles).

4. PARTHENOS AUDAESSA

1. βαδίζειν, παρέχειν ἑαυτὴν τῷ θεῷ: *On the Disappearance of Oracles* 50 (*Mor.* 437 D8–9). Εἰς ἀνδρὸς βαδίζειν/τῷ θεῷ σύνεστιν: *On the Oracles of the Pythia* 22 (*Mor.* 405C9–11). Note the use of the verb σύνειμι which unambiguously denotes sexual union in the strict sense. See note 3 below.

2. *On the Disappearance of Oracles* 50 (*Mor.* 437D9–11).

3. "That is why the Pythia is kept *pure of all* carnal union and completely *isolated*, throughout her life, *from all contact and all relations* with strangers"; ibid., 51 (*Mor.* 438C1–3). The Pythia's immaculate retreat may be compared with the behavior prescribed for the priestess and priest of Artemis Hymnia in Arcadia: absolute chastity, of course, but also a prohibition against washing and eating with strangers and against entering any private home (Pausanias VIII.13.1).

4. *On the Disappearance of Oracles* 40 (*Mor.* 432C10–D3).

5. Ibid., 46 (*Mor.* 435C–D).

6. In the story of Coretas, "who, according to the Delphians, was the first to point out the virtue of this place as a result of having chanced upon it"; ibid. (*Mor.* 435D3–5).

7. Pausanias X.5.7.

8. Diodorus Siculus XVI. 26.

9. The mythology of the oracle's origins is recounted primar-

ily in the *Homeric Hymn to Apollo,* as well as in Aeschylus, *Eumenides* 1–34, and Euripides, *Iphigenia in Tauris* (1245–81). It is repeated by Pausanias (X.5.5–6), Apollodorus (I.4.1), Aelian (*Varia historia* III.1), and Hyginus (*Fabulae* 140). These versions are well known to be different.

10. Diodorus Siculus XVI. 26. The same equivalence between virginity and regained chastity is found in the story of the priestess of Artemis Hymnia (Pausanias VIII.5.11). Plutarch narrates the biography of a widow who, having pledged to remain sexually abstinent, devotes herself to the service of the goddess; *On Love* 22 (*Mor.* 768B). Note, too, that Plato ascribes the choice of a mature woman instead of a young girl to Artemis in discussing that quasi-priestess, the midwife (*Theaetetus* 149).

11. E. Fehrle, *Die Kultische Keuschheit im Altertum* (Giessen, 1910), pp. 75–89. Among the texts cited in the valuable chapter on the cult of Apollo is a passage from Pausanias that deserves special attention. He describes the mantic method practiced at Argos in the sanctuary of Apollo Deiradiotes, founded by Pythaeus upon his return from Delphi. A woman who was not allowed to engage in sexual relations of any kind delivered the prophesies there. Once a month, at night, she sacrificed a lamb and tasted its blood, whereupon she was possessed by the god (Pausanias II.24.1). K. Latte, "The Coming of the Pythia," *Harvard Theological Review,* 32 (1940), 9–18: the figure of the Apollonian priestess may be comparable to that of the concubine.

12. Ovid, *Metamorphoses* XIV.140 ff.

13. Pausanias X.12.1–3.

14. Ibid., X.12.4.

15. Ibid., X.12.6.

16. On Cassandra and her iconography see J. Davreux, *La Légende de la prophétesse Cassandre d'après les textes et les monuments* (Liège and Paris, 1942); concerning her amorous misadventure, see ibid., pp. 30, 51, 68–69, 102.

17. Aeschylus, *Agamemnon* 1178ff.

18. Ibid., 1275.

19. Lycophron, *Alexandra* 4. On the symbolism of belts, see P. Schmitt, "Athena Apatouria et la ceinture: Les aspects féminins des Apatouries à Athènes," *Annales: Economies, Sociétés, Civilisations,* 6 (1977), 1059–73, esp. 1063.

20. Plutarch, *On the E at Delphi* 2 (*Mor.* 385C8); *On the Oracles of the Pythia* 76 (*Mor.* 397A4).

21. Callimachus, *Iambi* IV, fr. 94. 26–27 (Pfeiffer). Cf. G. Roux, *Delphes, son oracle et ses dieux*, pp. 123–129.

22. Pausanias VIII.20.3; X.7.8. Ovid, *Metamorphoses* I.452 ff. The fable of Daphne is the archetype of those analyzed by F. Dupont, "Se reproduire ou se métamorphoser," *Topique,* 3–4 (1971–72), 139–160.

23. Diodorus Siculus IV.66.

24. "The laurel branch, branch of Apollo, how it trembles, how it causes his whole house to tremble! Far, far from here, everything wicked! It is he, Phoebus. His handsome feet strike the gates"; Callimachus, *Hymn to Apollo* 1–3.

25. Cf. Lucan, *Pharsalia* 169–197, and Virgil, *Aeneid* VI.77 ff.: "But the prophetess, still resisting the god's embrace [*nondum patiens*], struggled in his cave like a wild bacchante and sought to shake the omnipotent god off her bosom." R. Pichon has noted these "scenes of hysteria and ecstasy" that echo Virgil in Lucan's work; *Les Sources de Lucain* (Paris, 1912), p. 186.

26. In the celebrated passage of the *Phaedrus* (251c6–e6) where he speaks of the pain caused by sprouting wings trapped in their obstructed pores.

27. Herodotus I.182, trans. de Sélincourt, p. 114.

28. "Many people think that Byzios is the same as Physios: this month does indeed mark the beginning of spring, the time when most creatures are born and grow. The truth is otherwise . . . This was the month during which the consultation with the oracle was held, and the seventh was considered to be the anniversary of the god's birth . . . Monthly consultations were not instituted until much later. Previously the Pythia prophesied only one day each year—that day, according to Callisthenes and Anaxandrides"; Plutarch, *Quaestiones Graecae* 9 (*Mor.* 292E). Cf. Hesiod, *Works and Days* 770–771: the seventh day of the month was the day on which Leto gave birth to Apollo.

5. OPEN TO THE SPIRITS

1. This is the conclusion reached by E. Will in "Sur la nature du pneuma delphique," *BCH,* 1942–43, pp. 161–175. The most de-

tailed analysis of Stoic influence on Plutarch's Platonism is G. Verbeke, "Plutarque," in *L'Evolution de la doctrine du pneuma du stoïcisme à saint Augustin* (Paris and Louvain, 1945), pp. 260–287.

2. This point is forcefully argued by P. Amandry, *La Mantique apollinienne à Delphes. Essai sur le fonctionnement de l'oracle*, chaps. 19 and 20. But see the objections of R. Flacelière in "Le Délire de la Pythie, est-il une légende?" *REA*, 52 (1950), 306–324.

3. Plato, *Phaedrus* 265b.

4. Plato, *Cratylus* 396d–e.

5. Plato, *Phaedrus* 262d.

6. Aeschylus, *Suppliants* 17, 45, 577.

7. Xenophon, *Symposium* IV.15; Plutarch, *Cleomenes* 3, 2; Aelian, *Varia historia* III.12.

8. On the propagation of epidemics through the air that people breathe, see J. Pigeaud, "La Contagion: Un problème épistémologique," in *La Maladie de l'âme*, pp. 211–226.

9. Strabo, *Geographics* IX.3.5, trans. Horace Jones.

10. In Plutarch's dialogue the existence of an exhalation is given as an accepted and shared belief, not as a hypothesis invented by a philosopher. Belief in Delphic vapors is reported by pseudo-Aristotle, *De mundo* 395; Cicero, *De divinatione* 38, 79, 115; Iamblichus, *De mysteriis* III.11.126; Longinus, *On the Sublime* XIII. 2; scholium to Aristophanes, *Plutos* 39; Pausanias X.5.7.

11. See L. B. Holland, "The Mantic Mechanism at Delphi," *American Journal of Archaeology*, 37 (1933), 201–214. The hypothesis of an artificial fumigation, with smoke rising to the Pythia through a hole in an omphalos, has been refuted by the discovery that the stone in question was not of ancient origin. See J. Bousquet, *Gnomon*, 32 (1960), 260–261 (review of H.-V. Herrmann, *Omphalos* [Münster, 1959]).

12. Pausanias X.5.8–9.

13. Plutarch, *On the Disappearance of Oracles* 51 (*Mor.* 438A).

14. Longinus, *On the Sublime* XIII.2.

15. For a recent account of the division of medical knowledge between Cos and Cnidus in the fifth and fourth centuries B.C., see A. Thivel, *Cnide et Cos?* (Paris, 1982).

16. See E. Nardi, *Procurato aborto nel mondo greco-romano* (Milan, 1971), for a useful though discreet summary.

17. Soranus, *Gynaikeia* I.30–32. See P. Manuli, "Elogio della castità. La ginecologia di Sorano," *Memoria,* 3 (1982), 39–49.

18. For a comprehensive survey of these aspects of the Hippocratic literature see P. Manuli, "Donne mascoline, femmine sterili, vergini perpetue," in S. Campese, P. Manuli, and G. Sissa, *Madre materia* (Turin, 1983), pp. 146–192.

19. *Nature of Woman* 3 (7:314 Littré).

20. Ibid. Cf. *Diseases of Women* 127 (8:272 Littré).

21. *Nature of Woman* 2 (7:314 Littré). Cf. pars. 8 and 35.

22. *On Sterile Women* 230 (8:444 Littré).

23. *Nature of Woman* 34 (7:372 Littré).

24. *On Sterile Women* 230 (8:438 Littré).

25. *De locis in homine* 47 (6:346 Littré). Cf. *Nature of Woman* 107 (7:422 Littré).

26. *Nature of Woman* 206. Cf. para. 195.

27. *On Sterile Women* 230 (8:445 Littré).

28. For examples see *Diseases of Women* 13 (8:51, 53 Littré); *Nature of Woman* 87, 88 (7:322 Littré).

29. *Diseases of Women* 12 (8:50 Littré).

30. Hippocrates, *Aphorisms* V.28.

31. *On Superfetation* 34 (8:501 Littré).

32. *Diseases of Women* 51 (8:110 Littré).

33. Ibid.

34. Thivel, *Cnide et Cos?* pp. 280–281.

35. *Diseases of Women* 133 (7:302 Littré).

36. Ibid. (7:286 Littré).

37. Ibid., 142 (8:314 Littré).

38. Ibid., 138 (8:310 Littré).

39. Ibid., 125 (8:268 Littré).

40. Ibid.

41. R. Joly, *Le Niveau de la science hippocratique* (Paris, 1966), p. 45.

42. Soranus, *Gynaikeia* III.29.

43. *Diseases of Women* 1 (8:12 Littré); *On the System of Glands* XVI.

44. Soranus, *Gynaikeia* III.26.

45. *Diseases of Women* 7 (8:32 Littré); *Nature of Woman* 3 and passim.

46. Euripides, *Hippolytus* 293–296; Plutarch, *On Curiosity* 7 (*Mor.* 518D); Hyginus, *Fabulae* 274.9–13.
47. Text in Joly, *Le Niveau*, pp. 62–63.
48. See Artemidorus V.73.
49. Plato, *Republic* 395e–396a.

6. THE TORTOISE AND THE COURTESAN

1. Consider a few examples drawn from the opening paragraphs of *Diseases of Women:* "Menstrual flow, though present, is less abundant than it should be; the uterine orifice [*to stoma tōn metreōn*] deviates somewhat from the direction of the genital parts or is sufficiently closed to obstruct the paths of transmission without preventing all flow. When the blood comes to the womb, it constantly presses on the orifice [*stoma*], and little by little it flows out" (8:24–26 Littré). "When the menstrual flow is more abundant and thicker than it should be, it is because the person has a body naturally given to flux and the uterine orifice [*to stoma tōn metreōn*] is located near the vulva" (ibid., p. 28). "When a woman who lives with her husband cannot become pregnant, she should be asked whether or not she had her period and whether the sperm flows out immediately or the next day or on the sixth or seventh day. If she says that it flows out immediately after intercourse, then the uterine orifice [*to stoma*] is not straight but is deviated and cannot receive the sperm" (ibid., p. 40). "If the man's semen flows out immediately after intercourse, the cause is in the uterine orifice [*to stoma tōn hystereōn*]. Treat this as follows: if the orifice is quite closed, open it with pine needles and leads" (ibid., p. 50). This is only a tiny sampling intended merely to show how constant the reference was. Post-Hippocratic gynecology faithfully followed the lead of the Hippocratic physicians. Oribasius, faithful compiler of the anatomy of Soranus and Rufus of Ephesus, assures us that the uterus opens into the genitals, or *kalpos*, like a mouth (*Collectiones medicae* III).

2. Aristotle, *De generatione animalium* II, 739a36. Concerning the closure of the mouth, consider this Hippocratic text: "In fact the womb, after receiving the sperm and closing up, retains it within itself, because its orifice clamps down in response to the

humor, and that which comes from the man is mixed with that which comes from the woman" (*On Generation* V.1.5, ed. and trans. R. Joly in *Le Niveau de la science hippocratique*). Receive, close, retain: conception was a result of this reaction of the uterine mouth, which Galen praised as one of the marvels of the human body (*De usu partium* XIV.III.146). Aristotle uses the same verb (*Historia animalium* VII, 583b29) to describe the same phenomenon. It is important, however, to note that this oral configuration concerns the uterus and not only the vulva (*aidoion*) or vagina. In Hippocratic and Aristotelian texts no detailed anatomical description is given of the visible sex organ—the shameful part. The lips that a woman must moisten with cedar oil or incense or white lead in order to allow the sperm to slip in easily are located at the place where the sperm arrives, that is, inside the genitals, at the bottom of the vagina (ibid., 583a21–24).

3. In *Laws* VI.

4. Plutarch, *Coniugalia praecepta* 32. This idea, introduced through the image of Aphrodite Urania, whom Phidias portrayed with her foot resting on the shell of a tortoise, derives from the idea of a mute animal that becomes a musical instrument in the hands of man. Here, however, it is the man's mouth that occupies the servile position of instrument, so Plutarch chooses to identify it with the nobler flute. The accent is therefore entirely on the *aulos*, a marvelous organ capable of transforming the female voice into music. Plutarch is more spontaneous in comparing a speaking woman with an instrument: the Pythia is a lyre, a mantic tortoise, in the hands of Apollo (*On the Disappearance of Oracles* 50 [*Mor.* 437D9–10]). Behind the image of the woman who requires an interpreter is the *kyrios*, her obligatory representative in the courts.

5. Plutarch, *Numa* XXV.10.77A9–B5. Wine, a beverage consecrated to Venus, is studied in R. Schilling, *La Religion romaine de Vénus depuis les origines jusqu'au temps d'Auguste* (Paris,1954), pp. 91–148. On the Greek tradition see p. 136: "This association of ideas (Venus/wine) was in no danger of being effaced when Rome was invaded by Hellenism. On the contrary, the ritual link between Venus and wine (the feast of the Vinalia) was mythologically 'justified' by the marriage of Aphrodite and Dionysus." Perhaps the most arresting comment on this much-commented-upon marriage

is to be found in a line of Aristophanes preserved by Athenaeus: "Delightful it is to drink wine, the milk of Aphrodite" (IX.463e).

6. Plutarch, *Coniugalia praecepta* 19.

7. Ibid., 15 and 16.

8. Ibid., 10. Plutarch alludes to the unhappy story of Candaules, his wife, and Gyges (Herodotus I.8).

9. Ibid, 46. Even naked and invisible, a wife's body is supposed to radiate virtue, fidelity, and affection. A married woman's body is not like other women's bodies but nameless and faceless.

10. Ibid., 29.

11. Ibid., 48.

12. Ibid., 145D–E. On the mole, or voluminous dermoid cyst, the medical literature has little to say, and what it does say is contradictory.

13. Aristotle, *Politics* I, 1260a30.

14. Ibid., 1253a9–10.

15. Aristotle, *Rhetoric* I, 1355a38–b2.

16. The image of woman as a clothed body whose nudity is never complete is a variation (in the key of conjugal modesty) on a very ancient and very misogynistic theme: the idea of woman as a creature whose truth can never be grasped. Ever since the first woman this body has offered itself to desire through the transparency of a veil: "The cloak is a trap, a trap with a very beautiful exterior. Does that mean it is a trap based on appearances? . . . To be sure, dissimulation is inscribed in the veil as the word *kalyptre.* In contrast to the 'veiled women' of the Indo-European myths studied by Dumézil, however, the creature in the *Theogony* does not wear a misleading disguise. Her veil does not hide the fact that she is something other than a woman: a god, a demon, a man. It hides nothing because the woman has no interior to conceal. To speak plainly, in the *Theogony* the first woman *is* her garment; she has no body. In any case it is as though the text were reluctant to give her one"; Nicole Loraux, "Sur la race des femmes et quelques-unes de ses tribus," in *Les Enfants d'Athéna,* pp. 85–86.

17. Aristotle, *Politics* V, 1313b34.

18. Sophocles, *Antigone* 690–700; 739.

19. Aristotle, *Politics* II, 1269b22–23.

20. Plutarch, *Lycurgus* XIX.1–3, 47E–F.

21. Plutarch, *Numa* XXV.9, 77A.

22. Ibid., 5.

23. Ibid., 11. There were two exceptions: the Vestal, a *virgo* whose concentration brought her the most extraordinary powers; and the woman who was the mother of three children. These women, who respectively embodied the highest female virtues in the sacred and private spheres, had the right to plead their own cases (ibid., X.5). Georges Dumézil, *La Religion romaine archaïque*, 2d ed. (Paris, 1974), p. 577, explains the prerogatives of the Vestals as follows: "In many so-called primitive societies, virginity, which is generally associated with special mystical and magical powers, is seen in [the Vestals] as constituting a state intermediate between femininity and masculinity—not mythologically as in other places but, as one might expect in Rome, legally: they were exempt from wardship (Gaius, I, 145; Plut. *Num.*, 10, 4 [*sic*]), allowed to bear witness, and permitted to dispose of their property as they wished by testament."

24. Plutarch, *Lycurgus* XIV.7.

25. Plutarch, *Numa* XXV.5.

26. Ibid., 6.

27. Plato, *Laws* VI, 78a; 781c2–5.

28. Ibid., VII, 806e1–10, esp. 4–7.

29. Ibid., VI, 781c7.

30. Isaeus, *On the Estate of Pyrrhus*.

31. Ibid., par. 14.

32. Ibid., par. 13. "At several points in this speech, and in accordance with a well-attested Greek opinion, it was alleged that for a woman merely to participate in a banquet with men was an irrefutable sign of a dissolute life." With this note L. Gernet glosses one oft-repeated item of testimony intended to convince the judges that Neera, a foreign woman who dared to pass herself off as the legitimate wife of an Athenian, was in fact a prostitute. Once, having coming to Athens for the Great Panathenian games, she "banqueted and feasted in a large company as a courtesan might do." The words "as a courtesan" echo those of one Euphliletus, also present at the banquet: see pseudo-Demosthenes, *Against Neaira* 24 and 25 (L. Gernet, ed., *Plaidoyers civils*, vol. 4 [Paris: Belles Lettres, 1960], p. 77).

33. Isaeus, *On the Estate of Pyrrhus* 16.

34. Isaeus, *On the Estate of Kiron* 19.

35. Ibid., 18.

36. Ibid., 20.

37. Claude Lévi-Strauss, *La Pensée sauvage* (Paris, 1962), p. 148. On the interconnections between food and sex see "Destins du cannibalisme," a special issue of *Nouvelle Revue de Psychanalyse*, 6 (1972). On maternal bodily appetites in African mythology see D. Paulme, *La Mère dévorante* (Paris, 1976), pp. 277–313.

38. Lévi-Strauss, *La Pensée sauvage*, p. 148.

39. Ibid.

40. See Jean-Pierre Vernant, "Manger à la table des hommes," in *La Cuisine du sacrifice en pays grec,* ed. Marcel Detienne and J.-P. Vernant (Paris, 1978), pp. 37–132; Loraux, "Sur la races des femmes" M. Arthur, "The Limits of Transcendence: Male and Female in Hesiod's *Theogony,*" in *La donna antica* (Turin: Boringhieri, forthcoming).

41. See P. Manuli, "Donne masculine, femmine sterili, vergini perpetue," in S. Campese, P. Manuli, and G. Sissa, *Madre materia,* pp. 146–192.

42. Plato, *Laws* VI, 773b4–6.

43. Ibid., 773a5–7.

44. Ibid., 775a1–e5.

45. Ibid., 775e2–5.

46. Ibid., 775e1–2.

47. Ibid., 775c1.

48. Ibid., 782c10–783b1.

49. Plato, *Timaeus* 90e1–91d6. The passage is of great interest because it deals with the origins of woman and of sexual procreation. In the beginning humans were all males, *andres,* and the female was a punitive and metaphorical mutation: "Of the men who came into the world, those who were cowards or led unrighteous lives may with reason be supposed to have changed into the nature of women in the second generation." Woman was thus born as a result of masculine *deilia* and *adikia,* and sexuality, which is obviously not necessary for genesis, since the first *andres* were born without mothers, appears only after the advent of woman. A result of meiosis in an originally homogeneous human race, sexual dif-

ference is reflected in a remaking of the body by divine surgery, with the spinal column extending into the genitals in man and the uterus being placed inside woman. Males bear marks of their original injustice on their own bodies, for their sperm and penis are living anatomical reminders of an animality that will remain with them forever. Desire, which in women is focused on maternity, in men takes the form of violence and madness, as if the male portion of humankind took part in reproduction by way of its defects, its bestial vocation.

50. *On the Control of Anger* (*Mor.* 452F–464D), *On Tranquillity of Mind* (*Mor.* 464E–477E), *On Curiosity* (*Mor.* 515B–523B).

51. Plutarch, *On Garrulousness* 17 (*Mor.* 511B).

52. Ibid., 7 (*Mor.* 505A).

52. Ibid., 3 (*Mor.* 503C–D).

53. Plutarch, *On Curiosity,* 9 (*Mor.* 519C).

54. Ibid. (*Mor.* 519E).

55. Plutarch, *On Garrulousness* 6 (*Mor.* 504D–E).

56. See above, page 54.

57. Plutarch, *On Garrulousness* 11 (*Mor.* 507B–D).

58. Because Fulvius, a friend of Caesar Augustus, was driven to suicide by his wife's indiscretion. Before killing herself at his side, the guilty woman reminded her husband how foolish he was to have confided in her: "As long as you have been living with me, you should have known me and protected yourself against my incontinence [*akrasia*]"; ibid. (*Mor.* 508B–C).

59. Ibid. (*Mor.* 507F).

60. Emile Benveniste, "Termes gréco-latins d'anatomie," *Revue de philologie,* 2d ser., 39 (1965), 8. These expressions, which are also found in the Greek of the New Testament, "come from the best classical language."

61. *Diseases of Women* 127 (8:272 Littré).

62. *On Sterile Women* (8:444 Littré).

63. Herodotus III.108.7–11.

64. Ibid., 109.8–11.

65. Ibid., 108.3–7.

66. The viper (*echidna*) is an animal whose mythology is emblematic for us. As a serpent, it makes us think of Delphi, for the monster that is associated with it in the land of the Arimi (Hesiod,

Theogony 295ff.) is the same Typhon who at Crisa protects the *drakaina*, the female dragon killed by Apollo (*Homeric Hymn to Apollo* 300–354). This interchangeability is highly indirect and does not warrant any assertion that the female dragon of Delphi is a viper. The feminine mark, the female visage of the viper, is worthy of attention, however. In Hesiod's *Theogony* Echidna appears in the lineage of Phorcys and Ceto: an irresistible monster (*amechanon*) like the later Pandora (*Works and Days* 598), in contrast to the first woman, who is all semblance (ibid., 60–78), she "in no way resembles either mortal men nor the immortal gods." She has a twofold nature: "Half nymph with sparkling eyes and pretty cheeks, half monstrous serpent, terrible and huge, mottled and cruel, who lies in the secret depths of the divine earth" (*Theogony* 295–305). Heracles encounters her in a region known as Hylaia: "There, in a cave, he is said to have found a viper that was also part maiden [*mixoparthenos*]. The upper part of her body from her buttocks up was that of a woman [*gynaikos*], the power part that of a reptile": Herodotus IV.9.1–5.

67. P. Chantraine, *Dictionnaire étymologique de la langue grecque*, vol. 1 (Paris, 1968), p. 211.

68. Ibid. In fact the word does not refer to a definite internal organ, but it does indicate sometimes one, sometimes the other digestive cavity. In Aristotle, for example, *gastēr* usually refers to the abdomen, but in some cases to the stomach (see *Historia animalium* 509a14–15). Similarly, *koilia* is not always the intestine (for which the word *enteron* was also used) but sometimes the stomach. As for *stomachos*, in classical Greek it was a synonym for *oisophagos*, the tube that carries food from the mouth to the *koilia*. Only later did *stomachos* come to mean stomach. See Benveniste, "Termes gréco-latins d'anatomie." This nomenclature is precisely defined in the brief treatise *On Anatomy* in volume VIII of Littré's edition of the *Corpus Hippocraticum*.

69. D. Lanza, *Lingua e discorso nell'Atene delle professioni* (Naples, 1980), p. 113.

70. On the relation between taxonomy and language in Aristotelian biology, see M. Vegetti, *Il coltello e lo stilo* (Milan, 1980), pp. 13–53.

71. Aristotle, *Historia animalium* 579b30 ff; *De generatione animalium* IV, 774a34 ff.

72. Aristotle, *Historia animalium* VI, 579a35–b6.

73. In one passage of *De generatione animalium* (IV, 775b29) concerning the mole, *gastēr* is used in a gynecological context: "the volume of the belly increased." But in this case Aristotle's point is precisely that the swollen abdomen is not due to pregnancy.

74. Aristotle, *Historia animalium* I, 493a17–18.

75. Ibid., II, 740a5.

76. Ibid., 745a19–20: "Those who claim that infants feed in the uterus by sucking on a bit of flesh are in error." Aristotle accordingly denies that the uterus is "a blood-swollen breast" (ibid., 746a3–4).

77. See G. Sissa, "Il corpo della donna: Lineamenti di un ginecologia filosofica," in Campese, Manuli, and Sissa, *Madre Materia*, pp. 83–139, which considers Aristotle's theory of sexual difference and generation in great detail.

78. Aristotle, *Historia animalium 585a25*.

79. Cf. H. Bonitz, *Index Aristotelicus* (Berlin, 1870), s.vv. συλλαμβάνω and σύλληψις (p. 711).

80. An example of this attention to the lexicon may be found in the attempt to define sperm as a residue rather than as a product of decomposition (*De generatione animalium* II, 724b21–725a3).

81. Ibid., III, 756b3–8, trans. Arthur Platt.

82. Herodotus II.93, trans. de Sélincourt, p. 163.

83. Ibid.

84. Aristotle, *De generatione animalium* 756b8–12.

85. Ibid., 756a33.

86. Ibid., 756a30–32.

87. Ibid., 756b13–16.

88. Ibid., 756b29.

89. Ibid., 756b33–a32.

7. VIRGIN BIRTHS

1. John Chrysostom, *De virginitate* I.1.

2. For an overview of the patristic literature on virginity see E.

Dublanchy, "Chasteté," in *Dictionnaire de théologie catholique*, vol. 2 (Paris, 1923). A brief history of this literature is sketched in T. Camelot, "Les Traités *De virginitate* au IVe siècle," in *Mystique et continence. Travaux scientifique du VIIe Congrès international d'Avon* (Bruges, 1952), pp. 273–292.

3. See G. Blond, "Les Encratites et la vie mystique," in *Mystique et continence*, pp. 117–130.

4. John Chrysostom, *De virginitate* I.1.

5. Blond, "Les Encratites," p. 120.

6. John Chrysostom, *De virginitate* VIII.2.

7. Ibid., V–VI.

8. Justin, *Apologies* I.33; Isaiah 7:4.

9. Justin, *Apologies* I.54.8.

10. Basil of Caesarea, *De vera virginitatis integritate* (*Patrologia Graeca* XXX.669–809). See also Camelot, "Les Traités *De virginitate*," p. 274.

11. Aelian, *De natura animalium* II.46; Basil of Caesarea, *In Isaiam prophetam capitulum VII* 529; *Homilia VIII in Hexameron* 76.

12. Claude Calame, *Les Choeurs des jeunes filles en Grèce archaïque*, vol. 1 (Urbino, 1977), p. 65

13. Angelo Brelich, *Paides e parthenoi* (Rome, 1969), p. 305.

14. Henri Jeanmaire, *Couroi et courètes* (Paris, 1939), p. 529.

15. Scholium to Theocritus II.66, mentioned by Jeanmaire, *Couroi et courètes*, p. 260.

16. Brelich, *Paides e parthenoi*, p. 286.

17. Aeschines, *Letters* X.

18. *Palatine Anthology* IX.444.

19. Pseudo-Phocylides 13.

20. *Palatine Anthology* V.79.

21. *Odyssey* VI.254. Diodorus Siculus VI.7.

22. Pollux, *Onomasticon* III. 39, 42. For defloration, see Aristophanes, *Thesmophoriazusae* 480.

23. Euripides, *Trojan Women* 979ff.

24. Aeschylus, *Prometheus* 898.

25. Or to the man who marries a virgin, that is, to a woman's first husband (Plutarch, *Pompey* 76).

26. Pausanias X.6.1.

27. Pindar, *Olympian Odes* VI.31.

28. Pindar, *Pythian Odes* III.34, 39.

29. Sophocles, *Trachiniae* 148. See also C. Segal, "Mariage et sacrifice dans les *Trachiniennes* de Sophocle," *Antiquité classique,* 44 (1975), 30–53.

30. Sophocles, *Trachiniae* 1222–26.

31. Ibid., 1219, 1275.

32. For Atalanta, maternity is a consequence of violent seduction and is not included in the tale of the marriage accomplished by way of the ruse of the apples. See, e.g., *Mythographi Vaticani* 174: "Atalanta a Meleagro per vim compressa."

33. Euripides, *Phoenissae* 1106–09, 1162.

34. Ibid., 145–153.

35. Sophocles, *Oedipus at Colonus* 1320ff., trans. Robert Fitzgerald.

36. Pierre Vidal-Naquet, "Les Boucliers des héros," *Annali del seminario di studi sul mondo classico,* 1 (1979), 95–118.

37. Aeschylus, *Seven against Thebes* 533 ff. Cf. L. Lupas and Z. Petre, *Commentaire aux "Sept contre Thèbes" d'Eschyle* (Bucharest and Paris, 1981), pp. 173ff. Late mythographers simply reduce Parthenopaeus' life to his birth and death: Hyginus, *Fabulae* 99; *Mythographi Vaticani* I.174; II.144.

38. Euripides, *Suppliants* 888–900.

39. Euripides, *Ion* 585ff.

40. *Mythographi Vaticani* I.206.

41. Pierre Vidal-Naquet, "Esclavage et gynéocratie dans la tradition, le mythe, l'utopie," in *Le Chasseur noir* (Paris, 1983), pp. 278–281.

42. Aristotle, *Politics* V.7, 1306b29–30.

43. Strabo VI.3.3, trans. Horace Jones.

44. Ion, in the tragedy that bears his name, line 593.

45. Strabo VI.3.3: "Now the Lacedaemonians divided up Messenia among themselves, but when they came back home they would not honor the *partheniai* with civic rights like the rest, on the ground that they had been born out of wedlock . . . Their fathers' influence was used to persuade them to leave the city and found a colony: if they found a territory that suited them, they were to remain there; otherwise they were to return home and would be allowed to divide a fifth of Messenia among them."

46. Ibid: "And they sent forth, found the Achaeans at war with the barbarians, took part in their perils, and founded Taras [Tarentum]."

47. Ibid., 3.2.

48. Euripides, *Ion* 594.

49. Cf. Aristophanes, *Clouds* 530ff., and scholium ad loc. In Menander's *Samian Woman* a comic plot turns on the story of a child born out of wedlock who is not exposed but turned over to the concubine of the house.

50. Pausanias VIII. 54.6.

51. Callimachus, *Hymn to Delos* 70.

52. Hyginus, *Fabulae* 99.

53. Aelian, *Varia historia* XIII.1.

54. Servius, *Ad Virgili Bucolica* X.57.

55. Marie Delcourt has given a lengthy analysis of the mythical motif of the exposed child in *Oedipe et la légende du conquérant* (Liège and Paris, 1944), pp. 1–65 (Telephus, pp. 5–6). Like G. Glotz she interprets this practice, which the stories describe as punishment, as an ordeal or trial.

56. *Homeric Hymn to Aphrodite* 6–35.

57. On the mythical trio of Hephaestus, Ge, and Athena, in which the city goddess *Parthenos* plays the role of putative and symbolic mother, see Loraux, "Le Nom Athénien," in *Les Enfants d'Athena*, pp. 119–153. Loraux sees the virgin who defends her body against impregnation and motherhood as the most emblematic figure of femininity that the Greeks of Athens could imagine. The mother who has not given birth (like the Pythia in Euripides' *Ion* 270 and 1324) and who did not herself emerge from a woman's womb allows one to conceive of procreation without the female body. The absolute virginity of Athena (which Walter Burkert, *Homo Necans*, considered essential for the city-goddess divinity, a potential victim in a city of latent hunter-sacrificers) was called into question by Theophilus of Antioch; see M. B. Keary, "Note on Ἀθηνᾶ φιλόκολπος in Theophilus of Antioch," *REG*, 84 (1971), 94–100.

58. Herodotus IV.180.

59. For a recent account see S. Ribichini, "Athena Libica e le *parthenoi* del lago Tritonis," *Studi storico-religiosi*, 2 (1978), 39–60. The author situates the ritual in Libyan tradition.

60. Aelian, *De natura animalium* XI.16.

61. Propertius says that the girls returned from their visit to the serpent in a fright. The poet speaks of the consultation with the reptile as if its purpose was to receive an omen of the harvest.

62. Achilles Tatius, *Leukippe and Clitophon* VIII.12.

63. Ibid., 6. Cf. P. Borgeaud, *Recherches sur le dieu Pan* (Geneva, 1981), pp. 125–127. "A twofold symbolic equation seems to be postulated here: while the nubile but virginal young girl is identified with a Nymph who refuses Pan's embrace, the girl who has lost her virginity prior to marriage is identified with a Nymph violated by the same god. In the first case, the music is equated with that which Pan obtains as a substitute for erotic satisfaction (cf. Ovid, *Metamorphoses* I.689–712), in other words that which traditionally accompanies the song of the Nymphs. In the second case, the plaint that emanates from the grotto resounds like the cries of distress mentioned by Euripides, the cries of a Naiad taken by surprise and forced against her will to submit to 'marriage with the goatlike god' (*Helen* 190). Thereafter, the pipes, now useless, are abandoned on the ground, while the young woman 'seduced' by Pan disappears" (p. 126).

64. Achilles Tatius, *Leukippe and Clitophon* VIII.12.

65. The ambiguity of the verb *lyein*, whose meaning falls somewhere between "loosen" (the belt of virginity) and "dissolve" (a body in water), is dispelled by stories of defloration by a river (*Odyssey* XI.254; Diodorus Siculus VI.7) and of the collective offering of *parthenia* to the current of the Scamander in the Troad (Aeschines, *Letters* X). As Strabo (X.2.19) explains, the very force and thrust of an impetuous river calls to mind an irresistible virility: a river with the power and horns of a bull. It ravishes a young girl and takes her virginity, not by penetrating her but by overcoming her defenses. Hence Artemis turns Rhodopis to water on the spot where her belt was undone. On the waters of Arcadian Styx see Herodotus VI.74 and Pausanias VIII.18.2. It is significant that in Greece these waters, which take the form of a deadly, destructive spring as well as of a sinister swamp, have the power to guarantee the oaths of gods but not of women.

66. Achilles Tatius, *Leukippe and Clitophon* XIII.6.

67. In this connection see Leukippe's touching letter to her prospective husband, who is gnawed by doubt.

68. Aristophanes, *Thesmophoriazusae* 480.
69. Pausanias X.19.2.

8.HIDDEN MARRIAGES

1. "Erubescerent": *Mythographi Vaticani* I.206.
2. See Plutarch, *Solon* 23, and A. R. W. Harrison, *The Law of Athens*, vol. 1 (Oxford, 1968), p. 73 n. 2: "There is no reason to doubt the existence of the law or its Solonian origin."
3. The verb used by Plutarch is *lambanein*.
4. Jean-Pierre Vernant, "Hestia-Hermès: Sur l'expression religieuse de l'espace et du mouvement chez les Grecs," *L'Homme*, 3 (1963), 12–50, reprinted in *Mythe et pensée chez les Grecs*, vol. 1 (Paris, 1971), pp. 124–170.
5. See P. Grimal, "Vierges et virginité," in *La Première Fois* (Paris, 1981), pp. 203–238, esp. 212: "One could multiply examples. They show that physical virginity is not a primary component of the notion of *parthenos* but most liklely an added condition."
6. On the paternal house as the locus of virginal life, see Vernant, "Hestia-Hermès."
7. Diodorus Siculus VIII.22.
8. The sale of a seduced girl may be compared with the burial of a living person, a form of execution for which the person who performed the act was not responsible: Antigone's punishment, for example. In certain stories the girl herself assumes responsibility for her death, as when a young woman shamed by a rape takes her own life. This was the case with the Leuctrides, who, after suffering a violation, hang themselves (Pausanias IX.13.5–6). In this instance the father later slits his own throat after failing to obtain justice from the Lacedaemonians, compatriots of the rapists (Plutarch, *Pelopidas* 20–22).
9. Harrison, *The Law of Athens*, pp. 35–36.
10. See, e.g., *De generatione animalium* II.5, 741b22–23: "Indeed generation goes from nonbeing to being, and destruction *goes back from being to* nonbeing."
11. I shall have more to say about the finality of marriage in Part III.

12. Harrison, *The Law of Athens,* pp. 19, 34–36. The ancient source referred to is pseudo-Demosthenes, *Contra Neera.*

13. Pollux, *Onomasticon* III.21:ἐκ τῆς δοκούσης εἶναι παρθένου.

14. "Tragic writers commonly call virgins women who have been seduced by violence and not in accordance with their own decision (*proairesis*)" (old scholia to Aeschylus, *Prometheus* 588 = p. 162 Herington). In the tragic interplay of will and destiny, a *parthenos* was a young woman who was as good as absent in sexual relations. Outside this context, however, the term *virgin* was not interpreted as a sign of innocence. On *proairesis* as decision see Jean-Pierre Vernant, "Ebauches de la volonté dans la tragédie grecque," in *Mythe et tragédie en Grèce ancienne* (Paris, 1973), pp. 41–74, esp. 48–53.

15. Think of the story of Callisto in the version contained in *Mythographi Vaticani* II.58: "[Jupiter] in Dianam mutatus compressit et gravidam fecit. Cuius quum crimen tumens uterus proderet, indignata Diana comitatu suo eam reppulit."

16. Like the newborn that fell from the womb of one of Dionysus' priestesses while she was leading an ox to sacrifice ("propter nimiam eius lassitudinem infans coactus excidit de vulva"), thus revealing a clandestine pregnancy (*Mythographi Vaticani* I.164).

17. Pollux, *Onomasticon* III.21; (Eubulos II, fr.140 Kock).

18. Herodotus V.6, trans. de Sélincourt, p. 342.

19. [Theocritus], *Oaristys* 65.

20. Aristotle, *Historia animalium* VII.1, 581b!1–16, trans. D'Arcy Thompson.

21. Ibid., 581b16–17.

22. Cf. Athenaeus X.437f. *Paidiskeion* was one of the Greek words for a bordello.

23. Herodotus I.93.

24. Euripides, *Ion* 1524.

25. Sophocles, *Trachiniae* 596.

26. See Chapter 9, text accompanying note 62.

27. The moral nonexistence of a secret sexual act is a wonderful illustration of what E. R. Dodds calls a "shame culture" in *The Greeks and the Irrational* (Berkeley: University of California Press, 1951).

28. Plato, *Laws* VI, 775a1–e5.

29. Pollux, *Onomasticon* III.36.

30. Pherecydes of Syros, in Clement of Alexandria, *Stromata* 6.9. Cf. M. L. West, *Early Greek Philosophy and the Orient* (Oxford, 1971), p. 16.

31. For an analysis of the unveiling ritual, see J. Toutain, "Le Rite nuptial de l'*anakalyptērion*," REA, 42 (1940), 345–353. On the Roman *flammeum* and the *velamen* of Christian virgins, see R. Schilling, "Le Voile de consécration dans l'ancien rite romain," *Revue de science religieuse*, 1956, pp. 403–414; reprinted in *Rites, cultes et dieux de Rome* (Paris, 1979), pp. 154–165.

32. Pollux, *Onomasticon* II.59.

33. Plato, *Laws* VI, 771e.

34. *Odyssey* VI.100.

35. Ibid., V.232.

36. Ibid., I.334.

37. In Hesiod, *Theogony* 573–575.

38. *Iliad* XXII.468–472, trans. Richmond Lattimore.

39. Euripides, *Phoenissae* 1485ff.

40. *Iliad*, XXII.460.

41. Euripides, *Phoenissae* 1436–37.

42. In scenes depicting the sacrifice of a virgin in tragedy, the tearing of clothes serves a dramatic purpose. Cf. Aeschylus, *Agamemnon* 231–240.

43. Euripides, *Alcestis* 1115–22.

44. Athenaeus XIV.644d = Evangelus, *Anakalyptomenē*, III fr. 376 Kock.

45. Pausanias IX.2.7. On this episode see F. Frontisi-Ducroux, *Dédale. Mythologie de l'artisan en Grèce ancienne* (Paris, 1975), pp. 193–216.

46. Pollux, *Onomasticon* III.37.

47. Ibid., 36 = II fr. 49 Kock.

48. *Anecdota Graeca* I.390 Bekker; Harpocration, s.v. Ἀνακαλυπτήρια; scholium to Euripides, *Orestes* 284.

49. Perhaps the anakalyptērion is alluded to in the metaphor that refers to the "premature disrobing of a virgin"; see note 17.

50. Toutain, "Le Rite nuptial."

51. This view was propounded primarily by Deubner; see ibid., p. 345.

52. This is the view of E. Pottier and S. Reinach; see ibid.

53. Ibid., p. 350.

54. Ibid.

55. An image found on a series of vases. See ibid., p. 347.

56. On the history of the Bodmer codex, the papyrus discovered in Cairo in 1956 and containing *The Samian Woman*, the *Dyskolos*, and *The Shield*, see O. Reverdin's preface to Menander, *Théâtre. La Samienne. Cnémon le misanthrope. Le Bouclier* (Geneva, 1974), pp. 9–18.

57. Toutain, "Le Rite nuptial," p. 348, cites a passage from Lucan in which cupids are shown unveiling Roxane as Alexander looks on.

58. Homer, *Iliad* XVIII.491–493, trans. Lattimore. Cf. [Hesiod], *The Shield* 273–276; Pindar, *Pythian Odes* III.30ff.

59. Scholium to Theocritus XVIII, cited by J. A. Hartung, "Hymenaios (Brautlied)," *Philologus*, 3 (1848), 238. This double representation of marriage as the celebration of a secret, with noise and light added to heighten the mystery, is reminiscent of the Spartan matrimonial ritual as an anti-*gamos*. For a Laconian warrior, the wedding day was no different from any other, and after dining as usual with his comrades the prospective bridegroom went without ceremony to the place where his bride was hiding. In total darkness he undid her belt, spent a brief time with her, and then withdrew to join his sleeping comrades. Plutarch, *Lycurgus* XV.5–9.

60. Pollux, *Onomasticon* III.44. Cf. ibid., 38.

61. Toutain, "Le Rite nuptial," p. 345.

62. Aristophanes, *Peace* 1076; Theocritus XXII.179; Pollux, *Onomasticon* III.37; Euripides, *Heracles* 834 (*anymenaios hē agamos*).

63. A virgin who knows nothing of the hymeneal is Lyssa, daughter of the night.

64. Sophocles, *Antigone* 876, 917.

65. Euripides, *Hecuba* 416.

66. Ibid., 612.

67. Euripides, *Ion* 1474–76.

68. Diodorus Siculus VI.7.

69. See Euripides, *Ion* 14.

70. Euripides, *Ion* 1523. Cf. Menander, *Samian Woman*, and Aeschines, *Letters* X.

71. Euripides, *Ion* 1543–44.

72. Ibid., 340.

73. Ibid., 1459–95.

74. Ibid., 957.

75. Ibid., 44–46 (my italics).

76. Ibid., 1365–67: "First find out whether a girl from Delphi, having given birth to you, would have abandoned you in this temple; and then search among the other Greeks." Note, by the way, the Pythia's ignorance in Euripides' plays.

77. Nicole Loraux, "Créuse autochtone," in *Les Enfants d'Athéna*, p. 253.

78. Ibid., p. 241 n. 185.

79. Ion to Creusa: 238, 244, 255, 263, 289 ("Woman, of what Athenian are you the wife?"), 309, 329, 333, 372, 379; Xuthus: 402, 422.

80. Recall Plato, *Republic* 395d-e: "We will not then allow our charges, whom we expect to prove good men, being men, to play the parts of women and imitate a woman young or old wrangling with her husband, defying heaven, loudly boasting, fortunate in her own conceit, or involved in misfortune and possessed by grief and lamentation—still less a woman who is sick, in love, or in labor." Plato is probably alluding to Euripides' characters and, for labor, to Auge. In Aristophanes' *Frogs* the chaste Aeschylus accuses his rival: "Of what woes is he not the author? Has he not represented procuresses, women who give birth in temples, have intercourse with their brothers, and say that life is not life?" (1078–82). On the prohibition against giving birth in a sacred place, see Aristophanes, *Lysistrata* 742; Thucydides III.104.2; Pausanias II.27.6: at Epidaurus in the sacred territory of Asclepius it was necessary to create a sacred spot where men could die and women give birth.

81. Pausanias VIII.47.

82. Ibid., VII.47.

83. Ibid., VIII.47.9. For a detailed history of the tragic and mythographic tradition concerning Auge, see F. Jouan, *Euripide et les légendes des chants cypriens* (Paris, 1966), pp. 226–227, 246–248.

84. Pausanias VIII. 47.2–3.

85. Diodorus Siculus IV.33.7–9.

86. Ibid., 33.9.

87. Apollodorus, *Bibliotheca* II.7.4. Here, Auge is the priestess

of the temple of Athena (III.9.1), and her father has forced her to accept this form of perpetual chastity so that he will have no descendants.

88. Euripides, fr. 266 Nauck. Cf. *Iphigenia in Tauris* 380–384: "I do not accept the subtleties [*sophismata*] of Artemis! What! If a mortal touches blood or a woman who has given birth or a cadaver, she bans him from access to the altars and holds him to be tainted. And she takes pleasure in human sacrifices!"

89. *Iliad* XVI.175–178.

90. Ibid., 179–190.

91. Pindar, *Pythian Odes* III.25–26, trans. Richmond Lattimore.

92. Ibid., 29–35.

93. Pindar, *Olympian Odes* VI.69, trans. Richmond Lattimore.

9. ANATOMY WITHOUT VEILS

1. Servius, *Ad Virgilii Aeneidem* IV.99.

2. C. Calame, *Les Choeurs de jeunes filles en Grèce archaïque,* 1:65.

3. Sappho, frs. 110–111 Lobel-Page; Euripides, *Phaethon* fr. 781.14 Nauck²; Euripides, *Trojan Women* 310, 314, 330; Aristophanes, *Peace* 1316–56; *Birds* 1736, 1742; Callimachus, fr. 461 Sch.; Theocritus XVIII.58; Bion, *Adonis* 87ff.; *Palatine Anthology* VII.407.5; Oppian, *Cynegetica* I.341; Nonnus, *Dionysiaca* XVI.290; XXIV.271; Pollux, *Onomasticon* III.37. See also J. A. Hartung, "Hymenaus (Brautlied)," *Philologus,* 3 (1848), 238–246; P. Maas, "ὑμὴν ὑμήν," ibid., 66 (1907), 590–596; R. Muth, "Hymenaios und Epithalamion," *Wiener Studien,* 47 (1954), 5–45; A. Jolles, "Hymen, Hymenaios," in *Realencyclopädie* XI (1914), cols. 126–130; P. Maas, "Hymenaios," ibid., cols. 130–134.

4. A. Severyns, *Recherches sur la Chrestomathie de Proclos, première partie: Le codex 239 de Photius,* vol. 2 (Liège, 1938), pp. 49–50 (see pp. 194–204 for the commentary).

5. Pindar, *Threnodies,* III Snell-Maehler.

6. Apollodorus, Περὶ Θεῶν, *F. Gr. Hist.* 244 F 139 Jacoby: OF 40 Kern: Apollodorus, *Bibliotheca* III.10.3.

7. A. Brueckner, *Athenische Mitteilungen,* 32 (1907), 90, cited by Muth, "Hymenaios und Epithalamion," p. 11.

8. Servius, *Ad Virgilii Aeneidem* I.651.

9. Artemidorus, *Oneirocritica* II.65.

10. Antonio Brelich, *Paides e parthenoi*, pp. 261–263.

11. Servius, *Ad Virgilii Aeneidem* IV.99 (my italics).

12. Ibid., I.651.

13. Cf. Eustathius, *Ad Iliadem* XVIII.493.

14. A. Mai is cited by G. H. Bode, "Proemium," in *Scriptores Rerum Mythicarum Latini Tres Romae Nuper Reperti* (1834: reprint, Hildesheim, 1968), p. x: "Christianum se fuisse, immo catholicum, p. 217 (III, 9, 7) ipsemet docet."

15. *Mythographi Vaticani* III.11.2.

16. Ibid., 11.3.

17. Ibid., III.1; Servius, *Ad Virgilii Aeneidem* IV.99.

18. Muth, "Hymenaios und Epithalamion," p. 9. Jolles, "Hymen, Hymenaios," col. 126: "Die Etymologie ist unsicher."

19. P. Chantraine, *Dictionnaire étymologique de la langue grecque*, s.v. ὑμήν. An interesting explanation was proposed by that great connoisseur of Hippocrates, Emile Littré, in his *Dictionnaire de la langue française*, vol. 2 (Paris, 1869), col. 2073: "Latin etymology *Hymen*, from Ὑμήν, god of marriage (a word which in Greek occurs only in the phrase ὑμὴν ὑμέναιος) and marriage song. Some etymologists associate it with the ὑμήν, membrane, which is not very probable, others with ὕμνος, hymn."

20. Owsei Temkin, *Gynecology* (Baltimore, 1956), p. xxxix.

21. Aristotle, *Historia animalium* III.13, 519a30 ff., trans. D'Arcy Thompson.

22. Ibid., 519b2–4.

23. Aristotle, *De partibus animalium* IV.14, 673a4.

24. Ibid., 677b14–19, trans. William Ogle.

25. Ibid., 677b37–678a19.

26. Ibid., 672a10–673a1.

27. Aristotle, *Historia animalium* 519b4–5.

28. Galen, *Anatomicae administrationes* 348–354, 549–567.

29. Ibid., 549.

30. Ibid., 591–593.

31. Ibid., 605, 708–716.

32. Galen, *Opere scelte*, ed. I. Garofalo and M. Vegetti (Turin, 1978), p. 303.

33. Galen, *De usu partium* XVII.346.

34. Ibid., 351.

35. Ibid., XI.13–14.

36. Ibid., XV.3.

37. Ambroise Paré, *De l'anatomie*, in *Oeuvres complètes* (1840–41: reprint, Geneva, 1970), 1:167.

38. Caelius Aurelianus, *Gynaecia*, ed. F. Drabkin and I. E. Drabkin (Baltimore, 1951); *Sorani Gynaeciorum Vetus Translatio Latina*, ed. V. Rose (Leipzig, 1882).

39. Soranus, *Gynaikeia* I.16–17 Ilberg.

40. Oribasius, Ἰατρικαὶ συναγωγαί III.378 Daremberg.

41. Soranus, *Gynaikeia* I.17.

42. Ibid., II.33 Rose = IV.17 Ilberg.

43. *Diseases of Women* 20 (VIII. 58 Littré).

44. This form of congenital, anatomical infertility is also described in *Nature of Woman* 67 (7:402 Littré) and *On Sterile Women* 223 (8:432 Littré).

45. Aristotle, *De generatione animalium* IV.4, 773a15–20.

46. Ibid., 773a20–29.

47. Soranus, *Gynaikeia* I.32.

48. Soranus' explanation of the blood of virginity is identical to the one that Ambroise Paré put forward in the sixteenth century. And the Chevalier de Jaucourt, author of the article "Virginité" in Diderot's *Encyclopédie*, would later repeat it, citing Buffon: "Anatomy itself leaves complete doubt as to the existence of the membrane known as the *hymen* and of the myrtiform carunculae whose presence or absence was for so long regarded as a certain sign of defloration or virginity. Anatomy, I repeat, permits us to dismiss these two signs as being not only dubious but also imaginary. The same is true of another more common yet equally equivocal sign, namely, the flow of blood. People have always believed that the flow of blood was authentic proof of *virginity*. However, it is clear that this alleged sign means nothing in any case in which the entrance to the vagina has been naturally relaxed or dilated . . . Before puberty there is no flow of blood in girls who have commerce with men, provided the disproportion is not too great or the entry too abrupt. By contrast, when they are in full puberty, and in the time when these parts are growing, there is often a flow of blood if they are even touched, particularly if they are plump and the menses are going well."

49. Can it be said that for the church fathers the concrete man-

ifestation of virginity was a membrane? They viewed the state of *parthenia* as involving such a total repudiation of the senses, such a total neutralization of desires, that they did not dwell on that last shred of innocence, the intact hymen. Consider this allusion to the genitals of a virgin: "The body is not holy just because its parts are intact, or because they have not undergone any handling. Those parts may suffer violent injury by accidents of various kinds, and sometimes doctors seeking to effect a cure may employ treatment with distressing visible effects. During a manual examination of a virgin a midwife destroyed her maidenhead, whether by malice, or clumsiness, or accident. I do not supoppose that anyone would be stupid enough to imagine that the virgin lost anything of bodily chastity, even though the integrity of that part had been destroyed" (Augustine, *City of God* I.19, trans. Harry Bettenson, p. 29). What practice is Augustine referring to when he speaks of an "obstetrix virginis cuiusdam integritatem manu explorans"? And how are we to interpret the *integritas* that a clumsy hand could destroy (*perdere*)?

50. Pseudo-Demosthenes, *Contra Neera* 72–84.

51. Apollonius Rhodius, *Argonautica* IV. 1105–1205.

52. Parthenius of Nicaea XXXV.

53. Sophocles, *Trachiniae* 308–309.

54. *Odyssey* XI.249–250.

55. Pausanias VII.25.13.

56. Pliny, *Natural History* XVIII.147. On bull's blood as poison, see Aristophanes, *Knights* 83.

57. Gustave Glotz, *L'Ordalie dans la Grèce primitive* (Paris, 1904), pp. 71ff.

58. Martin Nilsson, *Griechische Feste* (Leipzig, 1906), p. 367.

59. *Odyssey* XI.235–245, trans. Robert Fitzgerald.

60. Nonnus, *Dionysiaca* I.124. Cf. Diodorus Siculus VI.7.3.

61. Pausanias X.25.1.

62. Aelian, *De natura animalium* XI.2.

63. Diodorus Siculus XVI. 26.

64. [Galen], *De remediis parabilibus* XIV.478; 486 Kühn.

65. *Diseases of Women* I.1 (8:10 Littré).

66. *Nature of Woman* 3 (7:314 Littré).

67. Pausanias VIII.22.2; II.38.2.

68. Xenophon of Ephesus, *Ephesiaca* XIV.2.

69. Plato, Theaetetus 149b–c.
70. Plato, *Laws* VI, 759b9ff.
71. Sappho 139 Lobel-Page.

10. THE DANAIDES' ENDLESS CHORE

1. Valerius Maximus VIII.1.5. Yet another trial of virginity in Roman territory. On the "incest" of the Vestal see T. Cornell, "Some Observations on the *Crimen incesti,* in *Le Délit religieux* (Rome, 1981), pp. 27–37.

2. Pliny, *Natural History* XXVIII.1.2.

3. Livy, *Epitome* 20; Dionysius of Halicarnassus II.69.

4. Tertullian, *Apologeticus* 22.12.

5. Augustine, *De civitate dei* X.16.

6. In Ovid, *Fasti* IV.295–325, Claudia does not use her belt as in the versions mentioned but a rope from the ship itself.

7. A. B. Cook, "The Holed Vessel in Greece," in *Zeus* (London, 1940), 3:338–451.

8. The custom of pouring water into a pithos or pierced water pitcher as a "rain charm" was supposedly introduced into Greece by the Danai, a tribe that had waged a war against Egypt. But this ritual exists only in the exegesis of the punishment of the Danaides. Diodorus recounts that in the town of Akanthoi on the banks of the Nile "there was a pierced jar into which three hundred sixty priests poured water from the Nile every day" (I.97.2). For Diodorus, who is here reporting the testimony of Egyptian priests, this story constitutes the North African prehistory of Greek mythology. Besides the jar of the Danaides, the Egyptians are said to have practiced a ritual that anticipated the rope woven by Oknos and unwoven by her she-ass (I.97.3). From Homer to Orpheus, from Athena to Dionysus, all the religious traditions of the Greeks are said to have stemmed from this source.

9. Aristophanes, *Clouds* 373; Cook, *Zeus,* 3:333.

10. Cook, *Zeus,* 3:428.

11. C. Picard, "L'Eleusinisme et la disgrâce des Danaides," *Revue de l'histoire des religions,* 100 (1929), 48–84, esp. 54–56.

12. Pausanias X.31.11; Plato, *Gorgias* 493aff.; *Republic* 363d6–8.

13. For an exhaustive bibliography and in-depth discussion,

see C. Bonner, "A Study of the Danaid Myth," *Harvard Studies in Classical Philology,* 13 (1902), 129–173, esp. 164–173, on the punishment. Less detailed but useful is O. Waser, "Danaides," in *Realencyclopädie,* IV.2 (1901), cols. 2087–91.

14. E. Rohde, *Psyche*[9] (Berlin, 1886); J. Chevallier, *Etude critique du dialogue platonicien l'Axiochos* (Paris, 1915), p. 99; J. Carcopino, *La Basilique pythagoricienne de la Porte Majeure* (Paris, 1927), pp. 290–291; Picard, "L'Eleusinisme," p. 49. See also *Etymologicum Gudianum,* s.v. γυνή.

15. A. Dieterich, *Nekyia* (Leipzig and Berlin, 1893), p. 70 n. 1; Rohde, *Psyche,* p. 604. For the history of this hypothesis see Bonner, "A Study," p. 169 n. 4.

16. Rohde, *Psyche,* p. 604.

17. For the well-nymph thesis, see Jane E. Harrison, *Prolegomena to the Study of Greek Religion* pp. 619–621. They are water-bearers in S. Reinach, "Sisyphe aux Enfers et quelques autres damnés," *Revue archéologique,* 4th ser., 1 (January–June 1903), 154–200, esp. 190–91. Cook, *Zeus,* 3:426, denies that the Danaides were *agamoi* but views their punishment as the endless repetition of a fertility charm. Picard, "L'Eleusinisme," pp. 51, 54–56, sees them as water-bearing deities ("génies arroseurs").

18. Rohde, *Psyche,* p. 603.

19. Harrison, *Prolegomena,* p. 621. The reference to Frazer concerns his commentary on Pausanias X.31.9.

20. In contrast to Eva Keuls, who admits that her study is based on her belief that the water-carriers on Apulian vases look happy; *The Water Carriers in Hades: A Study of Catharsis through Toil in Classical Antiquity* (Amsterdam, 1974), p. 3.

21. Picard, "L'Eleusinisme," pp. 69–70.

22. Ibid., p. 62.

23. Cook, *Zeus,* 3:426.

24. Harrison, *Prolegomena,* p. 619. For another interpretation of the Danaides as victims of a "patriarchal deformation" that transformed their original power into a crime, see A. Pestalozza, "Il crimine delle Danaidi," in *Studi in onore di A. Calderini,* vol. 1, pp. 1–13.

25. Picard, "L'Eleusinisme," p. 61.

26. Ibid., pp. 50–51.

27. Harrison, *Prolegomena*, p. 620: "So does theology shift."

28. Stated by Bonner, "A Study," p. 170; Harrison, *Prolegomena*, p. 621; Keuls, *Water Carriers*, p. 55; Cook, *Zeus*, 3:426.

29. The archaeological sources used include A. Milchoeffer, "Gemälte Grabstele," *Athenische Mitteilungen*, 5 (1880), 164–184; P. Wolters, "Rotfigurige lutrophoros," ibid., 16 (1891), 371–405, and 18 (1893), 66; R. Vallois in REA, 28 (1926), 121.

30. Bonner, "A Study," p. 174. The author cites Milchoeffer, *Philologus*, 53 (1898), 397 n. 14; and Reinach, "Sisyphe aux Enfers," offers the same observation.

31. Rohde, *Psyche*, p. 604.

32. Harrison, *Prolegomena*, p. 621.

33. Demosthenes 44.18: "He died . . . never having been married: the proof [semeion] is that there is a loutrophoros on his tomb." See Pollux, *Onomasticon* VIII. 66; Hesychius; Photius, *Lexicon, Anecdota Graeca* I. 276.23: Bekker; Harpocration; Eustatius, *Ad Iliadem* XXIII.141: all s.v. λουτροφόρος *vel sim.* See also A. Herzog, "Eine Lutrophoros," *Archäologische Zeitung*, 40 (1882), 131–144.

34. Apollodorus, *Bibliotheca* II.1.5.

35. Aeschylus, *Suppliants* 750–752.

36. Ibid., 760.

37. Ibid., 1069.

38. Ibid., 426, 528.

39. Ibid.

40. Ibid., 742.

41. Aeschylus, *Prometheus Bound* 856–868, trans. George Burges. I agree with P. Mazon that line 865 should be construed as "one of the maidens was beguiled by desire to be a mother" rather than "one of the daughters was beguiled by (erotic) desire," as it is read by F. Ferrari in "La misandria delle Danaidi," *Annali della Scuola Normale Superiore di Pisa*, 1977, pp. 1303–21. That desire for children as well as erotic desire can be called *himeros* is attested in Mimnermus, e.g., fr. 2.

42. Danaus, the father who leads an army of daughters, is a *stasiarchos*, and the Danaides are themselves amazons. The warlike aspect of the clash between two groups of cousins was analyzed by Nicole Loraux in her 1980–81 seminar at the Ecole des Hautes Etudes en Sciences Sociales.

43. The figures of Io and Procne, which are present in the memory of *The Suppliants* (Procne: 57–63; Io:295) as victims of a fate they abhor, represent girls seduced by force.

44. Ancient scholia to Aeschylus, *Prometheus* 866d Herington.

45. Keuls, *Water Carriers*, pp. 54–55, collects and discusses the various versions concerning the sexual status of the murderesses.

46. Harrison, *Prolegomena*, p. 621; E. Des Places, "Platon et le langage des mystères," *Annales de la Faculté de Lettres d'Aix*, 38 (1964):16. Carrying water in a sieve was not in fact an ordeal of virginity, and, what is more, it did not orginate in Greece. In Italy, the actions of the vestal Tuccia are particularly striking in that she is not performing a ritual but *inventing* a gesture of her own, as if the demonstrative value lay in the very representation of such an object.

11. THE MATTER OF DESPAIR

1. Xenophon, *Oeconomicus* VII.18–40.

2. Jean-Pierre Vernant, "Hestia-Hermès: Sur l'expression religieuse de l'espace et du mouvement en Grèce," in *Mythe et pensée chez les Grecs*, 1:124–170, incorporates this text in an analysis of the contrast between the closed domestic space and the outside world open to a variety of people and activities.

3. Xenophon, *Oeconomicus* VII.18–32.

4. Ibid., 39–40.

5. Hesiod, *Works and Days* 699–701.

6. [Aristotle], *Oeconomicus* I.6, 1344b23–25, trans. E. S. Forster. J. Tricot, ed., *Aristote, Les Economiques* (Paris, 1958), pp. 7–9, accepts this work as Aristotle's, whereas B. A. Groningen, ed., *Aristote, Oeconomicus* (Paris, 1968), pp. vii–xii, challenges this attribution.

7. Aristotle, *Politics* V, 1320a31.

8. Although Tricot translates the passage from the *Oeconomicus*, which he considers to be by Aristotle, as "akin to drawing water with a sieve."

9. Confirmed by P. Chantraine, *Dictionnaire étymologique de la langue grecque*, πίθος: "Large earthenware jar containing various sorts of provisions such as wine, oil, etc." Vitruvius tells us of tanks

designed to catch rainwater in Italy. These cisterns are not described as dolia (*De architectura* VIII.6.14). Athenaeus mentions basins used for the same purpose (*lakkoi:* I.46d). But these were pits dug in the earth to form pools. Cf. Herodotus IV.175; Xenophon, *Anabasis* IV.2.22.

10. "When you visit the farm, see if there are many presses and jars," is Cato's recommendation to a novice about to buy a farm; *De agricultura* I.4. The presence of several dolia is a promising sign, a mark of generous soil.

11. *Odyssey* II.337.

12. Ibid., XXIII.305.

13. *Iliad*, XXIV.524, trans. Lattimore. Cf. *Scholia Vetera, Works* 94, cited by M. L. West in his edition of Hesiod, *Works and Days* (Oxford, 1978), p. 71, and the commentary ad loc. P. Mazon, in his edition of the *Iliad*, "We should think of these mythical jars as being like the enormous vases that we know particularly from the excavations of Crete and that were deeply rooted in the earthen floors of storehouses. Cf. *Athenische Mitteilungen*, II, 1886, p. 147"; *Iliade*, vol. 3 (Paris: Belles Lettres, 1949).

14. Xenophon has Ischomachus refer to "people who, as they say . . . pour into a bottomless jar" (*Oeconomicus* VII.40). Ὁ λεγόμενος τετρημένος πίθος repeats the author of the Peripatetic *Oeconomicus*. "This is the leaky jar": Aristotle, *Politics* VI.5, 1320a31–32. The expression is noted by Zenobius (I.6), Diogenianus (I.95; VII.27), and Apostolius (VI.79), who link its etymology to the Danaides and/or noninitiates, while Gregory of Cyprus, (I.48) and Plutarch (*Anecdota Graeca* I.394 Boissonade) limit themselves to interpreting it as "useless labor." My view is that the mythological interpretation is not necessarily implicit in every occurrence of the expression, particularly when the images of the Danaides and the noninitiates are not explicitly mentioned and when the context fully justifies the symbolic use of the pithos.

15. For the function and values attached to the jar in Hesiod's economics, see Jean-Pierre Vernant, "Manger à la table des hommes," in *La Cuisine du sacrifice en pays grec,* ed. Marcel Detienne and Jean-Pierre Vernant, pp. 37–132. See also West on *Works and Days* 47–105, 368, 475, and 819 (for the pithos as a container for storing provisions, see esp. at 368). For a more radical interpre-

tation of the analogy between the jar and a woman's belly, see Geneviève Hoffmann, "Pandora, la jarre et l'espoir," *Etudes rurales,* 97–98 (January–June 1985), 119–132.

16. Vernant, "Manger," p. 120.

17. Ibid.

18. Vernant, "Manger," p. 120; Hesiod, *Works and Days* 475; 600–608.

19. Cato, *De agricultura* 23.1; Pliny, *Natural History* XIV.134; *Geoponica* V, passim, "If you carefully repair or hoop it, if you fix the cracks with packing, and if you cover it well with pitch, you can use any kind of jar as a wine jar"; Cato, *De agricultura* 39.1; cf. ibid., 2.3.

20. For a vineyard of 100 *iugera* one needed "containers capable of holding two harvests, for a total capacity of 800 *cullei,* 20 containers for marc, 20 for grain, and stoppers and covers for all"; Cato, *De agricultura* 11. 1–2. Cf. Varro, *De re rustica* I.22.4. For an olive orchard of 240 *iugera* one needed "100 oil containers, 12 basins, 10 containers for grape marc, 10 for the lees, 10 for wine, 20 for grain, 1 for lupine"; ibid., 10.4. Pliny, who devotes an entire book of his *Natural History* to wine, says that wine cellars (*apothecae*) store a form of wealth that appreciates faster than any other (XVI.57).

21. Cato, *De agricultura* 39.2; Varro, *De lingua latina* V.137: "sirpata dolia quassa."

22. "Keep it in mind that even if you do nothing, expenses are still mounting"; Cato, *De agricultura* 39.2.

23. Jane E. Harrison, "*Mystica Vannus Iacchi,*" JHS, 1903, pp. 292–324. Although the *Suda* identifies winnowing basket and sieve (*liknon and koskinon*), the two tools were not exactly the same, and Harrison actually refers to a *cribrum areale,* a wicker sieve for separating the seed from the unwanted husk (cf. Servius, *ad Virgilii Georg.* I.65). Both the sieve and the winnowing basket are used for sorting, for separating what is good to eat from what is to be thrown away (Jane E. Harrison, *Prolegomena to the Study of Greek Religion,* p. 531). The *pais amphithalēs,* child whose two parents are living, who carries a *liknon* in the marriage ceremony utters the following words: "I have left the bad, I have found better." His basket-sieve filled with seed stands for the new life that awaits

the couple (cf. Zenobius III. 98; pseudo-Plutarch, *Proverbs of Alexander* I.16).

24. Harrison, *"Mystica Vannus Iacchi,"* p. 323.

25. Cato, *De agricultura* 10.5: "1 [cribrum] seminarium, 1 qui nucleos succernat." Cf. R. Goujard, "Etude critique de quelques passages de Caton, *De agricultura,"* *Revue philologique,* 46 (1972), 266ff.

26. Cato, *De agricultura* 11.2.

27. Baskets used for carrying grapes were also sealed with pitch. Ibid., 23.1.

28. J.-P. Vernant, "Le Fleuve *Amelēs* et la *meletē thanatou,"* *Revue philosophique,* 1960, pp. 163–179, reprinted in *Mythe et pensée chez les Grecs,* 1:108–123, esp. p. 116.

29. Xenophon, *Oeconomicus* VII.36.

30. [Plato], *Axiochus* 371e.

31. Hesiod, *Works and Days* 595–599. Hesiod's conception of food emerges from his reflections on *oikonomia*. Plato, who before Xenophon spoke of the man of jars in the *Gorgias,* cites Hesiod (e.g., *Republic* 363b-c) as the poet of agricultural good fortune.

32. Theocritus X.13.

33. *Geoponica* VI.

34. L. Deubner, *Attische Feste,* p. 40 n. 5; S. Eitrem, "Les Thesmophoria, les skirophoria et les arrhetophoria," *Symbolae Osloenses,* 23–25 (1944–1947), 32–45.

35. C. Picard, "L'Eleusinisme et la disgrâce des Danaides," *Revue de l'histoire des religions,* 100 (1929), 81–82.

36. Plato, *Gorgias* 493a1–494a3, trans. W. D. Woodhead. On this passage see E. R. Dodds, *Plato's Gorgias* (Oxford, 1959), pp. 300–306; I. M. Linforth, "Soul and Sieve in Plato's *Gorgias,"* *University of California Publications in Classical Philology,* XII, 17 (1944), 195–313; E. Des Places, "Platon et la langue des mystères," *Annales d la Faculté de Lettres d'Aix,* 38 (1964), 16.

37. Vernant, "Le Fleuve *Amelēs,"* pp. 116–117.

38. Plato, *Gorgias* 494b7.

39. See scholia to ibid.

40. Plato, *Gorgias* 492e5–6.

41. On the work of Polygnotus of Thasos, see A. Rumpf's article in *Enciclopedia dell'arte antica classica e orientale* (Rome, 1958–

1966), 6:292. The tables on pp. 235–237 reproduce C. Robert's reconstruction of the *Nekyia* fresco. The image is also examined in A. B. Cook, *Zeus*, 3:397.

42. Pausanias X.28.3.

43. Ibid., 31.10–11.

44. Ibid., 31.11.

45. Plato, *Republic* X, 621a5–6. See Vernant, "Le Fleuve Amelēs," pp. 116–118. Linforth, "Soul and Sieve," p. 303, makes the same connection.

46. *Republic* X, 621b1.

47. *Gorgias* 493c3.

48. On "degrees of initiation," see P. Roussel, "L'Initiation préalable et le symbole éleusinien," BCH, 54 (1950), 51–74, which raises the question of the ritual viewpoint in attempting to interpret a scene sculpted on the Lovatelli urn and on the Torre Nova sarcophagus, which depicts the purification or perhaps the *myēsis* of Heracles. The sarcophagus has been studied and reproduced in G. E. Rizzo, "Il sarcofago di Torre Nova, contributi alla storia dell'arte et della religione antica," *Römische Mitteilungen*, 25 (1910), 89–167; Rizzo is certain that the scene depicts the initiation of Heracles. For the semantic value of *myein* and *myēsis* relative to *teletē* in Platonic literature, see Des Places, "Platon et la langue des mystères," p. 13, which shows that "the gradation *myēsis, teletē, epopteia* is supported" by *Symposium* 209eb-210a2, but that the "metaphorical use usually precludes a sharp distinction" (p. 12).

49. Aristophanes, *Frogs* 372–375.

50. Ibid., 400, 456–457.

51. Ibid., 454–455.

52. Ibid., 145–150.

53. Plato, *Republic* II, 363c-d (my italics). On the beatitude of drunkenness, see P. Boyancé, "Platon et le vin," *Bulletin de l'Association Guillaume Budé (Lettres d'Humanieté)*, 1951.

54. Plato, *Republic* II, 363d5–9. On the Orphic and Eleusinian model for this representation of the punishment, see P. Boyancé, "Platon et les cathartes orphiques," *REG*, 55 (1942), 217–235. "Musaeus is an Orphic. But his son is Eumolpus the Eleusinian. Therefore Plato presumably already knew of these relations between Eleusis and the Orphics and of the accord that would be

emphasized a short while later" (p. 220). This is Boyancé's summary of an argument he sets forth at greater length in *Le Culte des Muses*, 2d ed. (Paris, 1972), pp. 21–30, 376. See also idem, "Sur les mystères d'Eleusis," REG, 75 (1962), 460–482, esp. 474–480 (review of G. E. Mylonas, *Eleusis and the Eleusinian Mysteries* [Princeton, 1961]; and idem, "Eleusis et Orphée," *REG*, 88 (1975), 195–202 (review of F. Graf, *Eleusis und die orphische Dicthung Athens in vorhellenistischer Zeit* [Berlin and New York, 1974]), Both Mylonas and Graf are skeptical about the supposed Eleusinian source of the condition of amyētos. Boyancé correctly draws attention to the Eleusinian roots of Orpheus and the explicit indications in Pausanias (X.31.10–11) and Aristophanes (in the *Frogs*, the initiates invoke Demeter and Iacchus while the air fills with smoke from the piglet sacrificed to Korē).

55. See Graf, *Eleusis*, pp. 103–107. For the meaning of προπηλακισμός, rolling in the mud, see G. Lozza, "Una immagine platonica—Nota a *Gorgia* 527 a," *Acme*, 32, fasc. 2 (1979), 269–274. In ritualist interpretations (Harrison, *Prolegomena*, p. 614), immersion in mud is seen as endless repetition of a neglected ritual of purification, but according to Plutarch it is apparently the opposite: to roll in the muck is, for a superstitious person, a form of mortification, of self-punishment. Admitting his errors, a man who practices both *propēlakismoi* and *katharmoi* humiliates himself in the moist earth (*On Superstition* VII, XII) as though in anticipation of a punishment that will be eternal in the underworld.

56. For a summary of the current state of research, see Graf, *Eleusis*, pp. 107–120, esp. 108 nn. 64–67. Graf does not cite Vernant, "Le Fleuve *Amelēs*," where the hypothesis that the Italian or Sicilian might be Empedocles is scrutinized by means of lexical and semantic comparison (pp. 117–120). Vernant's conclusion is that "the problem is obviously insoluble" (p. 119). Linforth, "Soul and Sieve," p. 306, points out the various ambiguities and allusive winks of the eyes in Plato's text, which are justified only because this is a dialogue. But even if Olympiodorus and the scholiast of *Gorgias* and the scholars who have followed them are correct, and even if Linforth's caution is salutary, the fact remains that the water jar in the underworld points to the jar for storing provisions in the *oikos* (but Linforth pays no attention to this second Platonic image).

57. Instead, Empedocles describes the use of a vessel with perforated bottom that made it possible to draw water without causing it to flow: the clepsydra. Compare J. Bollack, *Empédocle 3. Les Origines. Commentaire*, vol. 2 (Paris, 1969), pp. 470–494, tables 4 and 5: gloss to fr. 110 B. See also E. Gallavotti, *Empedocle. Poema fisico e lustrale* (Milan, 1975), p. 257. The long Empedoclean fragment is transmitted by Aristotle, *De respiratione* 7, 473b15–474a24 (cf. *De caelo* II.13, 294b; *Physics* IV. 6, 213a; pseudo-Aristotle, *Problems* XVI.8, 914b; II.1, 866b).

58. Empedocles, fr. 121 DK.

59. See Vernant, "Le Fleuve *Amelēs*," pp. 119–121.

60. Plato, *Gorgias* 483a5–6.

61. Plato, *Republic* II, 363a.

62. Ibid., 364e.

63. *Phronēsis:* Plato, *Phaedo* 69c1.

64. Plato, *Gorgias* 493c4.

65. Plato, *Phaedo* 112b.

66. Zenobius II.6.

67. Plato, *Phaedo* 110d-111a.

68. *Odyssey* XI. 582–592; Pindar, *Olympian Odes* I.58.

69. This transformation is not systematic: the Islands of the Blessed depicted by Pindar in *Olympian Odes* II. 123–136 are cooled and irrigated by a water that causes golden flowers to grow. In this country, in which the righteous live without toil, water, earth, and meteors spontaneously offer up their boons (cf. *Odyssey* IV.563–569; Plato, *Phaedrus* 249a; Hesiod, *Works and Days* 169). An equilibrium that reconciles abundance and measure is established in the islands of the golden age, where nothing is ever tiresome or futile. Cf. J. Bollack, "L'Or des rois," *Revue de philologie*, 2d ser., 37 (1963), 234–254.

70. Plato, *Republic* X, 621. The absence of water capable of sustaining life in the underworld was noted by J. Rudhardt, *Le Thème de l'eau primordiale dans la mythologie grecque* (Bern, 1974), p. 91: "We will find it far more difficult to tell whether these waters are of any use to the dead themselves . . . The proximity of infernal waters is therefore not a factor in their reanimation." On the other hand, M. Pensa, *Rappresentazioni dell'oltre-tomba nella ceramica apula* (Rome, 1977), pp. 37–45, casually asserts that the water of

the uninitiated and of the Danaides in the underworld stands for both fertility and purification.

12. THE JAR

1. Vitruvius, who devotes one book of his treatise on architecture to the problems of supplying water, praises the moist element in a way relevant to our subject: "The fruits of the earth offer an abundance of foods to satisfy even unnecessary desires and sustain and support living things. As for water, which is useful not only for drinking but for an infinite number of other purposes, its utility is particularly pleasant because it is free" (*De architectura* VIII.3). A living thing deprived of one or another kind of food can survive by eating something else, but when water is lacking, the danger to life is absolute (VIII.3.28). Water is thus the sine qua non of the comestible, a substance that does nothing to stem hunger yet is the indispensable principle of fertility: accordingly, the water of the underworld is the consummate symbol of unsatisfied desire. Its incessant leakage signifies aridity, penury, and the depths of hunger and thirst.

2. Isocrates, *Panegyricus* 28. For an interpretation of this passage see Boyancé, "Sur les Mystères d'Eleusis," *REG*, 75 (1962), 474–480, in which the author reaffirms, in opposition to G. E. Mylonas, the importance of Eleusinian eschatology and cites the *Homeric Hymn to Demeter* 480–482. N. J. Richardson, *The Homeric Hymn to Demeter* (Oxford, 1974), pp. 310–312, comments on these lines by recalling the tradition that attached to them from Pindar to Cicero. On the myth, function, and ideology of Demeter, the generous goddess who showed no mercy to the ungrateful, see I. Chirassi Colombo, "I doni di Demetra: Mito e ideologia nella Grecia arcaica," in *Mélanges Stella* (Trieste, 1976), pp. 183–213. On the "beatitude" made possible by the mysteries, see also P. Lévêque, "*Olbios* et la félicité des initiés," *Mélanges Delvoye* (Brussels, 1982), pp. 113–126.

3. See Marcel Detienne, "Démeter," in *Dictionnaire des Mythologies*, ed. Yves Bonnefoy (Paris, 1981).

4. Athenaeus I.40d.

5. And its mythological symbol, Pluto, is Demeter's offspring.

For a history of representations of Tartarus, see Alain Ballabriga, *Le Soleil et le Tartare* (Paris, 1986).

6. G. E. Mylonas, *Eleusis and the Eleusinian Mysteries*, pp. 237–238. The Greeks were of course obliged, as the Pythia reminded them, to offer each year's first fruits to Demeter. See. H. W. Parke and D. E. W. Wormell, *The Delphic Oracle*, vol. 2; *The Oracular Responses* (Oxford, 1956), pp. 164–165. Those who denied the goddess her due were stricken with famine.

7. See Liddell-Scott-Jones, *Greek-English Lexicon* (Oxford, 1961), s.v. *telos*.

8. D. Sabbatucci, *Essai sur le mysticisme grec*, French translation (Paris, 1982), p. 155.

9. *Homeric Hymn to Demeter* 268–274, 480ff.

10. Diodorus Siculus V. 68.1–2.

11. Ibid., 75.4.

12. Ibid., 77.1–2.

13. Lucretius, *De rerum natura* III.1003–10, trans. H. A. J. Munro.

14. Ibid., 935.

15. [Plato], *Axiochus*, 377b6–7: in this dialogue, which condenses and mimics Platonic themes, the eternal water-carrying of the Danaides, along with the futile labors of Tantalus, Sisyphus, and Tityus, is contrasted with the banquets of the blessed, who sojourn in a temperate land and drink from pure springs (371c-d). See F. Graf, *Eleusis und die orphische Dichtung Athens in vorhellenischer Zeit*, p. 113 n. 92; Hecataeus, in Diodorus Siculus I.97.2.

16. This vessel was discovered in 1972, as reported in A. D. Trendall, *Archaeological Reports*, 19 (1973), 37, fig. 8, and analyzed in *Festschrift für F. Brommer* (Mainz, 1977), p. 284, Taf. 75, 3, 9. E. Keuls mentions it in *The Water Carriers in Hades: A Study of Catharsis through Toil in Classical Antiquity*, p. 8. Cf. D. Adamesteanu, "L'hydria apula di Heraclea," in *Studies in Honour of Arthur Trendall* (Sidney, 1979), pp. 9–12; M. Schmidt, "Ein Danaidendrama und der Euripidische Ion auf unteritalischen Vasenbildern," ibid., pp. 159–169.

On Amymone, the Danaid whom Poseidon persuades to marry him see Hyginus, *Fabulae* 168, and Lucian, *Marine Dialogues* 6. Amymone shares the fate of Hypermestra but escapes the collective crime through a sacred marriage. Cf. "Amymone," in *Lexikon der Griechischen und Römischen Mythologie,* ed. W. H. Roscher (Leipzig, 1884–1886), cols. 327–328.

17. Keuls, *Water Carriers,* collects a large number of images relating to the Danaides.

18. M. Schmidt, "Ein Danaidendrama," p. 161.

19. C. Picard, "L'Eleusinisme et la disgrâce des Danaides," *Revue de l'histoire des religions,* 100 (1929), 49.

20. Note this juxtaposition in Plato's *Gorgias* and Lucretius' *De rerum natura* (935ff., 1006ff.).

21. On lost works devoted to the Danaides, see J. M. Edmonds, *The Fragments of Attic Comedy,* vol. 1 (Leiden, 1957), p. 643; and Keuls, *Water Carriers,* pp. 61–62.

22. Euripides, *Hercules furens* 1016ff.; cf. *Hecuba* 869, 886.

23. Zenobius I.6 (*Corpus Paroemiographorum Graecorum,* ed. E. L. Leutsche and F. G. Schneidewin [1838; reprint, Hildesheim, 1965], 32–33).

24. Keuls, *Water Carriers,* pl. 1.

25. Pausanias X.31.10–12: the *amyētoi* are situated between Sisyphus and Tantalus.

26. Scholium to Euripides, *Hecuba* 869; scholium to Aelius Aristides, *On Rhetoric* II.229; Hyginus, *Fabulae* 168.4–5.

27. *Bibliotheca* II.1.5.

28. Fr. 125 Mette.

29. Fr. 124 Mette: scholium to Pindar, *Pythian Odes* III.19.

30. Pindar, *Pythian Odes* IX.110–116; cf. Pausanias III.12.2.

31. Euripides, *Hecuba* 1016; *Heracles* 859.

32. In Aeschylus, *Suppliants* 5, the Danaides are said to have been banished from their homeland but not because of a crime of blood.

33. Scholium to Aelius Aristides, *Orat.* II.229. Pausanias gives a version intermediate between purification and punishment: in order to find husbands for his tainted daughters, Danaus was forced to exempt the suitors from the obligation to give marriage gifts (III.12.2). Only on this condition would anyone agree to marry the murderesses. Note that even here Pausanias does not allude to the Danaides' infernal fate.

34. As is pointed out by G. E. Mylonas, *Eleusis and the Eleusinian Mysteries,* pp. 247–248.

35. On Heracles purified of the murder of Pholus at Eleusis,

see H. Lloyd-Jones, "Heracles at Eleusis: P. Oxy. 2622 and P.S.I. 1391," *Maia,* 19 (1967), 206–229, esp. 211–213. As the author points out, Heracles was obliged to have himself initiated and therefore to purge himself of the murder he had committed before descending into the underworld.

36. Herodotus II.171.

37. On the Thesmophoria in Greece see L. Deubner, *Attische Feste,* p. 50.

38. Hesiod, *Works and Days* 94–99. M. L. West gives a detailed commentary on this passage on pp. 168–170 (see also pp. 164–166) of his edition. Cf. Jean-Pierre Vernant, "Manger à la table des hommes," in *La Cuisine du sacrifice en pays grec,* ed. Marcel Detienne and J. P. Vernant; and Nicole Loraux, "Sur la race des femmes et quelques-unes de ses tribus," in *Les Enfants d'Athéna,* pp. 75–118.

39. This is the interpretation given by a scholiast glossing *Works and Days* 94: he regards the line as proof of Homer's anteriority to Hesiod, who allegedly used the *Iliad* as his source. The scholium can be found in West's edition of *Works and Days,* p. 71. According to another scholium (to line 89): the satyrs. Cf. A. B. Cook, *Zeus,* 3:351ff.; Jane E. Harrison, *Prolegomena to the Study of Greek Religion,* p. 280.

40. This isolated and unusual image requires cautious interpretation. I nevertheless reject the hypothesis proposed by Erika Simon, who hesitantly suggests that the female head atop the vessel may be that of Elpis ("Pandora," in *Enciclopedia dell'arte antica classica e orientale,* 5:932). The man next to her would then be Prometheus. Harrison was not wrong, I think, to identify the squat, twisted figure staring at the object as Hephaestus admiring his work. Furthermore, it seems to me that Hope ought not to emerge from the mouth of the jar; in fact Hope remains a prisoner within, below the jar's lips. Cf. C. Bérard, *Anodos* (Neuchâtel, 1974), p. 161 n. 7; J. D. Beazley, "Groups of Campanian Redfigured," JHS, 63 (1943), 67 n. 3.

41. Hesiod, *Works and Days* 61, 70; *Theogony* 571. On the tradition of a chthonic Pandora, see West on *Works and Days,* pp. 164–166, and Loraux, *Les Enfants d'Athéna,* 89 n. 74.

42. Hesiod, *Theogony* 585–600. Cf. Loraux, *Les Enfants d'Athéna,* pp. 78ff.

43. Hesiod, *Works and Days* 376; *Theogony* 603–607.

44. *Theogony* 591–599; *Works and Days* 373–375, 702–705.

45. *Works and Days* 702–705.

46. *Theogony* 571–572; *Works and Days* 70–71. In the *Theogony* the choice between two types of woman is a foolish one: even a good wife is still a hungry mouth (608–610), throughout her life a burden, like a malady for which there is no cure.

47. *Works and Days* 95.

48. Ibid., 375; "He who trusts a woman trusts in thieves."

49. J. P. Vernant, "Hestia-Hermes: Sur l'expression religieuse de l'espace et du mouvement chez les Grecs," *Mythe et pensée chez les Grecs*, 1:124–70.

50. Note that Ischomachus, the prudent husband, assures Socrates that he has chosen a girl well-bred with respect to *gastēr;* Xenophon, *Oeconomicus* VII.6.

13. UNCONSUMMATED

1. I. M. Linforth, "Soul and Sieve in Plato's *Gorgias,*" p. 302. *University of California Publications in Classical Philology*, XII, 17 (1944), 195–313.

2. E. Des Places, "Platon et la langue des mystères," *Annales de la Faculté de Lettres d'Aix*, 38 (1964), 16–17: "In the passage from the *Gorgias*, Plato uses *amyētos* twice (493b1 and 5), perhaps in a play on the etymology, associating *muein*, 'to initiate,' with *muein*, 'to close the mouth, the eyes' or, more commonly, in the intransitive sense, 'to be closed'; the *amyētoi* would have no bottom, like the cask in the myth!" A certain resistance to recognizing Plato's etymological play on words is also evident in E. R. Dodds, *Plato's Gorgias* (Oxford, 1959), p. 302: "*Amyētous:* I doubt if we are meant to think of this as 'unstoppered' (as if from *myein*)." But why cultivate doubt with regard to Cratylism where this type of semantics is so learnedly employed in the Platonic text?

3. Scholium to Aristophanes, *Frogs* 459.

4. Suda, s.v. μύησις.

5. Eustathius, *ad Iliadem* XXIV, p. 1492 Basil, cited by Linforth, "Soul and Sieve," p. 301.

6. G. E. Mylonas, *Eleusis and the Eleusinian Mysteries*, p. 224, considers secrecy in the mysteries; silence had been a fundamental

aspect of initiation since the *Homeric Hymn to Demeter* (pp. 473–479). Sabbatucci takes an even more radical view of its function: mystical experience, he says, was nothing other than a journey through the profound void of the ineffable (*Essai sur le mysticisme grec,* pp. 142–143).

7. In Andocides, *On Mysteries,* it is clear that an *amyētos* was truly ignorant of the mysteries of Eleusis rather than a slanderer of those mysteries.

8. Artemidorus IV.28, 48; V.78–79.

9. See above, Chapter 2; Diodorus Siculus XVI.26.

10. Hippocrates, *Aphorisms* V.51.

11. *On Generation* V.1.

12. Aristotle, *Historia animalium* 583b29; Galen, *De usu partium* XIV.3.146K.

13. *On Generation* XV.1.

14. Ibid., 2–3.

15. Ibid., 4; this error was an inadvertent but invaluable form of birth control in ancient Greece.

16. See, e.g., [Hippocrates], *Diseases of Women* 41, 133.

17. R. Joly, *Le Niveau de la science hippocratique,* p. 75: "Unnaturally retained menstrual blood seeks to escape: it presses on the hips, the loins, and the bladder, in the latter case causing strangury. After a few months the blood turns to pus and may exit by forming a tumor in the groin."

18. *On Generation* XIV.1–2.

19. Any leakage is a sign of a difficult pregnancy (ibid., IX.1).

20. The teleonomic principle that determines the laws of sexual physiology is set forth at the beginning of book II of *De generatione animalium.* On this aspect of Aristotelian biology, see D. Lanza, "Introduzione a Riproduzione degli animali," in his edition of Aristotle, *Opere biologiche* (Turin, 1974); Giulia Sissa, "Il corpo della donna. Lineamenti di una ginecologia filosofica," in S. Campese, P. Manuli, and G. Sissa, *Madre materia.*

21. Aristotle, *De generatione animalium* I.19, 726b30–727a2, trans. Arthur Platt.

22. Ibid., 738a33–b4. On the notion of residue (*perissōma*), which though an Aristotelian creation should be viewed in the context of the medical physics of humors, see A. Thivel, "La Doc-

trine des *perissōmata* et ses parallèles hippocratiques," *Revue de philologie*, 39 2d ser., (1965), 266–282. And concerning the epistemological adaptation that Aristotle based on these medical models, see M. Roussel, "Physique et biologie dans la *Génération des Animaux* d'Aristote," REG, 93 (1980), 42–71.

23. Aristotle, *De generatione animalium* 744b16.

24. Aristotle, *Politics* I, 1260a13.

25. Aristotle, *De generatione animalium* I.22, 730a28–b32. Cf. ibid., 734b4–19. That is why the female does not engender life by herself; she needs a principle, a factor that imparts movement and determines its direction.

26. Ibid., II.3, 737a18–22: "Now semen is a secretion and is moved with the same movement as that in virtue of which the body increases (this increase being due to subdivision of the nutriment in its last stage). When it has entered the uterus it puts into form the corresponding secretion of the female and moves it with the same movement wherewith it is moved itself." The female blood moves either indolently or frenetically, but contact with the male causes it to follow a structural movement (*kinēsis*), which does not move but builds, fulfills its form. On the process of coagulation, see P. Demont, "Remarques sur le sens de *trephō*," REG, 91 (1978), 359–370.

27. Aristotle, *De generatione animalium* II.1, 734b4–19: "For the parts of [automatic machines] while at rest have a sort of potentiality of motion in them, and when any external force puts the first of them in motion, immediately the next is moved in actuality. As, then, in these automatic machines the external force moves the parts in a certain sense (not by touching any part at the moment, but by virtue of an external contact), in like manner also that from which the semen comes, or in other words that which made the semen, sets up the movement in the embryo and makes the parts of it by having first touched something though not continuing to touch it. In a way it is the innate motion that does this, as the act of building builds the house."

28. The theory of resemblances is developed at the beginning of *De generatione animalium* IV. To give birth to a male child identical with its father is the most discreet way for a female to fulfill her mission. If she gives birth to a female, the male *dynamis* was too

weak. Aristotle has already explained at length the need for the birth of this first form of monster (ibid., II.1).

29. See H. Bolkestein, Τέλος ὁ γάμος (Amsterdam, 1933).

30. Plato, *Laws* VI; see above, Chapter 1.

31. J.-P. Vernant, *Mythe et pensée chez les Grecs*, 1:140–142.

32. Pseudo-Demosthenes, *Against Neaira* 122: "The state of marriage is distinguished by the fact that one produces children, introduces sons into the phratry and deme, and gives daughters in marriage as one's own."

33. Aeschylus, *Prometheus* 865. For a completely different interpretation of these lines, see G. Ferrari, "La misandria delle Danaida," *Annali della Scuola Normale Superiore di Pisa*, 1977, pp. 1303–21.

34. The idea of an intermediate state, a marriage *interrupted* rather than omitted, was proposed by H. J. Rose, "Antigone and the Bride of Corinth," *Classical Quarterly*, 19 (1925), 148. Here again, however, it is the ritualist model that intervenes. These half-wives allegedly spend all eternity trying to get married. For a long time it was impossible to see the act of the Danaides as a symbol of failure rather than as a compulsive ceremony.

35. Empedocles, fr. 31a70 DK. See J. Bollack, *Empédocle 3. Les Origines. Commentaires*, 503: "Palpable, visible trees stand in the same relation to the earth from which they stem and of which they are composed as the embryo hidden in the belly stands in relation to the womb. They both draw their substance and their being from their mother. The species differ according to the regions, just as embryos differ according to place in the womb where they are attached."

36. M. Lonie, "On the Botanical Excursus in *De natura pueri*, pp. 22–27," *Hermes*, 97 (1969), 391–411, esp. 409–411.

37. *De natura pueri* XXVII.1. Cf. ibid., XXII.1: "Nutrition and growth of the child takes place when what originates in the mother is found in the womb. According as the mother's health is good or bad, so is the health of the child. Similarly, plants feed on the earth; and as the earth is, so too are the plants. When the seed is sown, it fills with the humor that comes from the earth."

38. Aristotle, *Historia animalium* V.8, 586a31ff.; *De generatione animalium* II.7, 745b23ff.

39. Hyginus, *Fabulae* 273.1 Rose.

40. Horace, *Odes* III.11–21; Ovid, *Metamorphoses* IV.462; Hyginus, *Fabulae* 168, 170. Plutarch, *Septem sapientium convivium* 16 (*Mor.* 160B): "But, just as the Danaides would not have known what life to lead or what to do had they been delivered from their duty and from the filling of the jar, we ourselves would not know what to do if we ceased to pour into our insatiable flesh everything that comes from the earth and sea together, for, ignorant of what is beautiful, we love life at the level of needs." Porphyry, *De abstinentia* III.27.8: "But, they [men] say, assume that everyone could surrender to these reasons [that is, renounce the passions], what would be the result? Obviously happiness, since injustice would be banished from man's abode and justice would become a citizen of this world as it is of heaven. Hence it is as if the Danaides were at a loss as to what their life might be once they were freed from the task of filling the perforated jar from a sieve. For they are at a loss as to what might happen if we ceased to give in to our passions and desires, which assail us constantly only because of our ignorance of beautiful things, enamored as we are of this life limited to necessary needs and devoted to searching for them . . . Similarly, then, you too, freed of the slavery of the body and the servitude of corporeal passions, as you gave them every sort of external nourishment, so you shall give yourself every sort of internal nourishment, again possessing in justice your own property without taking that of others by force."

41. S. Reinach, "Sisyphe aux Enfers et quelques autres damnés," *Revue archéologique*, 4th ser., 1 (January–June 1903), 188–192, argues that the appearance of male water-bearers is justified solely as an Orphic interpretation of the Danaid myth.

CONCLUSION

1. See M. Vegetti, "Metafora politica e immagine del mondo," in *Tra Edipo e Euclide* (Milan, 1983), pp. 41–58; J. Svenbro, "La Découpe du poème. Notes sur les origines sacrificielles de la poétique grecque," *Poétique*, 58 (1984), 215–232.

2. See Françoise Héritier, *L'Exercice de la parenté* (Paris, 1978).

3. Denis Diderot, *Les Bijoux indiscrets* (1748) (Paris, 1972), pp. 36–37.

4. Cf. E. de Fontenay, *Diderot ou le matérialisme enchanté* (Paris, 1981), p. 194.

5. Galen, *De usu partium* XV.3.

6. Cf. Dio of Prusa, *De Homero* 53.9.

7. E. Dublanchy, "Chasteté," in *Dictionnaire de théologie catholique*, vol. 2 (Paris, 1923), col. 2320.

8. See, e.g., the medical textbook by Garrey, Govan, Hodge, and Callender, *Ginecologia illustrata* (Rome, 1975), p. 19.

9. Ambrose, *Epistula* V (*Patrologia Latina*, XVI, cols. 891–898).

10. Ambrose, *De institutione virginis* (*Patrologia Latina*, XVI, col. 319).

11. First Gospel of James 19–20; pseudo-Matthew 13:3–5.

12. Augustine, *De civitate dei* I.18; Cyprian, *Epistula ad Pomponium de virginibus* (*Patrologia Latina*, IV, cols. 364ff.).

13. Augustine, *De civitate dei* VI.9 (trans. Henry Bettenson, pp. 245–246).

14. Catullus 32.11.

15. Ambroise Paré, *De la génération*, 49.

16. Ibid.

INDEX

235

INDEX

INDEX